The Sultan's Court

WO ES WAR

A series from Verso edited by Slavoj Žižek

Wo es war, soll ich werden – *Where it was, I shall come into being* – is Freud's version of the Enlightenment goal of knowledge that is in itself an act of liberation. Is it still possible to pursue this goal today, in the conditions of late capitalism? If 'it' today is the twin rule of pragmatic-relativist New Sophists and New Age obscurantists, what 'shall come into being' in its place? The premiss of the series is that the explosive combination of Lacanian psychoanalysis and Marxist tradition detonates a dynamic freedom that enables us to question the very presuppositions of the circuit of Capital.

In the same series:

Slavoj Žižek, *The Metastases of Enjoyment. Six Essays on Woman and Causality*

Jeremy Bentham, *The Panopticon Writings.* Edited and Introduced by Miran Božovič

Slavoj Žižek, *The Indivisible Remainder. An Essay on Schelling and Related Matters*

Slavoj Žižek, *The Plague of Fantasies*

Forthcoming:

Mladen Dolar, *The Bone in the Spirit. A Lacanian Reading of Hegel's 'Phenomenology of Spirit'*

Alenka Zupančič, *Kant with Lacan. Towards an Ethics of the Real*

The Sultan's Court
European Fantasies of the East

◆

ALAIN GROSRICHARD

Translated by Liz Heron

With an introduction by Mladen Dolar

V

VERSO

London • New York

This book is supported by the French Ministry for Foreign
Affairs as part of the Burgess Programme, headed for the French
Embassy in London by the Institut Français du Royaume Uni

institut français

First published by Verso 1998
This edition © Verso 1998
Translation © Liz Heron 1998
Introduction © Mladen Dolar 1998
First published as
Structure du sérail: La fiction du despotisme Asiatique dans l'Occident classique
© Editions du Seuil 1979

Verso
UK: 6 Meard Street, London W1V 3HR
USA: 180 Varick Street, New York NY 10014–4606

Verso is the imprint of New Left Books

ISBN: 978-1-85984-122-8

British Library Cataloguing in Publication Data
A catalogue record for this book is available from the British Library

Library of Congress Cataloging-in-Publication Data
A catalog record for this book is available from the Library of Congress

Typeset by SetSystems, Saffron Walden, Essex
Printed by Biddles Ltd, Guildford and King's Lynn

Contents

Translator's Acknowledgement   vii

Introduction: The Subject Supposed to Enjoy
    Mladen Dolar   ix

Part I   A Genealogy of the Monster

1   The Unnameable Threat   3
2   The Concept of a Fantasy   26

Part II   In Orient Desert . . .

3   The Gaze and the Letter   55
4   The Machine   71
5   The Sword and the Book   85
6   Mahomet Beside Himself   100

Part III   The Shadow of the Seraglio

7   The Anatomy of the Seraglio   123
8   The Guardian of the Thresholds   147
9   The Other Scene   166

Wo es war   185

    Epilogue   189

    Notes   193

Translator's Acknowledgement

Some of the work of this translation was done during a month spent at the British Centre for Literary Translation. The translator wishes to thank the Centre and the Council of Europe for the bursary awarded to her.

Introduction: The Subject Supposed to Enjoy

Mladen Dolar

At the end of the 1970s two books appeared, dealing with largely the same topic, though in a very different way; they were written independently of each other, and met with very different fates. Whereas Edward W. Said's *Orientalism* (1978) was an instant success and has been a major reference in English-speaking countries ever since, Alain Grosrichard's *Structure de sérail* (1979) acquired only a limited – albeit enthusiastic – group of admirers, making its way to general recognition only slowly.[1] In spite of numerous intersections, the two books are as different as can be in their scope, perspective, methods and ambitions. Both books, dealing with Western 'ideas' about the Orient, share the conviction that those ideas were largely gross misrepresentations ridden with prejudice, bias and ideological interests, so that they are ultimately indicative only of the state of Western societies, and not to be taken seriously as descriptions of the East.[2]

First there is the difference in the periods studied: although Said makes a number of general claims and gives a rough historical overview, he concentrates mainly on the nineteenth and twentieth centuries, taking Napoleon's expedition to Egypt (1798) as a sort of watershed of modern Orientalism (pp. 42, 76, 80 f., 122, etc.). This is where Grosrichard stops, confining himself to the seventeenth and eighteenth centuries ('the Classical Occident', as the original French subtitle specifies). Then there is the difference of the area concerned: Said consciously limits himself to the Arab world, the Near East, while Grosrichard's sources mostly treat the Ottoman Empire (still a very real threat at that time). Then there is the difference of aspect: while Said takes into consideration a wide range of perspectives – political, economic, religious, linguistic, historical, anthropological, cultural, etc. – Grosrichard focuses on the rather limited perspective of 'Oriental depotism' and its implications ('The fiction of Asiatic despotism', as again the original French subtitle specifies). Consequently, Said practically never mentions any of Grosrichard's major sources, and vice versa.[3] But more importantly, Said's principal ambition is to situate Orientalist ideas into a wider pattern of the Western hegemony over the East, implicating them into an extensive web of practices of cultural, political and economic imperialism and colonialism, of which the 'ideas' and 'fictions' were willing or unwilling accomplices ('never has there been a nonmaterial form of Orientalism, much less something so innocent as an "idea" of the Orient' (p. 23)). Grosrichard's concerns seem to be quite the reverse: he concentrates on a fiction which underlies a number of discourses on the East in a certain period, focusing on that fiction in its pure form – a distilled fantasy, as it were. Yet what he is doing is far from apolitical, or confined to some aseptic realm of pure ideas: it is in the fantasy and its logic, perhaps, that one can find the best clue to the strange efficacy of those ideas. It is perhaps in the fantasy that one has to look for the secrets of political domination and its mechanism, although it seems far removed from the more palpable social realities. And above all, fantasy is not some realm of pure ideas and representations, for it ultimately relies on enjoyment, the stuff that irretrievably sullies the supposed ideal purity; it is the mechanism of 'production' and canalization of enjoyment, and in this way it may hold the key to our status as subjects – both political subjects and subjects of desire – and to our practices. So ultimately, the opposition between the two approaches can be seen as the difference between a vast and encompassing concept, and a narrow focus on the logic of fantasy which underlies it. One could even make a tentative claim that behind every political concept there is a phantasmic kernel which effectuates it: it discloses a certain 'economy of enjoyment' that makes it function. It aims at what one can indeed programmatically call 'enjoyment as a political factor' (to quote another subtitle, that of Slavoj Žižek's *For They Know Not What They Do* (1991)).

The despotic fantasy that Grosrichard submits to painstaking scrutiny is historically precisely situated in the period of the Enlightenment. To be sure, it has a long prehistory[4] and an endless aftermath, reaching up to the present (as Said has convincingly shown). Yet the limited period of investigation has an overwhelming strategic importance: it is the time when the basic social and political structures of modernity were laid down and elaborated, along with its basic forms of subjectivity. It is the time of spectacular endeavours proposing a rationally based society, a new concept of state, civil society, democratic liberties, citizenship, division of power, and so on; but in a strange counterpoint, there was the image of Oriental despotism as the very negative of those endeavours, their phantasmic Other. This was nourished by numerous travellers' accounts and propelled by their fictional amplifications to hold sway over imagination at large, becoming one of the prevalent 'ideas' of the epoch, a commonly acknowledged fantasy. That counterpoint is essential to bear in mind as the background to all the detailed analyses; its symptomatic value is of exceptional and far-reaching significance. For this fantasy lays bare – unguardedly, in a sort of 'naive', immediate and outspoken way which has subsequently become obfuscated – the economy of enjoyment that necessarily accompanies modern structures of the social and the status of the subject; it sticks to them as their reverse side.

Grosrichard's method in dealing with this fantasy, while obviously firmly rooted in Lacanian psychoanalysis, is remarkably unobtrusive. Not only is Lacan practically never mentioned, there is also a conspicuous absence of the usual psychoanalytic jargon. The texts he explores are never translated into some well-known shibboleths of analytic theory, never treated through the lens of a metalanguage entitled to tell their truth, never reduced to some deeper meaning behind them. His interventions seem to be minimal, almost imperceptible: the texts are just disposed, rearranged, articulated, punctuated, pieced together in a pattern. This method is finally much more compelling in its result than some clamorous proclamation of Lacanian theses; it produces an 'estrangement effect' in which the texts, although apparently hardly tampered with in their original setting, are deprived of their seemingly natural and self-evident air – they unexpectedly show their contrived and contingent side. One could even venture to say that Grosrichard does not really engage in interpretation – not in the usual sense. There is a famous Lacanian dictum that 'one doesn't interpret the fantasy' (as opposed to the symptom which demands endless interpretation) – one has to 'go through' [*traverser*] the fantasy, and Grosrichard leads us by the hand in this going through, this 'traversing', showing us both its profound consistency and its total contingency.[5] Writing an introduction to a translation of his book is thus an uneasy task, since putting it into a wider perspective and translating it into some general theses risks breaking the spell and dissipating its principal charm.

The fantasy of Oriental despotism seems to be ruled by the maximum distance in relation to our European reality, yet at the same time strangely close. It is geographically far removed, and its features, as different as possible from those of our own society, seem to be permeated with an uncanny quality, both horrifying and appealing to fantasy by an irresistible attraction, pertaining, in Freud's words, to 'that class of the frightening which leads back to what is known of old and long familiar' (*Pelican Freud Library*, vol. 14, p. 340). Those features are remarkably obstinate and inflexible through a great number of discourses and over a considerable span of time: subjects who abase themselves before a despot, the sole possessor of all political power; their total compliance with the despot's whimsical will and their utter deindividualization, since in relation to the despot they all count for the same – that is, nothing; the despot's utter capricious arbitrariness, unbounded by any law or predictability; summary executions, tortures, mutilations, confiscations, and so on, for which a mere wink is enough and which are carried out and accepted by the victims with a self-evident equanimity, or rather, with relish and devotion; an incredible lust for goods, which constantly stream into the despot's court as into a black hole, that supposed paradise of supreme enjoyment; a political order which functions without any attempt at legitimacy, without regard for the will or welfare of the people or for talent, knowledge or valour, not even for ties of blood; the unfathomable structure of the despot's court, with the seraglio at its centre, displaying a highly codified hierarchy of viziers, janissaries, mutes, dwarves, eunuchs, and countless despot's wives; and, last but not least, the immense sexual lust, the supposed boundless *jouissance* at the core of this institution, the despot's endless copulation with an endless number of women. This world seems to be politically insane, rationally untenable, economically catastrophic, morally outrageous, monstrous in any human terms, presenting an image of infamy and degradation, the very negative of our own society. Yet it seems to be endowed with an incontrovertible and ageless existence in those conveniently remote countries; moreover, it seems to lurk around every corner of our own homely world.

To be sure, it is obvious that this fantasy, elaborated down to the smallest detail, does not correspond to any Asian reality.[6] It is easy to expose the unreliability of sources, the use of highly dubious hearsay, the blatant partiality and prejudice of the authors, their meticulous reports on things which they, by their own account, could not possibly have witnessed (first and foremost, the seraglio), and so on. This dubious credibility is already evident in the peculiar monotony and uniformity of the accounts, which appear to be written by one and the same invisible hand throughout the centuries, ridden with the same commonplaces and episodes, testifying to a stubborn persistence of a certain kind of reality strangely immune to criticism, historical probability and change. These accounts of despotism, implausible as they are, seem to be endowed with an immediate appeal and suggestive power – 'it strikes the eye', as Montesquieu would say. Even for the modern reader, this tale possesses the strange quality of being instantly

recognizable, like a stroll through well-known countryside, producing an immediate *déjà vu* effect, as though we have always known
it. Why does it seem so self-evident, timelessly elevated above
history? How come we have already been there?

There is a paradox that this fantasy, despite its maximal distance
from our world and its imaginary shape, displays a real kernel, a
curious reality not to be found in the Orient. This merely provided
a setting and a screen, a necessary background for fantasy, but the
clue to its functioning can be discovered only in our own social
reality. The fantasy, useless as a tool to explain its object, can shed
light upon its producers and adherents. It projects on to the screen
of this distant Other our own impasses and practices in dealing
with power, and stages them.

The despotic fantasy served as an ideological weapon at the time
of the Enlightenment, a handy weapon to strike the opponent, a
warning and a constant inner peril. The rising bourgeoisie could
denounce the proponents of the old order as riddled with the
despotic disease, bearers of an irrational privilege and perpetua-
tors of slavery. The aristocracy could present democratic demands
as an extension of despotic levelling, soulless deindividualization,
loss of rank and distinction.[7] In both cases it was exhibited as a
monstrous counter-nature, a spectre demonstrating what our
society could become unless we used some radical means to
prevent it, though the recommended antidotes were sharply
opposed. It was endowed with a curious ambivalence, both confined to the exotic Asian horrors and corroding our own social
structure from within, haunting our past, present and future, Asia
in the midst of Europe. It could effortlessly cross the boundaries
of inside/outside, far away/close, alien/familiar.[8] Strangely
enough, opposed ideologies and classes could use the same
panoply as a common background, a shared store of clichés, as if
the reality of fantasy were immune to class and status differences.[9]
And the more fantastic the fantasy seemed the closer it seemed,
displaying a strangely inert perseverance of the imaginary, the
secret, quasi-immutable kernel beneath the more tangible social
relations and their mutations.

The functioning of the despotic fantasy in our midst can first be approached by the well-known formula of fetishist disavowal: 'I know very well, but nevertheless . . .' This formula, pinpointed in a famous paper by Octave Mannoni (1969), embodies the split between knowledge and belief. The notorious paradigmatic Freudian example would be 'I know very well [that mother has no phallus], nevertheless I believe she does' (see *Pelican Freud Library*, vol. 7, pp. 351–7). The belief persists against our better knowledge – not just as an intimate conviction but materialized in a fetish, a substitute object supplanting the missing one. The embodied belief materializes as an object 'independent of consciousness', providing a curious sort of objectivity which can bind subjects together through their disavowal of castration. It can be shown that Marx's concept of commodity fetishism rests on an analogous structure: I know very well [that the commodity relations between things are just a disguise for relations between people, etc.], nevertheless I believe that the commodity is endowed with mystical qualities, 'abounding in metaphysical subtleties and theological niceties' (see Karl Marx and Frederick Engels, *Collected Works*, Vol. 35, p. 81). Here also the fetishist delusion is incarnated in a practical relation to objectivity.

One can venture to extend this formula to a comparable sort of fetishism designating the status of the despotic fantasy, which could be translated into the following formula: 'I know very well [that our society is based on rational foundations and serves common welfare], nevertheless I believe that power is based on the whim of the Other, that it demands unconditional subjection, that it is indestructible, that its bearers are untouchable and made of a stuff apart, that it is the place of an unalloyed enjoyment . . .' Or, even more bluntly, 'I know very well [that I live in a democracy], nevertheless I believe that power is despotic.' There is a sort of fetishism which pertains to the very exercise of power. The fantasy of Oriental despotism stages a practical relation of subjects to power, that part of belief (i.e. voluntary submission) which also precedes and supports the rational and democratic foundations of power; the part which rational legitimation does not dismantle but, rather, tacitly presupposes; the part which brings about the subject's subordination before power is ever grounded in knowledge, or opposed in the name of a better knowledge. As in analytic theory, the fetish, as the object of belief, comes to fill a void, the void of castration; this phantasmic belief disguises an irreparable lack: the empty place of power which a Master comes to fill; and whoever comes to occupy it (even if they are democratically elected) is endowed with a fetishist aura, a belief staged by the fantasy.

Grosrichard touches explicitly upon these implications only in passing, when he points out that the same logic which animates despotism perpetuates itself, *mutatis mutandis*, in the functioning of the modern state:

> What the concept of despotism enables us to think about ... is less the reality of a *political regime* than the ineradicable measure of the imaginary by which all *political power* is maintained. Despotism is the concept of a phantasm (pp. 30–31 below). This means that there are not two economies (on the one hand the despotic and totalitarian, on the other the bourgeois and liberal), but, rather, two interchangeable languages to describe the same deception, off which every variety of political power lives. (pp. 137–8 below)

As political subjects, we are prepared at a certain point to endorse the deception against our better judgement.

But what is it that makes subjects follow such a belief against their better judgement? Why do we fall into the trap? What profit can one hope to gain from such belief? The fantasy of despotism, with its mechanism of economy of enjoyment, offers an excellent clue. For what else is the entire despotic machine but a gigantic system of organization, regimentation, circulation of enjoyment, its infinite evocation? This power springs up from a certain flow and distribution of enjoyment.

The machine is fuelled by a one-way stream of goods, produced by an infinite self-sacrifice of all subjects, which rolls towards the despotic centre for the sole enjoyment of the despot. Ultimately, it is epitomized by the flux of the 'sexual goods' reserved for the exclusive use of the despot. Grosrichard points out that this machine can be conceived as a *perpetuum mobile* which consumes only what it produces: enjoyment. But this one-way flow is based on the following axiom: enjoyment is an 'intersubjective', social category. The despot is the master over enjoyment, but he can enjoy only in so far as his enjoyment is confiscated from others. The master's enjoyment is produced by the subjects who renounce it; the quantity of enjoyment on one side equals the quantity of the renounced enjoyment on the other. The renunciation of enjoyment produces 'surplus enjoyment', which accrues towards the master just as surplus labour produces the surplus-value which comes to augment capital – and capital, also, can be accumulated only in proportion to the surplus labour extorted. (It is well known that Lacan's notion of surplus enjoyment was coined precisely following the model of Marx's surplus-value.)[10] Thus the despotic mechanism turns out to be an articulate totality (in Marx's terms) of production, distribution, exchange and consumption of enjoyment: it is produced only by a renunciation of all for the benefit of one; its social distribution is such that one is allotted all at the expense of all the others; its exchange is such that subjects are supposed unreservedly to give all and get nothing in return; and consumption is ultimately restricted to one. This flow of surplus enjoyment demands and presupposes a certain social organization, a hierarchy, which is in turn supported only by the belief in the supposed supreme enjoyment at the centre.

So the subject's belief, the part which one has to pawn in relation to power, is precisely the belief in the enjoyment of the Other, the place of a full enjoyment whose consistency can be provided only by this belief. The subject can participate in it only in so far as she/he subjects him-herself, and the minimal gesture of subjection is supplied by belief. The fantasy provides the part of enjoyment which I hope to attain as the subject (i.e. as subjected); moreover, the belief itself fulfils the promise it offers. This is the advantage of belief over knowledge: I am prepared to believe in the enjoyment of the Other in order to participate in it, but this belief itself procures enjoyment which supports it. The tiny surplus of belief over knowledge is the precarious support of enjoyment. So the power can find its fragile base in a *subject supposed to enjoy* (if one can coin this phrase on the model of 'the subject supposed to know', Lacan's clue to transference), and the supposed enjoyment derives its consistency only from fantasy – its promise, its withdrawal and its paradoxical realization.

Lacan's concept of surplus enjoyment does not, of course, imply that the enjoyment is in fact transferred to the Other – for example the despot, who would actually enjoy at the expense of the subject. It means, rather, the opposite: by renouncing enjoyment, the subject does nevertheless get enjoyment, a supplementary, surplus enjoyment, and this is what sustains the gesture of sacrifice. Enjoyment is not so easy to renounce; indeed, one never gets rid of it; the very act of renunciation produces a residue, an unexpected surplus. So do the subjects of despotism enjoy? The mystery is that the enjoyment is not extorted or confiscated from them – they give it up gladly and voluntarily in what looks like the 'voluntary servitude' described by La Boétie, in a gesture of love. One can speak of 'what political theory has unceasingly rejected, refused to think of as political, which might well be something stronger than strength, something more seductive than ideology, more enticing than gain – the very source of political power: love' (p. 11).

The perplexing thing is that despotism turns out not to be a system of coercion at all. It is not based on force, and the submission it presents could hardly be labelled 'ideology'; nor can it be seen to serve an (egoistic, economic) interest. The duality of force and ideology, their opposition in our quotation, can immediately bring to mind the extended discussions provoked by Gramsci's concept of hegemony as opposed to external repression, where the ideological battle for hegemony – a battle of argument, persuasion, striving for consent – was contrasted with rule by constraint. The same divide, in a modified form, was later echoed in the Althusserian distinction between repressive and ideological state apparatuses. The despotic fantasy seems to present a reality which eludes both parts of this alternative – or, rather, is placed precisely at the hidden intersection of the two: the part of voluntary submission, brought about by love, which precedes both ideological strife and the use of force. And since this phantasmic model of power concentrates on this kernel alone, it seems to dispense with both coercion and ideology, making them superfluous. It marks the point where power affects the subjects in their innermost being, where they submit even before any devices of force or persuasion are used. This gesture of love, which allows the subjects to get their share of enjoyment, is based on a belief, a supposition which sustains it – that of a 'subject supposed to enjoy'.

According to Freud's notorious dictum, there are three impossible professions where one can be certain of an unsatisfactory outcome in advance: government, education and psychoanalysis. Those professions are impossible because they presuppose and imply a relation of transference – they are based on a belief in an 'illusory' supposition, an unwarranted assumption, a necessary delusion; and even though it turns out to be false, it nevertheless produces very palpable effects – just as Columbus, acting on erroneous assumptions, nevertheless discovered America, even though he didn't get to where he wanted to go.[11] Lacan has pinpointed 'the subject supposed to know' as the kernel of this transferential relation, the paradox being that this supposition, this unjustified conjecture, this belief in a presupposed knowledge, can actually produce knowledge. Yet in order for the subject to believe in this knowledge there has to be a moment of enjoyment which induces his or her belief. It is this enjoyment, not knowledge, which is at stake in the belief, while knowledge can be produced only by a longer, more tortuous and wearisome process opened up by belief.

Analysis starts with this supposition, but ultimately aims at its suppression. It aims to dismantle the transference which has made it possible in the first place and which it has used as its principal lever. It culminates in the invalidation, the abolition, of the subject supposed to know, which leads to the experience that the Other doesn't know, turning the subject back to the impasses of his or her own enjoyment. Lacan described this moment as the emergence of 'the lack in the Other', the falling out of the object – of that miraculous treasure, *agalma*, supposedly held by the analyst, that secret clue to enjoyment. If the subject's world was initially 'out of joint' – and this is what made him or her enter analysis in the first place – then it is even more 'out of joint' at the end, where the promised cure, embodied by the transferential belief in the subject supposed to know how to 'put things right', turns out to be a mirage. The result is what Lacan has called subjective destitution. The transferential supposition in analysis also necessarily, quasi-mechanically, produces the moment of love that Freud examined in his famous paper on transference-love (1915).

The other two transferential professions aim, rather, at maintaining and perpetuating the supposition. They can be practised only as long as the transference relation is upheld. Whereas the analyst strives for unemployment, the other two want to keep their jobs. Education is also based on a subject supposed to know, though in another sense – a supposition ascribed to a teacher. It can get started only by a belief – the paradox that Plato already touched upon in *Menon*: if I know, I don't need a teacher; if I don't know, then I am also unaware of what there is to know. The resolution of this disjuncture between knowledge and ignorance is the belief in a presupposed knowledge as a paradoxical intersection of both. The moment of enjoyment appears in the form of the illusory assumption that knowledge will ultimately yield enjoyment, which leads to a perpetuation of the transferential relation. The enjoyment continually escapes, knowledge demands more knowledge in order to reach it,[12] so that the vast edifice of knowledge can finally easily combine with relations of domination.[13]

Finally, the master presents the 'subject supposed to enjoy' in its pure form, as distinct from knowledge. This is also the sense of his doubling into the pair of despot and vizier: the master is the master only when he delivers himself up to enjoyment, leaving to the vizier all the business which requires some knowledge (this structural function of the caretaker was already well described by

Aristotle, *Politics* Book I, 1255b). The divide between despot and vizier is also the divide between belief and knowledge: the master's enjoyment is an object of belief, while the vizier can be apprehended by knowledge, although his authority is based not on knowledge but on the fact that he substitutes for the absent master. The enjoyment is thus reduced to its pure form, which turns out to be its most imbecilic and idiotic figure. The splendour of full enjoyment, if one observes it from close quarters (and this is what one can do in fantasy), coincides with the disclosure of this feeble-minded, fatuous, weak, effeminate, trivial, spoiled, cowardly being, lost in his lust and enjoyment; this half-human and sub-human being which the despot ultimately turns out to be. The hypothetical place of full enjoyment coincides with an absence.

So the fantasy, which appeared as the hidden core of ideological reality, itself discloses a paradoxical core: an impossible Real which it reveals and disguises at one and the same time. At the centre of the fantasy there is a hole; the place of the despot is a vanishing point, evoked and veiled by the double device of the gaze and the letter – the supposedly omnipresent and terrible despotic gaze, which nobody can see, and the senseless signifier (the name, the seal) endowed with a formidable mysterious power. Both function mechanically and automatically, obliterating the despot as irrelevant. If one examines the fantasy in its own terms (not by confronting it with reality), it – strangely – shows, as its own essential ingredient, that the despot's supposed omnipotence reveals simultaneously his total impotence and annulment. The horrendous despotic mechanism conceals a void at its core. Even the seraglio, this much-envied place of unalloyed enjoyment, ultimately reveals the contrary: the fantasy reveals the infirm and impotent despot, while homosexuality, lesbianism and all sorts of perversions flourish, a veritable obsession with substitute objects and ersatz enjoyment in place of the supposed 'real' one. Everything in the seraglio is designed to evoke the full enjoyment at its centre, as by a negative image (the mutes, the dwarves, the eunuchs, etc.), but all this only points to a central void, which is ultimately the void of what Lacan has called the absence of sexual relationship. In this universe of substitutes, the despot himself is but a substitute: the intimidating despot who makes the whole world tremble finally trembles himself in front of his mother – his only consistency being that of a substitute object, of a 'mother's phallus', a fetish that fills an irredeemable lack.[14]

Here we touch upon the Real of the fantasy: the fantasy stands in the place of an impossible Real, a void which it disguises and discloses in one and the same gesture. This is why fantasy is never simply a 'hallucinatory satisfaction of desire', as it has frequently been described. It contains an evocation of the lack which organizes and supports desire. It does not simply procure a phantasmic object to satisfy desire, it enables the subject to assume any desire at all. There is a strange loop, a circularity of fantasy: it itself fills the lack which it itself opens up and perpetuates. It opens it by filling it, and can fill it only by constantly evoking it. In a sense, one could say that the fantasy is its own constant 'surpassing', 'traversing', 'going beyond'.[15]

What is beyond fantasy? So far we have treated fantasy as a source of enjoyment and a support of desire – that which 'frames' and canalizes it. But Lacan also says: 'For desire is a defence, a prohibition against going beyond a certain limit in *jouissance*' (Lacan, 1989, p. 322).[16] So fantasy itself, paradoxically, while it procures enjoyment, can ultimately be seen as a defence against it. It is a way of sustaining the Other without a lack, and of keeping enjoyment at bay. It fills the lack in the Other, which it cannot do without eliciting it in the same gesture, thus rendering it sustainable. It 'domesticates' enjoyment and makes it bearable. So when the phantasmic framework crumbles and the lack in the Other appears – at the end of analysis – this can indeed result only in 'subjective destitution', the annihilation of the very subject of desire, and in the emergence of another reality, that of the drive (ultimately, the death drive). So the fantasy can procure enjoyment only by keeping at a distance, by providing the screen against the impossible Real, thus keeping the subject and his or her desire in an ambiguous in-between state: 'But we must insist that *jouissance* is forbidden to him who speaks as such, although it can only be said between the lines for whoever is subject of the Law, since the Law is grounded in this very prohibition' (Lacan, 1989, p. 319).

In so far as one is a speaking being, one must renounce enjoyment, yet it is only the supposition of enjoyment that allures the subject into speaking at all, and can offer the frail and elusive share of enjoyment which a speaking being may be allotted, between the lines, in his or her very subjection. It is through the supposition of the enjoyment of the Other that the subject may get his or her share of enjoyment, but if there is enjoyment of the Other, it can be brought about only through the subject's renunciation. The paradox of belief is thus that if I am to get enjoyment, I have to renounce it. This renunciation can give consistency to the phantasmic enjoyment of the Other (according to the economy which rules the flow of enjoyment), and even this part can be taken care of by the fantasy itself. The subject who is pinned to this fantasy does not have either to believe or to renounce himherself; one can delegate one's belief and one's renunciation to others: the despot's no less phantasmic subjects. Those subjects, the necessary counterparts in the despotic fantasy, those Asian peoples deprived of individuality and prepared to annihilate themselves before the despot, are the ones who supposedly 'really' believe and 'really' renounce. This is the handy and comfortable aspect of this fantasy: as a European subject, I don't have to pawn my own belief and offer any sacrifice; others do it for me; the fantasy takes care of it. I believe that they believe. One can believe by proxy – it is enough that one extends one's belief only to someone who is supposed to 'really' believe. 'The subject supposed to enjoy'[17] is thus complementary to a 'subject supposed to believe'; the one relies on the other. So we do not naively believe in the despot's enjoyment, all the panoply of the seraglio, and so on; it is enough that we believe that somewhere, in some distant Asian land, there are people who are naive enough to believe. An immediate belief in the Other and its enjoyment would probably entail psychosis, so this delegated belief can maintain my subjectivity, and at the same time it enables the belief to bypass censorship and retain practical effectiveness. My own unconscious belief is preserved by being delegated; it is repressed by the mediation of a proxy. So the phantasmic mechanism can trap the subject by enabling him or her to retain freedom, disbelief and autonomy, in sharp contrast with Asian slavery and blind subjection.

It seems that Hegel comes close to some aspects of the despotic fantasy with his notorious dialectic of master and servant, which presents some striking analogies: he constructs a phantasmic scenario of a life-and-death struggle, where the one who is prepared unreservedly to risk his own life for freedom can become master, whereas the other – who, in the face of death, rather chooses his life deprived of freedom – becomes the servant. In this cellular social organization, the first is allotted enjoyment, while the other's lot is labour and renunciation. Obviously, this scenario never happened as a historical event, yet one can retroactively reconstruct it as a phantasmic reality which has determinable effects. It is designed to explain, at a single elegant stroke, the genesis of self-consciousness and the genesis of work, along with the genesis of domination and 'ideology' as its 'internalization'. The phantasmic scenario has 'always-already' had to happen to have such consequences, though it is a purely logical reconstruction. There is a strange reversal of the Marxist perspective, in which domination and ideology result from a certain stage of the development of 'labour forces' (the division of labour, private property, etc.), while for Hegel they are the presupposition of the work process as such, the work being the result of a relation of domination which precedes it. Labour, as a relation of subject to object, the shaping of nature, presupposes a certain structure of relationship between subjects and a certain 'ideology': the servant's acceptance of domination. For Hegel, it is thus necessary to account for labour on the basis of domination, not the other way round. Work, at its core, depends on a fantasy. If anyone is to engage in work, he has to be already endowed with fantasy.

Intersections with the fantasy of despotism immediately 'strike the eye': the distribution of power and goods: one produces goods for the other, the stream of goods runs only one way; the economy of enjoyment: all enjoyment belongs to one, but mediated only by the restraint of the other; renunciation on one side produces enjoyment on the other.

Yet this analogy falls short, and can best serve to show how the fantasy in psychoanalysis differs from the Hegelian one. It may well be that the servant's renunciation is the precondition of the master's enjoyment, but the flow is paradoxically reversed: the master's enjoyment (or rather, the hypothesis of the master's enjoyment) becomes the support of the servant's enjoyment. The renunciation gives consistency to the master's enjoyment, but in the same gesture the servant gets his share of enjoyment as well. One could even say that in psychoanalysis the flow is one-way in the opposite direction: the servant gets both the hard work and the enjoyment, while the poor master, after the heroic beginning of intrepidly staking his life, is increasingly lost in dumb and effete pleasure – which is, after all, the very opposite of enjoyment; and becomes the very opposite of a master, an effeminate impotent creature – like the despot.

This reverse flow of enjoyment is the basis of Lacan's criticism of the Hegelian master–servant model:

> The work to which the slave is subjected and the enjoyment that he renounces out of fear of death, we are told, will be precisely the way through which he will achieve freedom. There can be no more obvious lure than this, politically or psychologically. *Jouissance* comes easily to the slave, and it will leave the work in bondage. [*La jouissance est facile à l'esclave et elle laissera le travail serf.*] (Lacan, 1989, p. 308)

The servant assumes that the master's enjoyment is what prevents him from being himself, but the real obstacle ultimately turns out to be his own enjoyment. This is the source of his internal self-blockage, and of his servitude – he is subject to his enjoyment, in both senses of the word. He gets his share of enjoyment easily – precisely because of his footing in fantasy. We started by treating the master–servant story as a sort of Hegelian fantasy, but it is more correct to say that it is rather, a framework which situates fantasy. Fantasy is to be placed on the side of the servant – and its kernel is precisely the master as 'the subject supposed to enjoy'. So if for Hegel renunciation (work) and enjoyment are opposed, for psychoanalysis they endorse each other: the renunciation of enjoyment yields the surplus enjoyment supported by fantasy. On the one hand the enjoyment is infinitely deferred (the servant waiting for the death of the master finally to get his share of enjoyment),[18] but on the other hand it is what the subject 'always-already' gets, or something one cannot get rid of, no matter how hard one tries to renounce it – and this will be the tenuous stuff which will suffice to maintain domination. Waiting to enjoy, the servant enjoys.

This is why the fantasy of despotism shows a different mechanism from the struggle between master and servant. The Hegelian model presents a choice: Hegel's master is prepared to choose death rather than a life of servitude, while the servant, fearing death, clings to the unfree life.[19] But for the subjects of despotism this dilemma does not apply: they are prepared to choose both death and servitude. The astonishing feature of despotism is that the subjects willingly accept a life deprived of freedom and, with equal devotion and equanimity, accept death. The despot's whim is justification enough; hence the proverbial fanaticism of the Muslim army. Their honour is to sacrifice both honour and life. They do not embrace servitude out of fear of death; they do not cling to their life and enjoyment, but attain supreme enjoyment in renouncing both. If Hegel's servant gave up something in order to retain something, the subjects of despotism give up everything to get nothing in return – except that elusive phantasmic bit of enjoyment. If Hegel's master staked everything and thus became master, the despot does not have to stake or sacrifice anything, he still becomes master. The fear of death which gave authority to the master does not count here: the subjects are strangely more free of it than the despot. Their voluntary submission seems to be purely gratuitous, an act of love. The economy fails.[20]

The clue to the paradox is no doubt in another kind of economy than the Hegelian one, the economy of enjoyment outlined above: the supposed enjoyment of the Other sustained by the constant abasement of the subjects, which turns out to be the support of a paradoxical surplus enjoyment, the delegated permanent sacrifice and the delegated belief that the mediated structure of fantasy takes care of it – it is only by this mediation, by a double supposition – a double disclaimer, as it were – that this fantasy can be upheld in the midst of modern society, and the despotism in its bosom maintained.

One may think that the fantasy of despotism, displayed in such a bare and naive form at the time of the Enlightenment, at the dawn of our fundamental social and subjective structures, is obsolete today, in so far as we have access to better information which restrains and curbs the fantasy. This is obviously not so. New impersonations easily spring up, from the more extreme cases of the Chinese Cultural Revolution, Gaddafi's Libya and Khomeini's Iran to the general persistent depiction of the Arabs, 'Muslim fundamentalism', the bizarre habits of the Japanese, and so on, the still unfathomable Oriental Other. Said has impressively shown how supposedly factual historical and present-day information continues to be highly biased, imbued with tacit presuppositions of Orientalism, and how the media, while divulging information, are continually providing new fuel for fantasy rather than dissipating it. The age of despotism is still our own age. The achievement of Grosrichard's book is to lay bare the very roots of this mechanism.

PART I
A Genealogy of the Monster

1

The Unnameable Threat

From the end of the seventeenth century and all through the eighteenth, a spectre was haunting Europe: the spectre of *despotism*. All the intellectual forces in France – whether they were defending the rights that its 'pure blood' conferred on the ancient nobility, with its claims to origins in the Teutonic forests,[1] or whether they dreamed instead of a society in keeping with the principles of a new political law where the people would be sovereign and free – all of them came together in a 'crusade to run this spectre to ground'. Whether they were nostalgic for the past or were builders of the future, all of them saw the *Absolute One* as the instrument of an always deadly uniformity – in the one case because it was a kind of levelling, in the other because it was a kind of servitude. In the eyes of the old nobility, the access of the bourgeois class to high office and the frenzy of ennoblements accorded to their new wealth – which, since Colbert's day, had become intolerable – had corrupted the royal function; it played off these posturing lackeys against its more venerable allies, its blood brothers, annihilating the true natural hierarchy in a specious uniformity.[2] On the other hand, a bourgeoisie which prides itself on being enlightened regards the upholding of privileges and the ordering of things that maintains them as aspects of an arbitrary condition which asserts itself with all the more arrogance the more it feels threatened. Thus from each side come accusations of being the servants of the monster which all of

3

them proclaim they abhor in the guise of despotism. And probably, on the one side and on the other, this is right.

Lexicon

The noun *despotism* entered the language fairly late. The first dictionary to refer to it is Trévoux's, in 1721. The dictionary of the Académie Française included it in its 1740 edition, defining it as 'absolute authority, absolute power', adding: 'despotism finds a place in States that long prevail'. In 1771, Trévoux's dictionary was to note that the term was by then more current than 'despoticity', giving a fuller and more precise definition: this was a

> form of government in which the sovereign is absolute master, with limitless authority and arbitrary power, having no other law but his will. Thus is the government of Turkey, of the Mogul, of Japan, Persia and almost all of Asia. The principle, the character and the evils incurred by despotism have been well enough elaborated by the best of our writers.

In fact – like de Jaucourt in the Encyclopaedia – the author of the article had Montesquieu principally in mind. Indeed, it was *The Spirit of Laws*, in 1748, which gave the term its theoretical accreditation as the name for a form of government, illustrating the concept with the example of the governments of Asia.

Let us observe, however, that the adjective *despotic* (and the adverb *despotically*) had already been in general use for a long time. We encounter it, for example, in Chapter 10 of La Bruyère's *Caractères*;[3] and ever since the Fronde – and even more so since the revocation of the Edict of Nantes – it had been used to describe the abuses of royal power of which the Sun King was guilty. But although the term *despotic* increasingly prevailed as a description of these abuses, and while the debate about the term and the idea of *despotic power* which was initiated during the period of the minority of Louis XIV assumed so much significance, the fact is

4

that the word insinuates that it is the essence of monarchy itself which is being called into question and, with it, the deepest springs of power, the reasons for which a people willingly bends to the absolute authority of one man.

When La Bruyère writes: 'to call a king Father of the people is not so much to praise him as to call him by his name, or to define him',[4] he is recalling the fundamental principle of a doctrine long held by the theoreticians of absolute monarchy (and reaffirmed by Bossuet in his *Politique tirée des propres paroles de l'Écriture sainte*): the source and legitimacy of royal power stem from the natural authority, established by God, which a father exercises over his children, and which entails mutual duties. Now it is precisely because royal power is rooted in domestic power that its abuse can be denounced by describing it as *despotic*. For the Greeks, what indeed was the despot if not, to be precise, the 'father of a family', as Voltaire would remind Montesquieu, who seemed to have forgotten this? Again we must make ourselves clear: if 'despotic' power is in its origins the power of the father of a family, this power, Aristotle explains, is *despotic* only inasmuch as it is exercised not over the children or the wife, but over the slaves. When we speak of the *despotic* power of the King of France we thereby preserve the essentially domestic nature of his power, which likens him to the father of a family. But we denounce him precisely as an unnatural father, in that he confuses his children (the people) with slaves. Moreover, to define the King as 'Father of the people' does not suffice; we also need to determine what a father is and what a child is, and what are their real relations, their mutual rights and duties, and how this specifically paternal power is distinguished from the power of the husband over the wife or that of the master over his slaves or servants. These were all questions which the eighteenth century would keep on probing, reinterrogating the old categories of authority, might and mastery. We shall see later how, from the end of the seventeenth century onwards, critiques were developed and applied linking the arbitrary nature of royal absolutism and new ideas about the family, and how representations of the function of the father and the king, of educator and legislator, and so on, would be modified in relation to one another, and even, to a large extent, *by* one another. Let us only stress here that with regard to these terms, *despot, despotic, despotism*, an extraordinary semantic reversal takes place. What originally had significance only in the domestic and private sphere comes initially to be used to describe the abuses and perversions of a royal power which is itself likened to paternal power. But when Montesquieu introduced the noun *despotism*, he was designating a specific form of political government: the 'domestic' was thereby definitively 'politicized'. At a stroke, the domestic category would cease to serve as a model for conceiving of the political, and the converse would be the case. Rousseau, for example, talks about 'the iniquitous despotism of fathers',[5] using a blatantly political concept in a figurative sense. The *Dictionnaire de l'Académie*, in its 1798 edition, would note that the term *despotism* 'is used to speak figuratively of authority that is assumed over men and things'. Thus we can say that 'the father establishes the greatest *despotism* in his house, over all his servants'.

What a strange path for meaning to take, becoming 'figurative' when, at the end of the eighteenth century, the head of a family is spoken of as a *despot*, whereas this was originally its only true meaning, and, according to Aristotle, every usage of the words *despot* or *despotic* in the political arena could be only by analogy, and inappropriate. But in this semantic chiasmus there is much more than a linguistic curiosity. Before interrogating the spectre that despotism was for the men of the eighteenth century, it is well worth going back to the terrain of its theoretical origins: Aristotle's *Politics*. This is in fact where the monster had its genesis, and there too it was endowed with the aspect under which it would reappear, at the dawn of the Classical era.

'ΑΡΧΗ ΔΕΣΠΟΤΙΚΗ

There are some people who would have it, writes Aristotle at the beginning of his *Politics*, that the power of the office-bearer (πολιτιχόν), of a king (βασιλικόν), of a household head (οἰκονομικόν) and of a master (δεσποτικόν)is one and the same power; this is to suppose that the difference between these powers is merely that of numbers, with no difference in kind (εἴδει). The whole of Book I of the *Politics* will set out to make a critique of this point of view, and to establish a real difference between these four types of powers. This is not the place to pursue Aristotle's analysis in detail. Let us, however, observe that if these four powers are specifically distinct from one another, they can be grouped two by two: that of the king and the office-bearer, which belong in the arena of *politics*; and that of the head of household and the master, which are exercised in the realm of what Aristotle designates as the *domestic*. But we can be inclined to compare them two by two in another way: what the royal power is to the power of the office-bearer (properly *political* power) is like the power of the master (*despotic* power) in relation to the power of the head of household. This analogy – which we have put forward, and shall interrogate – probably contains the seed of a great many of the problems which Aristotle's political theory must resolve, and with him as a starting point.

What is a master?

We see it taking shape at the point where Aristotle analyses the three forms of power of the head of the family, which is the social group fundamentally constitutive of the State. If these three powers are based upon a natural order and purpose, we can, however, compare them to the forms of political power. Thus the father of the family is the father of his children, and his authority therein is comparable with that of a king over his subjects, because the reasoning of children is still imperfect (ἀτελές). He is the husband of his wife, and his power in this resembles that of the aristocratic man of state over his fellow citizens, whose will and reasoning carry no force (ἄκυρον), like those of women. Lastly, he is the master (δεσπότηζ) of his slaves, and his power is despotic. We can see that the use of the political comparison is valid in the first two cases, but not in the third.

First of all, the fact is that there are relations of political power only in the City, which is a community of free men. And it is over free persons that the powers of the father and the husband, like those of the king and the man of state, are exercised, while despotic power is that of a free man over a person who, in the nature of things, is deprived of freedom.

Moreover, this political power – one in keeping with the principles of a just (ὀρθός) government – must always have as its goal the common interest of those governed, while 'rule of master over slave is exercised primarily for the benefit of the master and only incidentally for the benefit of the slave'.[6] 'That one should command and another obey is both necessary and expedient'.[7] It is nature which decrees that the living creature endowed with reasoning should command as master, and that the living creature who is able to carry out orders only by virtue of his bodily faculties should obey as a slave. To say that the interest of the slave coincides with the interest of the master only 'accidentally' does not, however, mean that the master ought not to concern himself at all with the interest of the slave, and that he may abuse his power with impunity, 'for the part and the whole, the soul and the body, have identical interests; and the slave is in a sense a part of his master, a living but separate part of his body'.[8] But this common interest is achieved only if each behaves exactly in accordance with the wishes of nature: 'she recognizes different functions and lavishly provides different tools, not an all-purpose tool like the Delphic knife; for every instrument will be made best if it serves not many purposes but one'.[9]

To say that a person is a master or a slave *by nature*, Aristotle adds, is to say that *knowledge* plays no part in the distinction: "Ὁ μεν οὖν δεσπότης οὐ λέγεται κατ᾽ ἐπιστήμην, ἀλλά τῷ τοιόσδ ᾽εἶναι.᾽ ('A man is not called master in virtue of what he knows but simply in virtue of the kind of person he is').[10] In other words, there is no need to learn in order to be a master, nor to learn how to be one, and the same goes for the slave. Doubtless one can learn how to command or obey – that is to say: learn or perfect the techniques of exercising these functions. But this knowledge of technique is in no way formative of the difference, and this difference cannot be effaced by its presence or its absence. It is altogether different from that form of authority 'exercised over men who are free, and similar in birth. This we call rule by a statesman (ἀρχὴ πολιτική)'.[11] In this case a man commands only because he is in possession of knowledge, and he learns to be a leader first through having learned to obey:

> It is this that a ruler must first learn through being ruled just as one learns to command cavalry by serving under a cavalry commander.... This too is a healthy saying, namely that it is not possible to be a good ruler without first having been ruled.[12]

There is a kind of inherent reversibility in political power which thus distinguishes it radically from despotic power, where 'the master has no necessity to know more than how to *use* such labour'.[13] If the master does possess knowledge, therefore, it is a 'knowing how to profit':

> A master's knowledge consists in knowing how to put his slaves to *use*, for it is not in his acquiring of slaves but in his use of them that he is master. But the use of slaves is not a form of knowledge that has any great importance or dignity, since it consists in knowing how to direct slaves to do the tasks which they ought to know how to do. Hence those masters whose means are sufficient to exempt them from the bother employ an overseer to take on this duty, while they devote themselves to statecraft or philosophy.[14]

Despotic domination is therefore all the more clearly to be seen as the master rids himself of all involvement in the work of the slaves, up to and including its management. This can go so far as his being master only in his absence, delegating the tasks of organization, supervision, and even punishment to a lieutenant.[15] The supreme figure of freedom is thus associated with the supreme capacity for deriving enjoyment, which is also to say enjoyment of what is supreme (this is the famous subject that opens the *Metaphysics*): engaging in philosophy or politics, even as an ordinary citizen. To the extent, as we know, that manual workers will be deemed unworthy of being citizens, because without the *leisure* to exercise and develop their minds, they are unfit.

In the domestic despot, Aristotle defines a figure and a structure of mastery based on what the ordering of all his political theory opposes. Having thus specified something like a relation of pure, absolute and natural power, he supplies himself, as we shall see, with the means to conceive of the gap, in the political domain, between just government and deviant government. But most of all he opens the way to what, for the mind of the Classical age, would be regarded only as a spectre. Of course, in Aristotle domination of this kind is taken for granted. A man is master because of 'the kind of person he is', because that is how nature would have it. But when, refusing to allow that there can be a natural order of masters and slaves, one none the less attempts to understand *why* they can exist, and above all why the relation of master to slave seems so *natural* – why it is so easy to be a master without the need to use force, or a slave without being subjugated by fear – and therefore why despotism is so formidable, explanations will necessarily have to be sought elsewhere. 'Let us then seek by conjecture, if such we can find, how it is that having rooted this stubborn will to serve, it should seem now that the very love of liberty is not so natural', La Boétie was to write in 1576. How can this come about? What name are we to give to what blinds men to such an extent that they seem *naturally* to serve those who have the semblance of masters? What – if it is no longer nature in the Aristotelian sense, which creates each individual for a single function – makes them play what is now no more than a role, but a role which clings to their skin?

Oh God in heaven! What can this be? What name are we to say it has? What evil is this? What vice, or rather what unhappy vice? To see an infinite number of persons not just obeying, but serving . . . with their necks beneath the yoke, no longer constrained by a greater power, but in no way (it seems) bewitched and charmed by the name of one alone?

10

We can no longer call it cowardice: 'What monster of vice can this be which is undeserving even of the name of cowardice, for which no name is vile enough, whose making nature disowns and which language refuses to name?'[16] In La Boétie's poignant idiom, in the ardour of these questions asked in the face of a shocking proof, we can already feel all the turmoil of the philosophers who were to come after him when they were confronted with what political theory has unceasingly rejected, refused to think of as political, which might well be something stronger than strength, something more seductive than ideology, more enticing than gain – the very source of political power: love.

King and tyrant: a pure politics

> From all this it is clear that there is a difference between the rule of master over slave and the rule of a statesman. All forms of rule are not the same, though some say that they are. Rule over naturally free men is different from rule over natural slaves.[17]

It will therefore only be inaccurately that we can speak of a despotic political power. Aristotle does, however, use the term 'despotic government', but by analogy and to designate a deviation (ἔκβασις) from governments which are 'correct in terms of absolute justice' (κατὰ τὸ ἁπλῶς δίκαιον). Thus tyranny, a deviation from royalty, oligarchy, from aristocracy, and democracy, from the republic (πολιτεία), are all forms of despotism, because those who hold power, whatever their number, seek, like the domestic master, only their own good, even if their subjects might profit from it accidentally: 'For tyranny is monarchy for the benefit of the monarch, oligarchy for the benefit of the men of means, democracy for the benefit of the men without means. None of the three aims to be of profit to the common interest.'[18]

Of these three forms of despotic deviation, tyranny is none the less the worst, for it combines the vices of democracy with those of oligarchy. We recognize in Aristotle's picture of tyranny the image

that will later be formed of despotism, despised alike by the
defenders of privileges and by the upholders of the people's
sovereignty:

> From oligarchy it [tyranny] derives two things: (1) the notion of wealth
> as the end to be pursued (certainly wealth is essential to it, as it provides
> the only way of keeping up a bodyguard and a luxurious way of living),
> and (2) mistrust of the populace . . . . From democracy is derived
> hostility to the notables, whom the tyrant brings low by open methods
> or secret, and sends into exile as being rivals and hindrances to his
> rule.[19]

But if tyranny thus combines all the vices, it does so 'fatally',
according to Aristotle, for it has deviated from the first and most
godly form, which is kingship. As if one could fall only from one
extreme into another, the power of a single man being either the
best or the worst of things.

Now it is here that all the ambiguities arise – ambiguities from
which Aristotle fails to extricate himself, and which are the
probable origin of all the debates which will thereafter be engaged
about the relationship between kings and despots, and of all the
shaky theoretical compromises which will be thought of, up to and
including the 'legal despotism' of the physiocrats, which Rousseau
would condemn as a conceptual monstrosity.[20]

The real question is this: should the most perfect and purest
form of kingship be regarded as the exercise of a *political* power,
in keeping with the principles of correct government? If we define
political power as power which is exercised only in the interest of
the ruled, then the power of the king is political, and we possess a
solid criterion for distinguishing it from the power of the tyrant:

> But a tyrant, as has often been said, does not look to the public interest
> at all, unless it happens to contribute to his personal benefit. The
> tyrant's aim is pleasure: the king aims at what is good. Hence they
> differ even in the advantages they seek: the tyrant grasps at wealth, the
> king at honour.[21]

12

But for Aristotle this kind of kingship appears unrealizable, unless the king is God himself, for no human soul would be able to free itself from passions. Hence the old question already asked by Plato: 'whether it is more expedient to be ruled by the best man or by the best laws'.[22]

Aristotle debates this at length in Book III, and does not solve the dilemma:

> Therefore he who asks laws to rule is asking God (τὸν θεόν) and intelligence (τὸν νοῦν) and no others to rule; while he who asks for the rule of a human being is importing a wild beast too; for desire is like a wild beast, and anger perverts rulers and the very best of men. Hence law is intelligence without appetition (ἄνευ ὀρέξεως νοῦς ὁ νόμος ἐστιν).[23]

– and to forestall objections here, he takes the example of medicine and the argument that 'it is a bad thing to practise medicine according to written rules'. The doctor acts unquestionably for the good of the patient, in the knowledge that he will be paid only once good health is re-established; while the man in power has nothing more to gain by not causing harm.

Yet in these same pages, and several times over, Aristotle rails against the laws which prevent the disproportionate growth of power by an outstanding man in the City. Doubtless, he says, such laws (like the Athenian practice of ostracism) are useful within deviant regimes, but they cannot be so in absolute terms. If there are one or more individuals:

> whose virtue is so outstanding as to outstrip that of all the rest, then it becomes just that this family should be royal and sovereign over all things, and that this one man should be king.... For while the part is not naturally superior to the whole, yet superiority is exactly the position of one so outstandingly excellent as I have described. There is therefore nothing for it but to obey such a man and accept him as sovereign, not in alternation but absolutely.[24]

There are therefore men whose innate qualities prevail to the point where they seem born always to command. Now this is

13

clearly one of the characteristics of the despotic master. Indeed, a king of this kind will not be a despot, since he will think only of the common good.[25] But he will be a despot in the sense that between him and his subjects there is a *de facto* inequality, that he is *different* by nature, and most of all that his power is neither the other side of nor the recompense for a knowledge of how to obey. Everything takes place as if genuinely kingly authority were not *political*, if one defines political authority – as Aristotle did when he contrasted it with despotic authority – as that 'exercised over men who are free, and similar in birth'.[26]

Might it then be that the most excellent kingship and the worst tyranny are two forms of despotism? It certainly appears that the model of the despotic master, who rules by nature, is applicable in each of these two cases. Of the one, Aristotle says: do not let the laws reduce the man who is born to rule to the level of the ordinary citizen, do not foolishly erase an inequality that is so clear: 'it would be improper that such a man should be put to death or exiled or ostracized or required to be ruled over in his turn'.[27] In the other case, he denounces the tyrant's claim for recognition of this natural superiority, whose outcome is to reduce the city of free men and equal citizens to a private household where a single man rules as master of his slaves, without any acquired knowledge playing the least part in this power:

> Those on the other hand who are greatly deficient in these qualities are too subservient. So they do not know how to rule, but only how to be ruled as a slave is; while the others do not know how to be ruled in any way at all, and can command only like a master ruling over slaves.[28]

Of course it can be said that the consent of all, founded on the evidence that the man who rules them truly serves their common good, is what makes the true king. Whereas an 'extreme' tyranny, which corresponds (ἀντίστροφος) to absolute kingship, is one where

> any sole ruler, who is not required to give an account of himself, and who rules over subjects all equal or superior to himself to suit his own

interest and not theirs, can only be exercising a tyranny . . . for no one
willingly submits to such rule if he is a free man.[29]

But in fact, when Aristotle examines the means tyranny employs to
set itself up and be maintained, he shows that it never takes this
monstrous form where the inferior would rule the superior.

In reality, the tyrant's actions are of two types, both leading to
the installation of that natural inequality proposed by the model
of domestic despotism: the tyrant can either debase his subjects or
elevate himself.

In the first case, the tyrant will weaken the spirits of his subjects
(for an impoverished spirit could not rise up against him), sow
distrust among them (for tyranny cannot be overthrown while no
one trusts anyone else) and render them powerless to act (for no
one undertakes the impossible).[30] To weaken, divide and disarm:
these are sure methods, as we still know very well today, of
transforming free men inclined to rebellion into docile slaves, and
at one and the same time assuming domination.

The other system uses almost opposing methods: here what the
tyrant does is set himself up as a superior, simultaneously reducing
his subjects to subservience, and 'in his every real or pretended act
he must be adept at playing in the role of a king'.[31] For example:

in his dealings he should always give the impression of dignity, not of
harshness, of being the kind of person who inspires not fear but respect
in those who meet him . . . . Neither he nor any of his entourage should
be seen to violate any of his youthful subjects, male or female'

– and should appear 'as someone who moreover makes friends
with the notables but is also the people's leader'. The theatrics of
morality, of sexual order, of paternalism – these are the tools of
every variety of fascism. But just as the first methods genuinely
transformed free men into slaves, here too the tyrant is genuinely
elevated, at least in part. To achieve his ends, indeed, 'he himself
will have either the right disposition or at least a half-good disposition with respect to virtue, a man not wicked but half-wicked'.[32]

It seems, therefore, that there is no such thing as *pure* tyranny, since in order to match the despotic model (this *de facto* power independent of all knowledge, and exercised for the sole good of the master) the tyrant must employ methods which in themselves remove him from it. In order to transform his subjects into slaves, he must deploy a whole science of power whose absence is what accurately distinguishes the master, and in order to elevate himself he must play the part of the good king, which compels him in part to serve the common good and to be only half-wicked. No more than kingship exists as the figure of pure political power does its converse, extreme tyranny, exist as pure despotic power. These two seem like positive and negative poles towards which political regimes incline, in either perfection or degradation. Each of them shares in the essence of the political, which is never actual, but always potential, kingship or despotism.

We can understand why, in Aristotle's eyes, the best *possible* government will be aristocracy, which maintains the happy medium in everything. But above all we can understand why, when he lists the forms of kingship in Book III, Aristotle cannot but also list what in Book IV he will recognize as forms of tyranny.

The Asiatic alibi – the purely apolitical

Alongside the 'absolute kingship' of the ancient Greeks' *aisymnetes* or the Spartan rule of generals, he cites the kingships of certain barbarians:

> All these have power approximating to that of tyrannies, but they are legally established and ancestral. For it is because Non-Greeks are by natural character more slavish than Greeks (and the Asiatics than the Europeans) that they tolerate master-like rule without resentment.[33]

Thus there are countries where men are slaves *by nature.* Aristotle speaks of them as 'kingships' because laws exist, as do blood heredity and the consent of subjects, but fundamentally the barbarians of Asia are at home only with servitude. All this was already made plain in Book I, which presented the barbarian as a slave by nature ("ταὐτὸ φύσει βάρβαρον καὶ δοῦλον ὄν") – a way of illustrating his remark on this nature which is not slavish and makes tools fit for one single use. Among the barbarians there are no distinct kinds of power such as one has to observe among the Greeks. They can know only one type of power: despotism. And Aristotle must regard Asiatic kingships as merely thinly veiled tyrannies for him to acknowledge that 'it is proper that Greeks should rule non-Greeks'.

But he has in mind first and foremost the *Asiatic* barbarians, as confirmed in Book VIII where, examining the influence of climate on political differences, he contrasts the peoples of the north of Europe and those of Asia; in the north they are full of spirit, but lack ingenuity; they are therefore able to preserve their freedom, but unable ever to dominate others: 'On the other hand the Asiatic nations have in their souls both intellect and skill, but are lacking in spirit; so they remain enslaved and subject.' This is why the Hellenic race, occupying the happy medium, and therefore possessing both spirit and keenness of mind, is called – if it is politically united – to dominate the world while remaining free.[34]

Here, therefore, is a place – Asia – where all political power seems to be reduced to an appearance thinly masking a despotism willed by nature. Despotism *in the strict sense*, and no longer by analogy, as if the Asiatic peoples were unfit to accede to a *political* regime, and had to be confined eternally to domestic relationships. While their only fate, thereby in keeping with their natural destiny, is to yield to the Greek master, in whose service they will find their best interest, albeit only 'accidentally'.

This Asia of Aristotle will by now be recognizable as the one which Europe was to reinvent with the Classical age and the onset of colonization. After centuries of oblivion or indifference, by what routes and for what motives did an Asia that was none the less profoundly different from that of the fourth century BC, and also better known, come to be sought out and found wearing the countenance with which the Greek philosopher had endowed it for his own expediency? And in the first place, by what obscure path did Aristotle's ἀρχὴ δεσποτικὴ travel through the language in order to re-emerge in the seventeenth century, Gallicized as *pouvoir despotique*, despotic power, to become *despotism*, that noun which Montesquieu would impose upon his century?

On this final point, we shall confine ourselves to a few observations: the Middle Ages, which had first used the Latin equivalent of the Greek term, eventually Latinized the Greek word as *despoticus*. But when Marsiglio of Padua or William of Occam contrasted the *principatus regalis* with the *principatus despoticus*, they had in mind the Roman pontiff, not the Oriental despot. Both Oresme, translating Aristotle's *Politics* into French (1489), and Jean Bodin, in the *Six Livres de la République* (1576), offer as an equivalent of the Aristotelian ἀρχὴ δεσποτικὴ the term *pouvoir seigneurial* (feudal/baronial power), contrasting kingly monarchy with a monarchy of feudal rights. Bodin writes:

> Kingly monarchy is one where the subjects obey the laws of the monarch, and the monarch obeys the laws of nature, with freedom remaining as a natural property of the subjects. The monarchy of feudal rights is one where the prince becomes lord and master of things and persons by force of arms and victory in war, ruling his subjects as does the father of a household his slaves.[35]

But there is a third form of kingship – tyrannical kingship – 'where the monarch, scorning the laws of nature, abuses free persons as if they were slaves, and the property of his subjects as if it were his own'. For Bodin, ἀρχὴ δεσποτικὴ or 'baronial kingship' is therefore not the worst form of unlawful kingship. In it the king remains 'the father of the family'; as in Aristotle, he has his slaves' interest at heart – unlike the tyrant, who has no rule other than his capricious will, and no goal other than his own ends.

From Bodin to Montesquieu, from the end of the sixteenth century to the middle of the eighteenth, 'despotic power' will become gradually muddled with what Bodin designates as 'tyrannical kingship' to become the form of extreme political corruption. The two will even change places in the end; thus, for Rousseau, the tyrant retains some appearance of legitimacy, and is roughly equivalent to Bodin's baronial king, while the despot assumes the aspect of the tyrannical king.[36]

Now, the history of the term and the idea it covers is inseparable from that of the State which, from the sixteenth century onwards, provided their illustration: the Ottoman Empire. It was to the Grand Turk that Bodin's contemporary readers turned when they sought out an example of baronial kingship. People still had him in mind when, in the seventeenth century, 'despotic power' began to be talked of in the clearly Gallicized version of the Greek term. And finally – as the supreme representative of the regimes of Asia – he it was whom Montesquieu had as his target when, in the *Spirit of Laws*, he introduced the noun 'despotism' to designate a specific form of government.

The Eye of Asia

The Turk had been a vague source of terror ever since the Crusades. But with the taking of Byzantium on 2 April 1453 by Mehmet II, the Ottoman Empire set itself down at the gates of Europe, to which it would be a constant military threat for more than two centuries. For the sixteenth-century European he would be a fearsome – not to say hated – though respected enemy; he was feared for a power that derived from the courage and discipline of his armies and the burning faith that drove them. One is struck by this strong and effective regime in which political, military and religious powers were combined in the hands of a single man, the Great Lord, of whom the first Western ambassadors have sketched portraits to fire the imagination.[37] Even those who pronounce themselves horrified by a religion of which little is known, whose traditions, partly inherited from Byzantium, emerge with the most caricatured features, can still admire the tolerance which reigns in those countries conquered by the Turks at a time when Europe was torn by religious wars.[38]

'This Aesopian crow . . .'

From the seventeenth century onwards, however, things change. The external threat remains, but it is judged differently; journeys to the Levant are made more frequently, the sojourns are longer and the accounts of them which appear are increasingly numerous and better informed. Progress is made in learning the history and geography of this empire[39] and the customs of its inhabitants. Efforts are also made to understand the nature of the political regime and the sources of a power which until then had been encountered only through its external manifestations.

It is, though, a regime already in decline, and threatened from within, which travellers are in the process of discovering. While the Ottoman sultans of the sixteenth century took an active lead in the affairs of the Empire, those who were to follow them would on the whole become detached from it and would not venture from their palaces, where they would remain under the sway of women or favourites. Bloody revolts multiplied; in the course of the seventeenth century, four sultans would be deposed or assassinated. Mantran notes[40] that between January 1644 and September 1656 seventeen grand viziers would succeed one another, with only one of them dying a natural death.

At one and the same time, without ceasing to be feared, Ottoman might became an enigma. 'It is a torrent, threatening us unceasingly, which has far overflowed and is making ready to flood the whole of Europe, as it has done the greater part of Asia . . .', wrote Jean Coppin in 1665.[41] In his eyes, such savagery was justification for a new crusade, which was long overdue. Like Pierre l'Ermite before him, he addressed himself to 'all the rulers of Christendom':

> How can you suffer with untroubled spirit that a brutal and barbarous nation should insolently sully with its abominations a land honoured with the sacred relics of the son of God? . . . Providence has allowed Turks to heap victory upon victory only in order to awaken your zeal, and the same justice which has punished the sins of Christendom with

the laying waste of so many Provinces is not insensible to the voice of their iniquity which cries out unceasingly before it, and can scarce any longer delay the dreadful punishments which are merited by so many vices and impieties.[42]

In his eyes, victory is certain if the Christian princes will agree to unite and readily heed the plan of war which he is offering them. For the vaunted Ottoman might is moribund: 'it lays itself open to ruin through the vastness of its territories and the extreme nature of its tyranny'. Referring to the sultan, La Boullaye le Gouz had already written: 'the Christian princes could easily pluck this Aesopian crow, were they but willing to recognize its flaws'.[43] It seems, therefore, that the Ottoman regime maintains itself only by a miracle. It is a challenge to political reason, and its existence can be explained only as something decreed by Providence, whose will it was both to punish the Christians for their divisions and to give them the opportunity to redeem themselves by annihilating this monster. This is a theme also taken up by Ricaut at the beginning of his *Histoire de l'état présent de l'Empire Ottoman*, which would be one of Montesquieu's major sources:

When I look closely at the constitution of the government of the Turks, and I see a power that is utterly absolute in an Emperor who is without reason, virtue or merit, whose commandments, however unjust they be, are Laws; whose actions, although suspect, are exemplary; and whose judgements, especially in affairs of State, are decisions which cannot be opposed. When I consider further that among them there is so little reward for virtue, and so much impunity for vices, from which profit is rendered to the Prince; in what manner men are suddenly elevated by the flattery, the whim and the mere favour of the Sultan to the greatest, most notable and most honourable offices of the Empire, with neither birth, nor merit, nor any experiences of the affairs of the world. When I consider how short a time they remain in such eminent offices, how the Prince has them put to death in the blink of an eye; how eagerly and urgently they hasten to acquire riches, more than any of the peoples of the world, while knowing that their riches are their chains, and that they finally must be the cause of their ruin and their downfall . . . , I cannot but attribute its steadfast endurance within and the fortunate successes of its arms without more to some supernatural cause than to the wisdom of those who govern it; as if God, who does all things for the best, had aroused, raised up and upheld this mighty nation for the good of his Church and to punish the Christians for their sins and their vices.[44]

When we read this page we can tell just how much the European observer of the second half of the seventeenth century saw the Ottoman regime as having become the overriding image of political monstrosity. *Despotism* – to give this monstrosity the name which it would bear henceforth – truly is a monster in so far as, being explicable only as some transcendental plan of Providence, it stands simultaneously as the threat of punishment and as a call to order (this being, moreover, in keeping with the interpretation of monstrosity offered by a long theological tradition). But the threat it contains, for all that it is geographically close and chronologically imminent, still remains an external one. It is a threat of aggression, not of subversion. And there are ready arguments, as old as the West itself, to provide reassurance on this point. Ricaut himself writes: 'One need not be surprised that [the Turks] are happy in servitude and that they live gladly under tyranny, since for them this is as natural as it is for a body to live and to be nourished on the food to which it has been accustomed since childhood.'[45] Since it is therefore from a natural necessity that people in those parts have given themselves over to servitude, the same natural necessity which has created different conditions in Europe will preclude things from being the same among us.

'The spy at court . . .'

Very quickly, however, this external threat will appear as if it were also, and even primarily, an internal one. The security that Europe found for itself in the monstrosity of Asiatic despotism gives way to an increasingly insistent anxiety about the nature and future of

22

the monarchy – that political power to which it had laid claim as its own; the proliferating travels of ambassadors, merchants and missionaries, and the accounts of these which they published, enabled the accumulation of varied but concurring information about Oriental regimes, and attempts were made to understand them by seeking to find in them disguised or denatured versions of politico-social structures familiar in Europe. Tavernier writes, for example:

> In the State of Persia we can identify, as in almost all the states of Europe, three distinct bodies or ranks. The first is that of the sword, which corresponds to the nobility and includes the house of the King, the Khans or provincial governors and all of the army command. The second is that of the pen, which embraces those who are concerned with the law and the courts, and the third is like our Third Estate, made up of Merchants, Artisans and Labourers.[46]

Bernier and Chardin do likewise, looking for equivalents in terms and in functions, striving always for understanding by comparing the unknown with the known, and foreign conduct with familiar rules. These are ethnocentric prejudices, but they endow the differences which are brought out by analogies (statutes regarding property and the family, the role of priests, sexual relations, etc.) with the significance of possible perversions, and therefore of internal threats to the political and social system which is the point of reference.

These threats seem the more stark the more the European monarchies – the French monarchy very much so – indicate a tendency to absolutism, centralization and arbitrary rule. This is a reverse movement from the earlier one, this time impelling the example of the regimes of Asia as a reference to draw analogies with the actual state of monarchies, and to draw conclusions on the fate in store for them. As if, by learning to decipher the structures of an impossible power from the outside, Europeans were discovering that they had equipped themselves with the best key for interpreting their own present. An endoscopic fantasy, in a sense, one in which novels and drama would find an inexhaustible source.[47] The opening up of the seraglio, with its violent or unnatural amours, its mutes and eunuchs, its blind princes and veiled sultanas – a space in which pleasure and death are experienced within a time made up only of disconnected moments without duration, a master who is ever absent and everywhere present, and above all that language of silence, absurd yet supremely effective, consisting of signs which refer only to themselves: this is the stripping bare (a nudity of dream or delirium) of what the whole century fears and, perhaps, secretly desires.

It might be said that the same goes for travels among the savages of the New World, and Bougainville would also provide Diderot with the stuff of dreams. Certainly – and we shall see later how the West Indies manage eventually to meet the East Indies in the imagination. But there is at least one point where this symmetry fails: it is that we can see ourselves in the Turk or the Persian, and they can see themselves in us. But the Savage disappears, and as for us, we can no longer find ourselves upon his island.

Thus, while the despotic Orient is indeed the *Other* held up for us to see, it is also the one that *regards* us, in every sense of that word. Ever since the envoy from the Sublime Porte visited Louis XIV in 1669, the gaze of the Oriental has haunted France and Paris.[48] And this vast literary output (which keeps on growing up until the middle of the eighteenth century) is not just the mere result of fashion (or at least, it demands explanation). From the 'Turkish spy'[49] to the 'Chinese spy',[50] how many spying eyes have been imagined in order to strip us of our own secrets! Have we inquired deeply enough into the strange and complex relation that is at the root of this literature's success? An entire century took pleasure in making itself seen through what it burned to go and see; in revealing to itself the truth about its princes, its obeisances, its way of making love – in short, all its madness – through the artifice of a gaze which, it tells itself, is foreign. This gaze, which to me is other, knows more about me than I do myself. And when I attempt to go and look behind what I believe to be the point from which, over there in that other world, it looks at me, it is myself and our world that I find in the end.

2

The Concept of a Fantasy

The Secret Chain

No one made better play with this subtle trading of looks than Montesquieu, in the *Persian Letters*. Having left behind a seraglio where the artifice of epistolary exchange allows us to cast a glance as if behind their backs, Usbek and Rica, each in his different way, are able to see in the everyday life of the years 1712–1720, which they spend in France, things to which we remain blind. It has often been said of Louis XIV, observes Usbek in 1713,[1] that 'of all the types of government in the world, he would most favour either that of the Turks, or that of our own august Sultan, such is his esteem for Oriental policies'. Surprise is perhaps something these Persians experience most of all through its absence, when they finally realize that they are in a land that is familiar, and that the French king's dream is in the process of coming true before their very eyes. If 'as their stay in Europe goes on, the customs of this part of the world come to seem in their minds, less wonderful, less surprising',[2] it is because, Montesquieu implies, their eyes adapt and become Parisian. But is it not just as much that the world they see before them assumes the form of what they have always known, and that it is the French who in certain respects become Persians? While we are anticipating the dramas at Ispahan, they – who, in their shrewd innocence, are witnessing the final years of the *Grand Siècle*, the Regency, and the bankruptcy of John Law's system – are also discerning the all too clear signs of a nascent despotism: the gradual levelling of French society (letters 75, 84), the swift turns in the fortunes and power of the *nouveaux riches* (letters 98, 138), the decline of the parliaments (92, 140), of the authority of fathers (86, 129), of honour swept away by the rule of favouritism (24, 88), the rapt imitation of the Prince (99), and so on.[3]

Woven into the same complex fabric whereby the exotic becomes familiar while the habitual takes us by surprise, the philosophical satire of Parisian customs and the narration of intrigues in the seraglio are at first given mutual resonance and emphasis, bringing out the differences between an Asia that remains despotic and a France that is still monarchical. But interest in Oriental fiction and the feelings it arouses overflow in some way into the social and political analysis, colouring the latter with passionate overtones. As if, by exciting terror and pity for characters in the novel, Montesquieu had wished to find a means of provoking anxiety about the threat to a vain and unthinking epoch; here the novelist uses the technique of a musician skilled in counterpoint in order to lend drama to the reflections of the philosopher, and the philosopher uses the same technique to give an exemplary value to the twists and turns of the novel – making it possible to 'connect everything together with a secret chain which remains, as it were, invisible'.[4]

One could try to locate each link of this 'secret chain' which thus joins Paris and Ispahan, Oriental fiction and Occidental reality, novel and history, and, letter by letter, travel along it as far as that double catastrophe to which it leads. Let us confine ourselves here to its furthest reaches.

'You know that I spent a long time travelling in India', writes Usbek, who has just spent eight years in France.

There I saw a whole people, among whom magnanimity, probity, frankness and good faith have always been taken for natural qualities, suddenly changing into the most worthless of nations; I saw the disease spreading until it affected even the healthiest parts of the organism; the most virtuous men committing shameful deeds and violating the first principles of justice, on the empty pretext that they had been victims of a similar violation.[5]

This is September 1720. It is Usbek's final 'philosophical' letter, and by this time he has seen everything of the present generation in France, and 'the appalling state of nothingness to which it has committed itself',[6] and it is the last link in a historical chain which suddenly makes it plain that everything was connected from the start, and that each letter had its own place in an 'order of reasons' which was hidden but necessary.

But the work continues, and concludes with the picture of another catastrophe, this time a fictional one, which allows us a glimpse of another nothingness: the seraglio plunged into a 'terrible lamentation', where 'horror, darkness and dread rule'.[7]

These two catastrophes, although they are presented one after the other, are exactly contemporaneous.[8] Clearly, we can see nothing more than a coincidence in this. But everything invites the reader to give a meaning to this coincidence, by the setting up of a parallel between the history and the fiction: the one then becomes an encrypted allegory of the other.

At the moment when Usbek sets out the gloomy reckoning of a regency where, since the place of the too-well-loved king remains empty, power is in the hands of the 'body of lackeys' and the running of affairs is handed over to a minister, a foreigner who 'corrupts the morals of an entire nation, debases the noblest souls, sullies the prestige of high office, blots out virtue itself, and involves the highest nobility in this universal degradation'[9] – in other words, the very moment when Usbek observes that what is the essence of kingship – morality – has disappeared – his seraglio is already close to annihilation; love has given way to hatred, trust to lies, modesty and virtue to shame and all manner of foulness. Once Usbek, the beloved master, had gone, the order of the seraglio, which was upheld only by his presence, disintegrates inexorably. In his absence, all his power passes into the hands of his lieutenants, the eunuchs, who will now command his harem in his name, without which they are undoubtedly nothing, but which likewise is nothing without them; Usbek will realize this too late, and it is as an enraged but powerless despot that he will address himself to both the women and the eunuchs. In place of the firm but gentle absolute power formerly exercised by the gaze of an ever-present master, adored by the women, respected by the others, there is the mute, blind violence of the letter: 'May this letter be like a thunderbolt amidst lightning and storms!', he writes to his wives.[10] And to the First Eunuch: 'This letter gives you unlimited powers over the entire seraglio. Your commands have as much authority as my own. Let fear and terror be your companions.'[11]

The disorder which increases in the seraglio, 'in proportion to the length of Usbek's absence; that is to say as passions become more uncontrolled and love declines',[12] is the very image of the degradation of absolute power into despotic power, when the too-well-loved monarch is no longer there. This is perhaps the purpose of the secret chain which links historical analysis with the fiction of a novel in the *Persian Letters*, and gives the work's conclusion its true meaning. Fiction has the last word: it is fiction which can spill out over the present historical conjuncture, which at this point is nothing more than the corruption of monarchical morals and the vacancy of power. An imaginary link is joined to the final historical link. As if the novelist had wanted to lead us to imagine, in the features of the Oriental seraglio, a future which the historian dare not foresee.

It will be objected that it is very difficult to give serious support to the analogy sketched out here, and that the seraglio, whose inhabitants are women and eunuchs, cannot stand as an allegory of the French monarchy in decline. Undoubtedly. Admittedly, the seraglio does not have the form of a political *regime*, but if such a form is taken as a space of classification which makes it immediately readable, it is a *structure of power* which any kind of monarchical government turned corrupt will come to resemble – that is to say, when it ceases to be *moderate*, as Montesquieu will say further on.[13] That this structure assumes and imposes a rigorous economy of desire and of the relation between the sexes, that the despot rules only over a harem, through a love that is inseparable from fear and through the intermediary of castrated men, is worthy of reflection. In any case, in the *Persian Letters* Montesquieu never ceases to invite reflection. What is at stake for political power in the relation between the sexes? This will be one of the big questions openly tackled in *The Spirit of Laws*, and one which will go on being asked throughout the century – underlying the problems of population, education and the policing of morality, and so on.

On this point we shall have to interrogate the seraglio anew, in order to bring to light the hidden springs of power it encloses. But first we must inscribe it within what it is the heart of: Oriental despotism. And in order to do that, we must examine the work which gives it life within political thought: *The Spirit of Laws*. Here the literary game becomes a theoretical system, and we shall see the stark lineaments of that 'secret chain' which it pleased the author of the *Persian Letters* to conceal.

Asiatic Despotism

In gathering together the scattered, but to his mind convergent, observations of an entire generation of travellers returned from Asia,[14] Montesquieu endows this vast range of material – which is truly the stuff of all manner of dreams – with the form of concept. *Despotism*, as defined by the author of *The Spirit of Laws*, and with the *Asiatic* features which he gives to it, will be the obligatory – albeit controversial – reference for the whole of political philosophy in the second half of the eighteenth century.[15] From Rousseau to Sade, the unvarying nature of this reference can probably be explained by the rigour and depth of the system in which it is rooted, but this also has a connection with what we might call a fascination that emanates from the concept itself. What the concept of despotism enables us to think about, what is given form by it, is less the reality of a *political regime* than the ineradicable measure of the imaginary by which all *political power* is maintained. Despotism is the concept of a phantasm.

'A hideous phantom . . .'

This, at any rate, is certainly how Voltaire understood it, in reproaching Montesquieu: 'It is a delicate enough thing to seek out physical causes for governments, but one should not, above all, seek the cause of that which does not exist.'[16] In other words, it is rash enough to start with to offer climate, physical geography, and so on, as what lies behind the difference in actual forms of government. But in Montesquieu uncertainty becomes deception. Did the author – 'a man of much humour' – mean merely to jest 'by including despotism among the natural forms of government'?[17] No, he was aiming at something else: he 'made for himself a hideous phantom in order to fight against it', and at the same time fight against the regime of monarchy 'which is that of fathers in a household'.[18] As an admirer and defender of Louis XIV, Voltaire very clearly grasped the use which could be made of Oriental despotism, against what – in the eyes of a conservative nobility which was jealous of the rights it had enjoyed under the old feudal order – seemed like a perversion of the monarchy; an absurd fiction is concocted, it is proved that it exists in Asia and its horrors are laid bare with great relish, all in order to pass off a thesis which serves the reactionary ambitions of a caste attached to its privileges of blood inheritance.[19] Look where monarchy leads us when we have a Louis XIV at its head!

This is why Voltaire attacks Montesquieu simultaneously on the grounds of word, idea and evidence:

> Hitherto, this went no further than identifying two species of government, and setting down the one and the other under separate headings. Now it has gone so far as to imagine a third form of natural administration, to which has been given the name of despotic State, in which there is no other law, no other justice, but the whim of one single man.[20]

The measure of the idea's incoherence is to be found in the violence done to its etymology:

> The Greeks and then the Romans understood the Greek word *despotēs* to mean the father of a family, the head of a household . . . . It is my view that no Greek or Roman ever used the word *despotē*, or any derivation of *despotēs*, to signify a king. *Despoticus* was never a Latin word. Medieval Greeks took it into their heads in the early fifteenth century to give the name *despotēs* to Lords who were very weak, and dependent upon the power of the Turks, despots of Serbia and Walachia, who were regarded as no more than household heads. Now, the emperors of Turkey, Morocco, Hindustan and China were called despots by us; and we attach to this title the idea of a ferocious madman who heeds only his own whims; of a barbarian who has his courtesans lined up to prostrate themselves before him, and who, for entertainment, orders his satellites upon a riot of strangulation and impalement.[21]

Voltaire takes the view that this inversion of the original meaning can be explained by a distortion which is to be found in the history of the languages of nearly all nations, with the result that words 'no longer convey the same ideas that they once did'. But what happens here is that the distortion is not an innocent one; an interpretation of the word everywhere in its recent sense will ensure that 'despotism' is to be found everywhere in history, giving alleged content to an absurd concept.

For the concept of despotism, as it is understood by Montesquieu, is merely the container for an absurdity, since this would be an 'administration which would destroy itself'.[22] Despotic government does not exist, because it *cannot* exist: 'It is a great untruth that a government of this kind exists and it seems to me a great untruth that a government of this kind could exist.'[23] Therefore: 'there is no State which is despotic by nature. There is no country or nation which has told one man: "Sire, we give your gracious Majesty the power to take our women, our children, our possessions and our lives, and to have us impaled for the sake of your own pleasure and your adorable whims."'[24]

Facts, on which a claim is based to show that a regime of this kind exists and that from this one can deduce that it is possible: in other words, that the idea of it contains no contradiction – facts of this kind prove nothing. An objective perusal of the documentation furnished by the travellers, however cursory, will show that the Ottoman regime, which is taken as a model of despotism, in no way corresponds to the definition of despotism:

> The Ottoman Empire is not a monarchical government tempered by moderate customs, as France and Spain are today ... but we must not imagine that it is in every respect an arbitrary government, where the law allows the whims of a single person to sacrifice great numbers of men to his pleasure, like wild animals kept in a park for entertainment.[25]

Certainly, it is a false claim that there are no laws: 'The Koran and its approved commentaries are the laws of the Muslims, which the Sultan swears to observe.' It is a false claim that no form of private property exists there, and that all men are slaves: 'Not only are all the Turks free, but they have no distinctions of nobility between them. The only difference of standing known to them is that of employment.'[26]

It is precisely this equality, this absence of inherited privilege, Voltaire implies, that Montesquieu abhors. This is what allows him to make a distinction between monarchy and despotism: '[But] I should have liked the author, or some other writer of his weight, to have shown us clearly why nobility is the essence of monarchical government.'[27] Even if it means distorting the sense of Montesquieu's text, Voltaire here is clearly targeting the political intention of *The Spirit of Laws*: the restoration of the privileges of the old nobility.

Moreover, Voltaire's critique in no way suggests that he is aiming to defend Oriental regimes, nor even the absolutist tendencies of the French monarchy. He himself acknowledges having used the term despotism in relation to them on more than one occasion. But what he was describing, he points out, was not a *form of government* but a *way of exercising* monarchical power which can lead to abominable excesses, but these remain excesses and do not constitute a new kind of government. Montesquieu should have recognized that everything he was describing as characterizing the essence of despotism was only 'abuse of the monarchy, just as in free States, anarchy is the abuse of the Republic.'[28] A monarchy can therefore slide into despotism without thereby becoming denatured:

> I am obliged to say that what I meant by the despotism of Louis XIV was his ever-firm-handed and sometimes overextended use of his legitimate power. If on these occasions he bent the laws of the State beneath this power, for all his duty to respect them, posterity will condemn him on this point; it is not for me to judge. But I challenge anyone to show me a monarchy on earth in which laws, distributive justice and the rights of humanity have been less trampled underfoot, and where greater things have been done for the public good.[29]

Thus despotism is not the negation of monarchy; furthermore, it is not necessarily a source of evils. It is on this point, in fact, that Montesquieu and Voltaire diverge: what is an abuse of power? Is it or is it not an abuse of monarchical power when its exercise occurs without intermediaries? Can abuse have good effects? And so on. These are questions which reopen the Aristotelian problematic (which will be an issue throughout the second half of the eighteenth century) and where, specifically, the debate about 'legal despotism' versus 'enlightened' despotism will be situated.

Nature and principle

There is plainly no question here of splitting Voltaire and Montesquieu. On the level of evidence, Voltaire is right, and without doubt the analysis of the Asiatic regimes developed by Montesquieu – be it the Ottoman, Persian, Mogul or Chinese empires – rests on partial information and partial interpretation.[30] Correct though these criticisms may be, however, it seems to us none the less that they in no way detract from the force of the *concept* of despotism as elaborated and deployed by Montesquieu.

When it is defined first as a form of government, despotism is distinguished from each of the two other forms – republican and monarchical – by its nature and its principle. Though they are distinct, these three forms of government are not altogether without connections. We need not examine how the process of transformation from one to another has been effected historically in order to sketch out the rules of this transformation with some certainty.

As for their *nature*, governments are distinguished by two criteria: the number of those who rule, and whether or not there are laws. Thus we move from republican government – whereby all (democracy) or several (aristocracy) govern according to laws – to monarchical government, which is the power of a single individual subordinate to laws, and finally to despotic government, where a single individual exercises absolute and arbitrary power without laws.

But the same goes for *principles*: virtue, honour and fear are not merely juxtaposed by Montesquieu, but *deduced* in succession from one another in accordance with a movement of supplementarity or representation. Thus, in monarchy: 'Honour, that is, the prejudice of every person and rank, supplies the place of the political virtue . . . and is everywhere her representative.[31] But fear subsequently takes the place of honour, excluding it absolutely in despotism.[32]

At this point, there are two observations which seem imperative.

In the first place, the principle of a government is what enables it to *act*. It is the mainspring of the whole machine.[33] Montesquieu speaks aptly of the '*whole* machine', implying that the principle is something which ought to be as present in the rulers as among the ruled, in those who command as much as in those who obey. In democracy: 'the person entrusted with the execution of the laws is sensible of his being subject to their direction;'[34] this person, therefore, has great need of virtue. Although it is not 'so absolutely requisite', it is also needed in the 'nobles', in the

35

aristocracy. For 'they who are to execute the laws against their colleagues will immediately perceive that they are acting against themselves. Virtue is therefore necessary in this body, by the very nature of the constitution'.[35] The monarch has need of honour, since a large part of his authority rests upon the opinion his subjects have of him.[36] Lastly, the despot, whose whole power rests upon the fear he inspires, is himself unceasingly subject to fear. A 'principle' of government is therefore not exclusively either that by or through which one obeys, nor by or through which one commands. It always designates a mutual relation, and functions only inasmuch as it is reversible and able to be universally applied. Once it ceases to be so, it is corrupted, and the government will perish.[37] One must therefore recognize that in the principle there is a *mechanism of power* which is the condition whereby command and obedience are connected.

Furthermore, we have not sufficiently stressed that the three principles (virtue, honour and fear), which appear to be very distinct, are in fact three forms of a single 'passion', which we can equally call love or fear, according to whether we refer to its root or its expression. Thus virtue is based upon *love of the homeland*; honour upon *amour-propre*; fear, lastly, upon *amour de soi*, which corresponds to the basic instinct for self-preservation. But in one form or another fear is likewise inscribed in the principle of each government. In despotism, this is the *fear of death*; in monarchy, it is the *fear of opinion*; and lastly, in a republic, it is the *fear of the law*. Each principle therefore has two sides, a positive and a negative, love and fear, and can be regarded as a specific form of a certain unique principle, one which functions in every kind of power, that of the *love-fear pairing*.

These observations were necessary in order to draw out the paradoxical character of despotism as a form of government.

The fact is that at first sight despotism appears to be merely a corruption of monarchical government – and there are certain chapters in *The Spirit of Laws* which tend in this direction. Yet it is important to Montesquieu to distinguish them radically from one another, by making a radical distinction between their nature and

36

their principle: despotism is plainly a distinct *form* of government whose *nature* is that a single man rules without laws, and whose *principle* is fear.

A government of this kind is absurd, asserts Voltaire. It cannot exist. Now the strange thing is that this is something which Montesquieu would readily acknowledge. That there can be no pure despotism was something already stated in his *Considérations*:

> It is erroneous to believe that any human authority exists in the world which is in every respect despotic; there never has been, and there never will be; the most vast of powers is always bounded at some confine or other . . . . A king of Persia can easily compel a son to kill his father, or a father to kill his son; but he cannot compel his subjects to drink wine.[38]

In religion or customs, *The Spirit of Laws* would see the props of arbitrary power, and at the same time the brake and limitations on it which take the place of 'fundamental laws',[39] illustrating the observation: 'Within each nation there is a general spirit, and power itself is founded upon it; whenever it offends this spirit, it offends itself, and it necessarily comes to a stop.'[40]

To say that there is not and cannot be such a thing as pure despotism is to say that it is a form of government which is always necessarily imperfect in relation to its essence, and always undergoing a process of self-destruction. What brings about the ruin of a government is the corruption of its principle. And 'the principle of despotic government is subject to a continual corruption, because it is in its very nature corrupt.'[41] If there cannot be any such thing as pure despotism it is because there is no form of government whose principle can be pure fear, since fear is always necessarily subject to corruption.

What Montesquieu means here is not that despotism is a fragile regime because its principle is corrupt, but quite exactly the opposite. A despotic government based on the principle of pure fear would immediately collapse. Because the defects of the principle are compensated for by those institutional appearances which are always to some extent present in a despotic regime, and give it 'some order' and 'some rule',[42] a despotic regime can maintain itself, and the despot can preserve his position as more than momentary, only *because* the principle of the regime is corrupt.

Thus – contrary to the two other forms of government, whose ruin is the result of the corruption of the principle – the survival of the despotic regime rests upon the essential corruption of its principle.

The 'corruption of fear'

Why, though, is this principle necessarily subject to corruption? And first of all, *what is the 'corruption of fear*? The corruption of virtue or of honour is something we can understand – and Montesquieu explains it. But the corruption of fear? Montesquieu has nothing clear to say about this. Or rather, we can see two contrasting kinds of answer outlined, depending on the texts we consult.

This is the first: the specific fear involved in despotism is the fear of death, a manifestation of self-love. It is therefore a passion which in a certain sense is in a raw state. We might say, in consequence, that it 'is subject to corruption' (on condition that this does not assume a pejorative meaning), when it changes from being merely a fear of death into a fear of opinion – which assumes men led by self-esteem, not only by self-love. Or men whose actions are determined by a certain idea of themselves which they are afraid of seeing distorted or obliterated. From this point of view, a proposition such as 'fear, in despotism, is subject to a continual corruption' would mean that there is no self-love which is not reflected in self-esteem, and no fear which does not contain an irreducible kernel of honour. Furthermore, we must add: that is to say, in men worthy of the name – *free* men.

This is how Usbek explains to Ibben, the Persian, what honour (or the 'desire for glory') is for a subject of the king of France. Honour is not in opposition to self-preservation; it is, he says, 'no different in kind from the instinct for self-conservation which every creature possesses'. It is even, in one way, its highest expression, since it is the desire to preserve oneself in and through the opinion of others: 'We seem to be adding to what we are when we are able to impose ourselves on the memory of others; we acquire a new life, which becomes as precious to us as the one we receive from Heaven.' But, Usbek goes on, honour or 'the desire for glory increases in proportion to the liberty of the subject, and diminishes similarly; glory is never coupled with servitude'.[43]

If, in despotism, fear is always 'corrupt', this would imply that it never enslaves men completely, and that they are capable of behaving like men who are worthy of the name. This would explain the endless revolutions within despotic regimes, given the visibly stubborn opposition of men to a form of power which assumes the negation of their being, by reducing them to the state of savage beasts. If honour is rooted in self-esteem, and if self-esteem begins at the point in life when one is able to choose reasons for living,[44] therefore preferring death to the loss of liberty, then despotism, where we can see so many kinds of revolt and such great willingness to accept death, would be a form of monarchy – one, of course, that is permanently diseased, but always has a tendency to restore itself, since the corruption of its principle, honour, is never entirely accomplished. This would be the real reason for the impossibility of pure despotism: in addition to its absurdity as a political concept, it would contain a metaphysical absurdity. Total power over men is impossible, since it always comes up against the confine of their freedom. From here to the conclusion that despotism is itself continually 'degenerating' into monarchy, there is but one step, which Montesquieu, it seems, refused to take. Monarchy is no more a 'diluted' version of despotism than despotism is merely a degenerate version of monarchy. Between the two there is an ineradicable difference of essence. No doubt they resemble one another in many respects,[45] but this resemblance is a mere simulacrum. If the corruption of its principle forces despotism to 'follow order and some rule', by these things '*its nature is forced without being changed*; its ferocity remains; and it is made tame and tractable only for a time'.[46]

Nature and human nature

How does it come about, then, that despotism can never coincide with monarchy except by simulating it? In other words, how does it come about that despotism *exists* as a form of government that is irreducible to others? We have just seen that the paradox of this form of government is that its *nature* is not fulfilled unless its *principle* is corrupt. But if what we understand by the 'corruption of fear' is its socialization, its acculturation – in short, something akin to its humanization – we can no longer understand the existence of despotism; its nature enters into contradiction with the corruption of its principle, precisely to the degree that through it is affirmed – albeit in a form that remains frustrated – a *human nature* defined by liberty. So that, under the pressure of this 'corrupt fear', either despotism preserves itself only by changing its nature and transforming itself into monarchy, or – since human nature cannot tolerate a government of this nature – it collapses. In both cases, therefore, it is denied: either in its nature, or in its being.

Now, these are the facts:

> After what has been said, one would imagine that human nature should perpetually rise up against despotism. But, notwithstanding the love of liberty so natural to mankind, notwithstanding their innate detestation of force and violence, most nations are subject to this very government.[47]

How does one take into account the existence of a despotic government in keeping with its nature? – which is to say: how does one take into account a form of government whose *nature* is in contradiction with *human nature*? We know Montesquieu's answer: 'This is easily accounted for ... a despotic government offers itself, as it were, at first sight; it is uniform throughout; and as passions

40

only are requisite to establish it, this is what every capacity may reach.'[48]

Only passions are required – and fear first and foremost – to establish it; it is in this that its natural, violent and barbaric character consists, and in this consists its difference from other regimes, which assume artifice, culture and foresight. But the real problem is not so much knowing why it exists as how it preserves itself.

It preserves itself because it is 'in that part of the world where absolute power is in some measure naturalized, namely, Asia'.[49] In order to escape the contradiction between the nature of despotism and human nature, Montesquieu therefore makes an appeal to *physical nature*. There are places in the world where nature gives rise to such unnatural beings as men who are naturally slaves and able to tolerate a government of this nature:

> As all men are born equal, slavery must be accounted unnatural, though in some countries it be founded on natural reason; and a wide difference ought to be made between such countries, and those in which even natural reason rejects it, as in Europe, where it has been so happily abolished.[50]

And this applies to civil and domestic slavery, and to political servitude.[51]

In these chapters on slavery, where Asia appears as the natural site of despotism, Montesquieu seems, then, to concur straightforwardly with Aristotle's opinion. Nevertheless, he makes a point of distinguishing himself from it: while Aristotle allows the presence of domestic slaves in 'healthy' (ὀρθοι) political regimes, Montesquieu rejects this. All forms of slavery are condemned wholesale, in the name of *human nature*. But they are cast out of Europe and into Asia, in the name of *nature*. Thus Montesquieu can say at one and the same time that there is no slave *by nature*, contrary to what Aristotle maintains, although there is slavery *'founded on natural reason'*.[52] Nature and human nature, which overlap in Europe, are opposed in Asia, where nature, as a domain

41

of physical causality, contradicts human nature as a metaphysical determination shaping a destiny.

Long live death!

This contradiction allows us to understand what is meant by the 'corruption of fear' in despotism, and why this corruption stands simultaneously as a necessary condition for the preservation of a species of despotism in keeping with its nature, and as an obstacle to this nature achieving its full realization.

The fact is that whereas in other places fear – which is rooted, like all passions, in a physical instinct – is always inclined to outstrip this purely physical origin, in Asia all passions remain essentially *physical*, which is not the same as *natural*, since it is precisely the purely physical determination of passion which becomes the very cause of its corruption, as we shall see.

Let us take the example of love:

> In northern climates the animal part of love scarcely has a power of making itself felt. In temperate climates, love, attended by a thousand appendages, endeavours to please by things that have at first the appearance, though not the reality, of this passion. In warmer climates it is liked for its own sake, it is the only cause of happiness, it is life itself.[53]

In these climates, where 'the soul is most sensibly moved by whatever relates to the union of the two sexes', where 'everything leads to this object', polygamy is an institution which can be explained 'by natural reason', since it multiplies men's opportunities to satisfy this passion. Now, this is the very thing which dampens it,[54] or even goes to the point of corrupting it by some radical perversion: 'May I not say that a plurality of wives leads to that passion which nature disallows? . . . .' Where is the proof? 'In the revolution which happened at Constantinople, when Sultan Achmet was deposed, history says that the people, having plundered the Kiaya's house, found not a single woman; they tell us that at Algiers, in the greatest part of their seraglios, they have none at all.'[55] One 'depravity', Montesquieu observes, 'always draws on another'. Physical passion without any constraint leads to the despotism of one sex over the other, and ends up being corrupted into indifference towards the other sex, then into love against nature for objects of the same sex.

The very same thing goes for that other fundamental passion which is fear. If fear is continually in the process of corruption in Asia, it is not because men there are naturally courageous. The climate, softening their fibres, makes them instead 'like old men, timorous', excessively sensitive to the least threat of danger. So they are naturally made to be slaves. There, slavery is even so natural that fear, in extreme instances, is something the despot no longer needs in order to make himself obeyed. The force of habit takes its place, prolonging into apathy an upbringing which relies at first upon physical fear and is then reduced to the simple techniques of animal training:[56] the corruption of passion into apathy.

A better way of putting it: among the peoples of Asia the fear of death is replaced by a kind of joy in, or even a frenzied passion for, suffering and dying. Thus, the Indians are 'naturally a pusillanimous people', yet 'how shall we reconcile this with their customs and penances so full of barbarity? The men voluntarily undergo the greatest hardships, and the women burn themselves: here we find a very odd compound of fortitude and weakness.'[57] We find the same paradoxical behaviour among the Turks, who are garrotted without a word of protest on an order from the Sultan, and whose armies are capable of throwing themselves over a precipice if their general has so commanded. It may be said that in this contempt for death there is something akin to the 'love of glory' or the honour of our European monarchies. But this would be to let ourselves be dazzled by what is a mere simulacrum, without understanding, as Montesquieu explains, that 'the very same sensibility induces them to fly and dare all dangers'.[58] As in the case of love, the same cause, which is pure physical passion, gives rise to two opposing effects. In Europe, fear is 'corrupted' into

43

something higher, because men scorn death for the sake of an idea they have of themselves. In Asia, it is degraded to the point where it blots out every manifestation of that love of self which is allotted to every man, simply inasmuch as he is an animal. Hence the 'courage' of the Asiatics, which is the opposite of real courage: 'The difference between French troops and your own', a Frenchman 'of sense' explains to Usbek,

> is that the latter consist of slaves, who are naturally cowardly, and can overcome the fear of death only by the fear of being punished, which causes a new kind of terror in their souls and virtually stupefies them; whereas ours gladly face the enemy's attacks, banishing their fear by a satisfaction which is superior to it.[59]

The outcome, therefore, of the Asiatic corruption of physical passion (be it love or fear) through the very process of natural necessity is against nature – nature being understood in the most radical sense. For here we have not just a contradiction between men and human nature through the perversion of men, which is expressed by that of their government; it is life which contradicts itself – either by refusing itself the means of self-perpetuation (sexual indifference or loves against nature) or by its own ruination in that which denies it (contempt for life). This contempt for life goes even as far as love of death, just as sexual apathy extends to love against nature. 'The countries ravaged by despotism are those where depopulation is also the greatest,' observed Usbek.[60] This depopulation, of course, has political causes which are themselves closely connected to custom. But they are also, more deeply, the result of a certain unheeding denaturing of human nature: 'As I scan the earth, all I find is ruins; I seem to see it recovering from the ravages of plague and famine ... there is some internal defect, some secret, hidden poison, some wasting disease, which is attacking human nature.'[61] From where, then, does this disease of human nature come, if not from a disease of nature itself, which seems to wish for death? In the past it was rent apart by violent catastrophes. The tranquillity we see in it today must worry us all the more, instead of reassuring us. For 'destruction does not always happen violently; we can see that in several regions of the earth the provision of nourishment for mankind is being exhausted. How do we know that there are not generic causes of exhaustion, gradual and imperceptible, applying to the whole world?'[62]

Death is despotism's element, to the extent that its necessary impulse is towards death rather than its avoidance, and to the extent that the physical corruption of fear is the means by which despotism achieves its greatest stability. Foë (Buddha), 'the legislator of the Indies, … placed mankind in a state extremely passive'; he taught: 'We have eyes and ears, but perfection consists in neither seeing nor hearing; a mouth, hands, etc., but perfection requires that these members should be inactive.' The fact that he favoured the vices of the climate made him a bad legislator.[63] Or rather, he did not legislate, but only legitimated an unhealthy nature which already tends to reduce the heart to a pure vacuum, movement to immobility, life to death and any strictly political power relation to a kind of physical determinism.

This is an extreme case: despotism becomes 'naturalized' to such a point that the making of its nature seems to disappear altogether. Laws alone hold sway, but they are the laws of a moribund nature which, having turned against nature, is its own despot. But it is in its every excess that the corruption of the principle reveals its true meaning, which is not self-love corrupted into self-esteem, and the reasons for living chosen in preference to life. We can now see that if fear is that wild passion which sacrifices everything to the imperative of the individual's survival, its corruption – beyond impassivity and indifference – is that absurd passion for dying which we find in all the despotic regimes. The subject of the Oriental despot always in some way desires that death which he should fear above all (if the principle were functioning), and if 'the arm of the despot, ever raised to bestow death',[64] is a threat, it is also a promise.

Interrogating that mysterious political object we call despotism,

45

therefore, means engaging with a string of perplexities which lead us, in the end, to a naturalist postulate.

Or the fact is that despotic government is perfect in its nature, and then its principle is pure fear. But since the nature of its principle is precisely to be impure, a despotic government which is in keeping with its nature is contradictory; it cannot exist. Or one pushes to the limits what nature requires from its principle, and the corruption of fear is 'perfect'. But then the nature of the government is transformed into the government of nature, which contradicts the very idea of political government; here again it cannot exist.

There is only one way of escaping from this dilemma: by saying that despotism never *exists* except in an *imperfect form*. Here again there are two arguments: either one posits that this imperfect form is only a *degenerate* form, the outcome of a deviation from the normal class of the species – in other words, that despotism is simply the monster of monarchy. But then it ceases to be a specific and distinct form of government, and we can think of monarchy and despotism as having a common basis (a Hobbesian position, one might say, which is rejected by Montesquieu). Or one can maintain that it is a distinct form of government; but then it must be conceived as both essence and accident, species and monster – in other words, as the monster of itself. That such a monster should be a viable one in Asia – as Montesquieu sees as being proven by facts – assumes the monstrousness of men themselves in their love of servitude in that part of the world. This monstrousness is itself traced back to a nature which is monstrous in its origins, in that it produces living beings who live for death. Despotism is therefore a monstrous regime where, in the last analysis, the essence of power lies in that ineradicable absurdity of desiring what one fears and loving what kills you.

A GENEALOGY OF THE MONSTER

The Sun King's Medusa Head

All the time he is stating the difference in *nature* between despotism and monarchy, Montesquieu presents despotism as the *internal threat* faced by each of the two other governments:

> As democracies are subverted when the people despoil the senate, the magistrates, the judges of their functions, so monarchies are corrupted when the prince insensibly deprives societies or cities of their privileges. In the former case the multitude usurp the power, in the latter it is usurped by a single person.[65]

Despotism is therefore contrasted not only with monarchy, as the government of a single person in the absence of laws, but with all politically healthy forms of government.[66] A healthy government is a *moderate* government, and the republic (be it democratic or aristocratic) is a moderate government, like monarchy. As a result: 'The danger is not when the State passes from one moderate to another moderate government, as from a republic to a monarchy, or from a monarchy to a republic; but when it is precipitated from a moderate to a despotic government.'[67]

For France, and for the greater part of Europe, this threat principally involves monarchies. This is probably why there is a tendency to see despotism only as a degenerate form of monarchy, but, through monarchy, despotism calls into question the essence and the existence of the *political as such.*

We can understand, then, why Montesquieu lays such stress on distinguishing despotism from monarchy. Between the two, there is not just a difference of nature between forms of government, there is the gulf which separates the political from the non-political. But the paradox – to which all the difficulties which we have encountered are attached – is that this radical perversion of the political is achieved as an *existing form of government.* In other words, for Montesquieu it is a matter of giving a positive aspect to the negative. He does this, as we have seen, by recourse to nature.

But then if we are to connect the existence of despotism to the

47

contingencies of geography and climate, how are we to state at the same time that despotism is a threat inscribed in the midst of the States of *Europe*? The argument with which Montesquieu equips himself to make despotism exist as a form of government seems to backfire on him when he tries, instead, to make it the form assumed by the corruption of the political in any form of government.

Perhaps foreseeing this objection, he writes:

> Most of the European nations are still governed by the principles of morality. But if, from a long abuse of power or the fury of conquest, despotic sway should prevail to a certain degree, neither morals nor climate would be able to withstand its baleful influence: and their human nature would be exposed, for some time at least, even in this beautiful part of the world, to the insults with which she has been abused in the other three.[68]

Of the two hypotheses envisaged, only the first was in earnest at the time when Montesquieu was writing,[69] since he was thinking of the 'lengthy abuse of power' of Louis XIV[70] and the corruption of the constitutive principles of the French monarchy which was exacerbated after his death.

In the final analysis, Montesquieu sets out this possibility on exactly the same basis as he did for Oriental despotism – upon some *natural* order – although he does this in a symmetrically inverse manner. In Asia, the existence of despotism is explained by the fact that nature impels men to deny the demands of human nature. In Europe, on the other hand, it will be the demands of human nature which will instead go so far as to contradict natural determinations, cancelling out even the empire of climate, which is none the less defined as 'the first, the most powerful, of all empires'.[71]

Indeed, in temperate climates nothing in physical nature contradicts the demands of human nature, which can freely deploy all its potentiality. What are these demands? The rejection of servitude, to be exact. But also the desire for total mastery, which Montesquieu, like Hobbes, sees as an essential feature of human nature, in that all men, in private, would surely enjoy mastery over others' lives, honour and possessions, and that all passions must surely be stirred by this thought.[72]

Admittedly, Montesquieu writes elsewhere: 'The natural impulse or desire which Hobbes attributes to mankind of subduing one another is far from being well-founded. The idea of empire and dominion is so complex, and depends on so many other notions, that it could never be the first which occurred to the human understanding.'[73] But this objection is valid for the state of nature, not for civil society. For 'As soon as man enters into a state of society he loses the sense of his weakness; equality ceases, and then commences the state of war.'[74] This means that it is in and through civil and political society that the desire and the possibility of exercising absolute power have their genesis.

We must conclude from this that the seeds of despotism necessarily exist in every civil and political society, since it is from this that the desire for mastery in human nature arises: 'Constant experience shows us that every man invested with power is apt to abuse it, and to carry his authority as far as it will go.'[75] These limits upon power are never internal, always external. Power is always limited by some other power. Likewise, the *abuse of power* is not some accidental perversion of power occasioned by the temperament of its holder. The abuse of power is the natural modality by which power tends to be exercised among men who are not reduced by either climate or geography to that natural slavery which we find in Asia. What makes despotism almost necessary in Asia is a kind of 'abuse of obedience' (servitude) occasioned by nature, which is the symmetrical inversion of the abuse of power which is a property of human nature in society, making it possible in Europe. As a result, in order to avert despotism, that fearsome outcome of two opposing causes, it will be necessary in Asia – as the Chinese understood[76] – to legislate *against* the natural determinations which lead to immobility, apathy and servitude. In Europe, on the other hand, it will be necessary to do everything – as did the English, who are like the

Chinese of Europe – to temper the inevitable abuse of power. In both cases, the 'soul of government' is *moderation* – whether of nature, or of human nature. A never-ending task which is always threatened, since although one can act upon the effects, the causes remain. A good government is therefore nothing other than despotism well tempered, but never overcome.

Thus this monster, which sleeps beneath the skies and in the deserts of an Asia which gave birth to it, is continually engendered without being recognized in the States of Europe – because this is where one finds men worthy of the name. At first it seemed to designate only a perversion of monarchy; then, more radically, to represent the *other*, the negation of the political as such. But is it not, much rather, what reveals its essence and its truth? Despotism as a figure of political power in the pure state? This is a paradoxical proposition, but one which becomes clear if we reread the beginning of the essay entitled *De la politique* (which should have been Chapter 13 of the *Traité des devoirs*). Despotism is politics itself, if we understand by 'politics' that irreducible area of immortality, irrationality and violence which 'will always persist so long as there are passions independent of the yoke of laws'.[77]At the heart of every State, politics is the passion which clashes with the passions in an interplay 'which is repugnant to morality, to reason and to justice'. In which *politics* must be distinguished from *government*, even though the one is never without the other, and vice versa. Which explains both that human societies have a history (a history which is always unpredictable) and that they contain hidden utopias.

The eighteenth century produced a lot of utopias. But usually, we keep sight only of the 'happy' ones. These are, one might say, utopias of *government*, in so far as what Montesquieu calls 'politics' is kept away from them; here the passions are not 'independent of the yoke of laws', but instead espouse them, leaving nothing for politics to predict – history evaporates. It will be the West Indies or islands washed by warm seas which will provide the unspecified location for these utopias.

But there are other utopias, erroneously named 'counter-utopias' or negative utopias. None the less, they have the same positive value as the first kind in that they, too, offer the stripping bare, in a fully fantastical form, of the other element in this impure mixture which is political power in societies destined for history. These are utopias of *politics* in its pure state. In them, too, history is abolished and time immobilized. Montesquieu would give them Asia (and Africa too) as their chosen site, and despotism as their feature.

Despotism, then, appears very much as the negation of all forms of *government*, but this is all the better to highlight the kernel of *political power*, which is always masked and covered up in existing governments, where the laws and the passions unceasingly provoke one another.

By defining despotism as that regime which is sustained by pure passion, and as that power which is so 'plain' that it can be said to appear 'at first sight', Montesquieu is, however, forging no utopia. A despotism of this kind in the pure state is impossible, he insists; there will always be some semblance of laws – which is to say, of morality, reason and justice – in the midst of the clash of passions, just as there will be speech – albeit in the form of a faint murmur – to maintain the fascination of the gaze. Which means, conversely, that there is no such thing as pure government: the Prince who governs us never fails, whether deliberately or otherwise, to seduce us.[78] And if fear, which is the principle of despotism, never exists without a fatal love of what kills you, Montesquieu leads us to understand that we must keep in mind that in the extreme love we bore towards a king who, 'directing everything entirely to himself, called the State to his capital, the capital to his court, and the court to his own person',[79] we too had reasons to fear, for by then the principle of monarchy was corrupted. It is altogether corrupted when the Prince 'puts, like the Roman emperors, a Medusa's head on his breast'.[80] Let us beware of some day seeing, beneath the emblem of the Sun King, the emergence of a Medusa head. The very same one with which Usbek, once the only object of passionate love in his seraglio, finally armed himself against the surging of desire among his disillusioned women in revolt. 'In

51

their guilty confusion at all their crimes they will fall to the ground beneath your gaze', he writes from his distant exile, to the one who, without the least doubt, is the most fitting figure of Medusa: Solim, the black man who is his new Grand Eunuch.[81]

Here we are led back into the seraglio, the heart of that Oriental despotism which we spoke of as having become – with *The Spirit of Laws* – the idea of a phantasm. This phantasm of pure power gave an underlying consistency to the plot of the *Persian Letters*. We now propose to examine it for itself. This will not, therefore, be a matter of pursuing long-standing Voltairean practice, and taking an interpretation of the facts which is judged to be partial while, against it, seeking to re-establish the political reality of those Asian regimes which Montesquieu, for the sake of his own argument, mistakenly set under the generic and derogatory idea of *despotism*. A critical attitude of this kind is clearly a necessary one, and it has led to work which, on this point, clarifies things with definitive precision. Here, instead, we would like to try to draw out the structure of this despotic power in all its purity – not as it must have been in reality, but as it was *imagined* at the beginning of the eighteenth century. It seems to us that it is primarily in the accounts of travellers in the Orient[82] that we can see the workings of this despotic apparatus, which, for all that it belongs to the realm of the imaginary, is no less revealing about the reality of power.

'For a short time, then, allow your thoughts to wander beyond this world to view another, wholly new one, which I shall cause to unfold before it in imaginary spaces.' It is time to follow the travellers on to the despotic stage, to see the machinery behind its stage sets at work, before we enter deep within the machine, into the seraglio – in order to submit to the fabulous proofs we find there, through which, as Descartes wrote, 'I hope that the truth will not fail to come out sufficiently and that it will be no less agreeable to see than if I were to set it forth wholly naked.'[83]

PART II
In Orient Desert . . .

3

The Gaze and the Letter

The King gives a written order for a certain child to be blinded and this order is given to the first chance comer, for in Persia there is no official executioner. . . . Once the order is carried into the seraglio, it is quickly understood, provoking cries and weeping; but at last the child must be released. The eunuchs take him to the cruel messenger, who throws them the order, or as you would call it, the lettre *de cachet, and then squatting down, he seizes the child, puts him across his knees with his face upturned and grips his head with his left arm. Then with one hand he opens his eyelids, and with the other takes his dagger by the tip, and rips out the pupils one after the other, still whole, and undamaged, as one does with an unripe walnut. He puts them in his handkerchief and takes them off to the King.*[1]

This is the despotic scenario.

Everything in this text by Chardin delineates despotic power in the manner that struck the European traveller in the seventeenth century. The order: an unspoken signifier to be carried out immediately, on sight. The goal to be achieved: to take possession of the gaze. The messenger: the first chance comer, invested with all power, but existing only through and for the order which makes him the executioner. The present tense of the narration, in which we see obedience that is both prompt and without commentary; the repetitive character of the operation, its unvarying and ineluctable ritual, for no room is allowed here for even the smallest subjective initiative. And then, between two commas, the analogy with the *lettre de cachet* . . . .

The gaze, the letter: here we have the two key terms, the two driving elements, of despotic power in the Orient. Admittedly, in Turkey the sultan does not inflict blindness; he abducts, frequently assassinates. Admittedly, too, in Persia or elsewhere, the order is not always written; a blink, the motion of a finger or a foot, or the pursing of the lips are all that is required. But the gaze and the letter, and the intertwining of imaginary and symbolic registers which maintain their interplay, assume a paradigmatic value in this world of silence and transparency, which is centred upon an Idol and cut through with signifiers which are law, burning with passions yet cold as a machine which is incomprehensibly simple beneath the profusion of phantasmic forms which it engenders.

The Two Definitions of Despotic Power

Putting out eyes

A despotic government offers itself, as it were, at first sight.[2]

If we want an accurate idea of the function of the gaze in the economy of despotic power, we need only comprehend this definition by Montesquieu in all its meanings, first of all in the strictest meaning: the despot puts out eyes:

> There is a very specific thing in Persian Law, which is that the law of the State directs that no blind man should be raised to the throne. Although there are those who maintain that this law should be understood in a moral sense, it has been used to uphold the prevailing custom in Persia of blinding male children of royal blood.[3]

Therefore, to be master is to see. The despot can be stupid, mad, ignorant, drunk or diseased, but what does it matter so long as he sees. Not seeing means being condemned to obey. Under the despotic regime, where obedience is always 'blind', the blind man is the emblematic figure of the subject.

Xenophon said of Cyrus: 'The good ruler he regarded as a law with eyes for men, because he is able not only to give commandments but also to see the transgressor and punish him',[4] and he recounts how the King of Persia established the policing of his realm by multiplying spies throughout its length and breadth.[5] Things do not seem to have changed at all since then. Tavernier notes that the 'superintendent of all the King's property' is called the *Nazar*, which means the 'Seer'. In the Persia crossed by Paul Lucas or Chardin, everywhere they feel 'the eyes of the King' directed upon them; this is the phrase the Persian language uses to designate spies. But it is not merely a question of spies; wherever one is in the despotic space, one can never know whether it is the eye of the master himself that watches. In Turkey, according to Gedoyn, the Great Lord can be present at ordinary meetings of the Divan, 'through a trellised window looking into the room, by which means he holds his officers in a state of fear and stricture, always with the suspicion that their master is present at their deliberations'.[6] But it is in his power to watch anyone anywhere – for example, by assuming the guise of an anonymous passer-by in a Constantinople street. Thévenot tells us:

> Sometimes he would go to a baker's, where he would buy bread; and sometimes to a butcher's, where he would buy a piece of meat; and one day, when a butcher had tried to sell him meat above the price that he had set, he signalled to his executioner, who cut off the butcher's head straight away.[7]

Oriental despotism is the empire of the gaze which is simultaneously everywhere and nowhere, unique and without number.

The gaze as master, in the first place because he is the master of the gaze. From his seraglio, Amurat would watch what was happening outside 'with an excellent telescope which had been the gift of the Venetians; and one day when he was engaged upon this, as was his custom, he saw in Pera a man who was also looking through a telescope at the sultans who, at that moment, were walking in the garden'.[8] Whereupon he sent his mutes to kill him and hang him from his far-off window, in offering to the gladdened eye of the sultan. The blinding of royal children in the seraglio at Ispahan is the exemplary illustration of this mastery of the gaze; it is precise but simple work, demanding not so much the skill of the goldsmith or the surgeon as the care of the zealous servant preparing some delicacy for his master. And it is not the eye – the organ and the envelope of sight – which he brings him, but the pupil: the gaze itself. This is mastery attained, probably the master's crowning *jouissance*, for he can gaze upon the gaze itself as he holds it in his hands,

True service, therefore, means showing the master that he holds the monopoly of the gaze. In the early seventeenth century, Michel Baudier made the point that in the seraglio at Constantinople – 'now the principal seat of the arrogance of Princes' –

> any man who dares to lift his eyes and gaze upon the visage [of the Great Lord] is guilty of a great crime, so that all the bashaws of the Court, with the exception of the Vizier, the Mufti and the doctor, have their hands joined and their eyes lowered as they make their way to revere, or rather to adore him; and in this posture, bowing deeply to the ground, they greet him without setting eyes upon him, although he is before them.[9]

The same thing was repeated by Du Vignau, at the end of the century: the Turks 'take care never to fix their eyes upon those of His Highness, nor even anywhere close to his face . . . . They must not be so bold as to look upon him, and it is enough that they be looked at.[10] The same goes for Siam: 'If the King should appear, all doors and windows must be closed, and all the people prostrate themselves upon the ground without daring to cast their eyes upon him.'[11]

With this power over the gaze, the master can and does make play with it. Although he is all-seeing but invisible, he does show himself. But the appearance of the despot always comes down to a matter of theatrical staging.[12] Cyrus knew that grandeur is a thing of artifice and optical illusion when he adopted Median dress:

for he thought that if anyone had any personal defect, that dress would help to conceal it, and that it made the wearer look very tall and very handsome. For they have shoes of such a form that without being detected the wearer can easily put something into the soles so as to make him look taller than he is. He encouraged also the fashion of pencilling the eyes, that they might seem more lustrous than they are, and of using cosmetics to make the complexion look better than nature made it.[13]

As for the Great Mogul, he gives audience on certain days:

> The King sitts in a little gallery over head; ambassidors, the great men and strangers of qualety within the inmost rayle under him, raysed from the ground, covered with canopyes of velvet and silke . . . the meaner men representing gentry within the first rayle, the people without in a base court, and soe that all may see the King. This sitting out hath soe much affinitye with a theatre.[14]

This calculated representation of the despot has, moreover, a solemnity and regularity which makes it akin to some astronomical phenomenon.[15] In Ethiopia, the despot shows himself only four times a year, and that veiled. According to Gaultier Schouten, the king of Arraka appeared only every five years, at the full moon of the last month in that year. And Thomas Roe describes the appearance of the Great Mogul twice a day at a window of his palace overlooking a great square where the people would assemble to see him: 'For, as all his subjects are slaves, so is he in a kynd of reciprocall bondage, for he is tyed to observe these howres and customes so precisely that, if hee were unseene one day and noe sufficient reason rendred, the people would mutinie.'[16] The despot bends to laws as strict as those of nature. But nature itself seems to obey him in return – as in Japan, where, before the motionless Daïri, 'his smallest movements and gestures were observed and from them predictions would be made of whether the day would be a happy or an unhappy one; according to the season and according to the circumstances of the time, his movements were also regarded as presaging plenty or barrenness, peace or war',[17] or again as in Siam, where the king can lower the waters of the river with one look.[18]

Chardin writes: 'the Kings in Persia and the rest of the Orient are kings for display'. But they are so, one might say, *through* display. Whether he appears, at regular intervals, framed by a window, or hides; whether it is obligatory to show oneself to him when he emerges, or instead prostrate oneself out of sight – the despot tends always to be constituted as a pure 'being of the gaze', simultaneously peripheral and central, enclosing and enclosed, since he is this gaze which is imagined to look upon everyone else, and this unique gaze which, from the centre of the Palace, is cast down upon the City, the Empire and the World.

Despotic power is therefore characterized by what is 'at first sight' – in every sense, if we are willing to go along with the semantic game for which Montesquieu's definition provides the opportunity. But there is a second definition which we find in Montesquieu, one which emphasizes another, equally characteristic feature of this kind of power.

'The will of a billiard ball'

'When once the prince's will is made known, it ought infallibly to produce its effect,'[19] writes Montesquieu, 'just as one billiard ball hitting another must produce its effect' – a new metaphor, deliberately borrowed from a Cartesian universe, and one whose pertinence we ought now to value.

As the empire of the gaze, it is not surprising that despotism is also the empire of signs. As Rousseau wrote: 'The most vigorous speech is that in which the Sign has said everything before a single word is spoken. Tarquin, Thrasybulus lopping off the heads of the poppies . . .'.[20] But there is an even more vigorous form of speech, where the sign itself is exhausted in the very materiality of the signifier. 'Alexander putting his ring to his favourite's mouth' – here is the true language of the Absolute Master: the one where the sign has said everything, without it even being necessary, or even possible, to follow it with spoken words that would interpret it. Not because its meaning is clear, but because it has no meaning. Using the language of 'signs', even to signify death, is to allow the existence of an interpreter, who might betray, even in explaining the order, thereby legitimating it, and causing the master to seem dependent on something other than himself (truth, law) and subject at least to reason: 'In a despotic government, it is equally pernicious whether they reason well or ill; their reasoning is alone sufficient to shock the principle of that government.'[21] It seems that the more arbitrary an order is, the more it is obeyed, as if the only thing that mattered was its materiality as signifier, stripped of all other reference but itself: 'As soon as the Prince commands, everything he says is done straight away, and even when he knows not what he does nor what he says, as when he is drunk.'[22] Which is to say that the despot's very person matters little; obedience is given less to this person than to the signifier of his will. There is no doubt that the despot is master of the signifier, as he is of the gaze, and he is master through the signifier, as he is through the gaze. But we have to go further. A moment ago the master merged with the gaze itself; now he merges with the signifier.

We said earlier that obedience to the despot is 'blind'. Despotic states need vast desert plains: transparent space without obstacles, without secrets, open on every side to the gaze. Let us add that this space is a silent desert. Noise is an obstacle to the power of the signifier, which can circulate well – without interference   only in silence.

Obviously, there is little difficulty in establishing this silence in those vast deserts. What is striking, though, is that it holds equal sway in the city. According to the majority of the travellers, Constantinople is the biggest city in Europe, even more populous, they say, than Paris.[23] Yet Tournefort states: 'there is more noise made in a single day in a Paris marketplace than in a whole year in the entire city of Constantinople'.[24] Enter the first courtyard of the seraglio, where a crowd presses close: 'You could hear a pin drop, so to speak, and if someone broke the silence with a voice just slightly raised . . . he would be beaten with sticks straight away by the officers on patrol; it seems that even the horses know their place . . . .'[25]

Although his ears, like his eyes, are imagined to be everywhere, the despot is not spoken to, and words are always and only addressed to the one among his servants who has the privilege of passing on the message.[26] Whatever the content or meaning of the message, it is not that what might be said would be likely to displease. The prohibition has nothing to do with the meaning, but with the very employment of speech. Taking the initiative, even in order to tell the master that one loves him or one is his slave, would already constitute revolt, since the subject is therefore flaunting his claim to dispose likewise of the signifier. As Usbek wrote, in despotism: 'there is never a minor rebellion, nothing between protest and insurrection'.[27]

As for the despot himself, when he opens his mouth it is to make his voice heard, but never with meaning. Since it has no reference to anything other than itself, the word of the despot is not meant to be understood, verified or legitimated; with every instance it creates a new truth, just as it posits a new law, as valid for nature as for his subjects. When the sultan sails out on the sea in his ceremonial vessel:

> he savours long and deep the flattering pleasure of seeing a multitudinous people that obeys his voice, and this awesome element subordinate to his laws and, it would seem, holding back the fury of its waves, so that its calm surface might express the respect due to his might.[28]

This is why no dialogue is introduced between the despot and his subjects; there are no misunderstandings to be clarified, no consequent meanings to interpret, no time for understanding. Thus no answer is ever given to the despot; he is *echoed*. Each word he releases comes back to him, multiplied and magnified by a thousand mouths. The answer is always there already in the proposition put forward, however absurd it may be – precisely because it is absurd: 'If the King says at noon that it is night, it must be said that the Moon and the Stars are up in the sky.'[29]

The voice of the master can stupefy to this degree only because he is sparing of it.[30] It resonates as the gaze makes itself visible – in flashes, between two silences. The shorter the flash, the better it works. The outcome is that in order to make himself heard, the best thing of all is for the despot never even to open his mouth: 'To be a good Sultan, one must never speak, but by one's extraordinary gravity, make men tremble with a blink of an eye.'[31] By its fleeting interruption of the gaze which is fixed upon you, the *blink of an eye*, which sends death, is probably the master-signifier in its pure state.

The Flying Letter

But in the despotic world, absolute power is exercised usually by means of the graphic signifier: 'The Ottoman kings convey their commands almost always in writing, and the style which they use in writing is very particularly theirs', observed Baudier.[32] Chardin points out that in Persia the king is always accompanied by his 'chief scribe' (the *Douader*), who goes around with a roll of paper on his person, ready to 'write down straight away everything which the King tells him to'.[33] The fact is that in Muslim Asia the respect given to the letter *per se* is extreme. All the more so when the letter is guaranteed as issuing from the king by the mark of the Great Seal – which in Persia is hidden in a casket within the seraglio, with the queen mother as its titular custodian. And the Persians considered it 'a great impudence, and indeed disrespect, to touch the King's Letters. They enclose these letters of their King in pearl-embroidered bags or in some other way, for fear that hands will touch them.'[34]

Later, we shall consider the reasons which authors of the period give to explain this extraordinary power of the written word in the Ottoman and Persian regimes.[35] For now, let us merely stress the wonderful effects of these written orders [*Hatchérif*] which, says Du Vignau: 'were the principal means for preserving Ottoman authority, since a sheet of paper with five or six lines on it written in the hand of His Highness, does more than could substantial armies'.[36] It is as if the signifier itself flies, strikes and kills by being materialized in the letter. It is at one and the same time the sentence, the axe and the executioner. Unleashed from a single central spot and carried by a messenger whose prototype is a mute from the Grand Seraglio, it ploughs a soundless and unimpeded furrow to reach an unfailing target which the whim of the master has set for it. For example, the death of a pasha is decided: 'A messenger arrives and shows him the order he has to bring the man's head; the latter takes this order from the Great Lord, kisses it, places it upon his head as a sign of the respect he bears for the order, makes his ablutions and says his prayers, after which he freely lays down his head.'[37] All efficacy is thus concentrated into nothing more than the material of the sign, to the point where a blank sheet of paper can be all that is needed to prompt obedience. During a revolt of the ispahis at Andrinopolis, Du Vignau records, Suleiman Aga, chief of the janissaries, 'went in the midst of the rebels, escorted only by ten janissaries, with a paper in his hand, on which nothing was written. Seizing the leader of the rebels by the neck, and showing him the paper, he said: "The Emperor commands."'[38]

But the letter can annihilate in this way because it has the power to create. In the despotic state, where all are equally nothing before the unique One who is and has everything, no grandeur of birth or merit is attached to the person. Elevation or downfall, existence itself and its obliteration, are always the effect of the signifier: 'There is no protection from the extravagances of the whim of Despots, neither in probity, nor in zeal, nor in services rendered; the passage of an idle thought, marked by a movement of the mouth or a signalling of the eyes'[39] – or, more usually, by a letter – makes and unmakes viziers and pashas, or raises a humble cook to the highest office. The only greatness is the ephemeral one conferred by *hic et nunc*, momentary preference. As Montesquieu would observe: 'if those who are not actually employed were still invested with privileges and titles, the consequence must be that there would be men in the state who might be said to be great of themselves; a thing directly opposite to the nature of this government'.[40] In other words, all the value – and the only value – that individuals have depends upon how the seal of the master is marked upon them. It needs only this simple seal to be taken away again for the subject it rendered powerful to be immediately obliterated: 'Once the death sentence has been issued by the Prince against whomsoever it be, the Turks no longer accord him any station and when they speak of him they treat him like a dog.'[41]

Charles XII told an unyielding senate in Sweden that he would send one of his boots to command them, Montesquieu records, adding: 'This boot would have governed like a despotic prince.'[42] He meant that despotic power is not shared. Nor is it delegated. To say that 'in a despotic government the power is communicated entire to the person entrusted with it'[43] is to say that it is *transmitted*: the language of the physician rather than of politics, referring not so much to a society of men jealous of their freedom as to a mechanical world peopled by machine-animals and governed only by the laws of shock. But if this power can thus be transmitted entire, without loss or friction, without the resistance of 'intermediary bodies' (like the nobility in a monarchical regime), it is because it resides always and entirely within a signifier which passes silently from hand to hand: 'The Vizier himself is the despotic prince; and each particular officer is the Vizier.'[44] But this complete transmission of power is possible only because each man is nothing in himself, and can be merged with the signifier with which the master desires to mark him and make him serve as a neutral and transitory aid. How, then, is a vizier created in the Turkey that was visited by Ricaut?

No other ceremony is carried out that I know of . . . but that of placing in his hands the seal of the Great Lord, on which the Emperor's name is inscribed and which he carries always on his person. By virtue of this seal he is invested with all the power of the Empire, and can, without formality, remove every obstacle standing in the way of his free administration.[45]

It is therefore 'in the name of the despot' that the vizier commands. 'In the name of the despot' here means strictly *through his name*, which is itself reduced to the interlaced letters inscribed on his seal.[46] This name is what allows the prince's will 'infallibly to produce its effect just as one billiard ball hitting another must produce its effect'. It slips at lightning speed along the chain which, from despot to vizier and from vizier down to the lowest of subordinates, links the centre of the Empire to its periphery. The metaphor of the billiard ball evokes the *immediacy* of the order's transmission, which means that a part of its effect is almost *instantaneous*, but also that what is written 'in the name of the despot' is never a *means* of saying something to someone. There probably is a message, for there is a messenger. But the message is merged here with the code, and is itself the code. In the despotic world, what circulates is a name, and what is communicated is movement, never meaning. And the laws of this world are those of shock, which delivers life or death. So that we can echo Montesquieu in saying that despotic power is exercised entire, like the power of a name: 'The inhabitants of those countries need only the name of a prince to govern them.'[47] The despot's name is itself the despot.

A world of deserts and silence, sufficiently resembling the one Descartes fashioned for himself in the Second Meditation, the better to tear himself away from it; a creation which is not 'continued' by a God whose constancy would be a proof of benevolence, and would allow men to transform nature by dominating it, to enrich themselves and prosper – but a creation called into question at every moment by a capricious and perverse Evil Genius. Truths that are created, but with nothing to assure them, absurd and contradictory truths that are never the same, yet stand as law. And nowhere are there men ('others'), but 'hats and coats'[48] covering automata which the master's name can animate or paralyse. In other words, a world from which any kind of truly subjective relation seems to be absent, one reduced to the blind efficacity of a name – of a letter – animated by a descending centrifugal movement, and governed only by the impulse of efficient causality.

The essential feature of despotic power is a name as efficient cause – this is how we might characterize it at its most schematic if we were to rely on the travellers' accounts. But also, in a movement that is exactly the opposite of this, introducing another feature of power which this time assumes all too human relations: a gaze as final cause.

The Idol

The despotic space is thoroughly concentric and centralized: 'When the prince, directing everything entirely to himself, calls the State to his capital, the capital to his court, and the court to his own person',[49] he is bound to turn himself into a despot, wrote Montesquieu.

Despotism makes its home in deserts, but it unceasingly creates them and expands them around itself. By contrast with the Romans at the height of their greatness, it maintains itself only by depopulating its confines, by creating around itself a void in which nothing could survive:

> From there we can see ... those lands of Mesopotamia, Anatolia, Palestine and the wondrous plains of Antioch and so many other lands once so well cultivated, so fertile and so populous, now half wildernesses, uncultivated and abandoned, or turned into pestiferous and uninhabitable swamps.[50]

Geographically, the despotic state tends to reduce itself to one vast single city, surrounded by an infinity of ruins and fallow land. This is more or less how Du Vignau sees Turkey:

> That which has grown and become greatest in its centre and in its capital serves to prove all the more its ruin and decay. And it is almost impossible to imagine the number of its towns and villages where nothing more remains but the walls.[51]

All the wealth the country contains flows towards the despotic City, which will swallow it up in its centre, from where it will never emerge. This is an absurd economy, its only goal the *jouissance* of the One, not the country's enrichment; its principle is *coupure*, the cutting-off of all that circulates (blood, merchandise, currency). This, according to Montesquieu, is 'the idea of despotism': 'When the savages of Louisiana are desirous of fruit, they cut the tree to the root and gather the fruit. This is an emblem of despotic government.'[52] Bernier, like the others, is aware of this centripetal movement, which is so much in opposition to the most obvious principles of a healthy economy that assumes the exchange of merchandise and the circulation of currency. The title page of his *Voyages* through Asia tells his readers that they will learn 'how silver and gold, after circulating throughout the world, enter Hindustan, from where they never return'. Tavernier speaks in the same way about the Grand Turk's treasure: 'I shall discover all the rivers which make their way towards this sea, like those which enter the Caspian Sea and which we never see come out of it.'[53] Referring to the King of Persia's treasure, Chardin states that it is 'a true abyss, for everything in it is lost, and very few things come out of it'.[54] What strikes Chardin is that the Treasure is like women immured in the seraglio. Moreover, 'the Treasure House always adjoins the seraglio', and no one can enter to see it, except the black eunuch (the *Aga Cafar*), who is its guardian: 'He is the most brutal, the coarsest and the ugliest of persons one might see, always berating and always in a rage, except when in the presence of the King.'[55]

Most of the travellers attribute this internal haemorrhage of wealth – which is ruinous to the country – to the fact that under the despotic regime 'there is no Mine and Thine', as Bernier writes, making an endless catalogue (and no doubt he has in mind the France of the end of Louis XIV's reign) of the ravages of a regime where everything belongs to the One, where nothing exists except for his exclusive *jouissance*. Everyone, from the lowliest peasant to the governor of a province, is fearful of appearing rich. All the possessions they have are buried. They have no children, they do not work, they make no improvement in anything, 'since the peasant tells himself this: why should I work so hard for a tyrant who would come and take it all away tomorrow...',[56] harvests, children, money? No inheritance, neither in goods nor in titles: 'The fortune of the bashaws, which for a time is dazzling, is a shaky fortune upon which nothing can be founded, neither by father nor son, however much credit it might have.'[57] The despot takes everything, and everyone is left naked and alone, sinking with everyone else into nullity. It happens most often, besides, 'that no one expects the Great Rulers to die of a natural death, nor that they should have the time to hide their treasures; their gold, their silver, their jewels and their heads are carried inside the seraglio'.[58] Without forcing the metaphor, one might well say that 'the blood of the bashaws is one of the rivers which enter this great sea of treasure'.[59]

The movement of possessions towards the centre where everything converges is also a movement of bodies. But the despotic city, however populous it is, is itself a silent, dismal desert, haunted by a flock of dispirited victims. At the beginning of the nineteenth century, Chateaubriand visited Constantinople on his way to Jerusalem, and found what he already knew through the travellers' accounts which he had obviously absorbed. For all his affirmation that everything has been said already, and he will add nothing, as if in confirmation of what he has read about the capital of despotism, he cannot prevent himself evoking its dumb terror:

As scarcely any person walks abroad but in slippers, as there is no rumbling of coaches and carts, as there are no bells and scarcely any trades that require the aid of the hammer, a continual silence prevails. You see around you a mute crowd of individuals, seemingly desirous of passing unperceived, as if solicitous, to escape the observation of a master.[60]

And indeed, in the heart of the city – albeit cut off from it, as the despotic State is cut off from the world and the city is cut off from the country –

Amidst prisons and bagnios rises a seraglio, the Capitol of slavery: 'tis here that a consecrated keeper carefully preserves the gems of pestilence and the primitive laws of tyranny. Pallid votaries are incessantly hovering about this temple, and thronging to offer their heads to the idol. Hurried on by a fatal power, nothing can divert them from this sacrifice; the eyes of the despot attract the slaves, as the looks of the serpent are said to fascinate the birds on which he preys.[61]

The gaze of the despot lures and compels; as the principle and goal of an ascending, centripetal movement, this sun[62] could be compared to that of Aristotelian cosmology if it were not, in fact, its parodic double. When this gaze is held, it becomes one with death. The despot's gaze is an object of love and a source of desire, concealing and disclosing the abyss where everything in the Empire that can be deemed to be enjoyed is swallowed up, down to the very last shred.

A gaze as final cause; a name as efficient cause; thus, when despotic power is reduced to its most striking features, it appears in two opposing – not to say contradictory – guises. So we can equally say that only passions are needed to establish it,[63] and that it functions like a cold machine, with unfailing efficacy. As something which is simultaneously too human and fundamentally inhuman, how can it maintain itself except by a miracle?

What we shall now see is that this very contradiction is the paradoxical essence and strength of despotic power. Its two aspects are inseparable because they are complementary, and the two movements we have just described, instead of opposing and negating one another, are mutually productive and sustaining, so that Oriental despotism becomes like some extraordinary machinery of power which is able not only to keep running, but to keep on running perpetually, indefinitely reproducing the conditions of its own movement.

4

The Machine

Judged by the criteria of a market economy, the despotic economy is patently absurd. Instead of promoting the growth of national wealth by allowing the circulation of goods and the accumulation of revenue and commercial capital – in other words, fostering production in order to become rich, and enrichment in order to produce more – it leads to the widespread impoverishment of all and the exclusive enrichment of a single man, who hoards, consumes and squanders without the smallest profit to the nation. Since the despot's subjects are the owners neither of their means of production nor of what they produce – even in the minimal case of producing their own offspring – it can be said that they do not belong to themselves. They are nothing; they exist only for and through the despot.

Yet as soon as one judges the despotic economy according to its own norms, relating it to the type of government in which it is described, it ceases to seem absurd. We can then see that just as a liberal, capitalist, market economy can function properly only within a given political structure, so what we can call an economy of *jouissance*, which is characteristic of the despotic regime, is simultaneously the *raison d'être* and the necessary effect of a certain type of exercise of power which, as we have tried to show, could be reduced to the pure form of a mere communication of the master's name.

The Paradox of the Vizier

In Oriental despotism, the relations between the economic and the political take the following form: upon a whim, the despot elevates this or that subject, who a moment before was nothing, to the highest office. By marking him with the seal of his name, he instantly transmits the whole of his power to him. The vizier becomes the despot: 'He is called the lieutenant of the Great Lord, or the Vicar of the Empire, because effectively the whole of the Sultan's might and authority reside in his person.'[1] As the holder of the signifier which gives him absolute power, the vizier therefore desires *like* the despot, which assumes that his will, like that of the despot, is made manifest arbitrarily, suddenly and absolutely. But the exercise of this absolute power depends at every moment upon the good graces of the despot, who can reduce it to nothing by taking back his seal. The vizier must therefore avoid displeasing the despot. He may well desire *like* him, but we must now realize that he will desire everything the despot desires. And since the will of the despot merges with his wish, and this wish is, by its nature, unpredictable, the vizier will be careful of any personal initiative; for him, this is the only way of continuing to be loved, which is to say of responding to the wishes of that Other, of whom it is a characteristic that nothing can be known or predicted. In other words, the vizier must simultaneously desire *like a* despot, and *like the* despot, which is plainly contradictory – as Tavernier, for example, points out: the power of the Grand Vizier is

so absolute that in all the Empires and Kingdoms of the world there is no prime minister whose authority can be compared with that of the Grand Vizier . . . but he is above all someone who merits close study, for since only the Grand Vizier has the right to put forward all matters of importance, he must take care to make no proposal which might displease the Great Lord; for according to that maxim of the Ottoman Court that nothing must be proposed to the Prince which might anger him, without a word in answer, the Great Lord could on the instant have him strangled.[2]

Thus the vizier is torn by a dilemma which seems irresolvable, since he is compelled both to be reckoned with and to obliterate himself, to be and not to be the despot, to exercise all power alone and to exercise none. If he does not act, he displeases, since he is failing in the function of 'vicar' for which he has been named, therefore risking his head. But if he acts, he still risks his head, since he exposes himself to displeasure. This is an impossible situation, one which ought to discourage all ambition. But this is not so: 'This office is a very hard one, and a Grand Vizier has very little time of his own, yet all aspire to this office with great fervour, although they know almost for certain that within a short time they will die.'[3] But if death is the only way out of the dilemma in which the vizier is locked, it is because this dilemma is itself the expression of a more radical choice: in the despotic State, either one lives but counts for nothing, or one counts, but on the condition of giving one's life. In these terms, freely offering his head to the despot when he demands it is not the vizier's failure. It is his triumph. This death must be seen as the only moment when the vizier knows with absolute clarity that he is the Other's wish, and when he is fully in control of responding to this wish. He can finally desire *like him*, in both senses simultaneously: 'The highest officers in the Empire are in agreement that the peak of happiness and glory is to end life by the hand or command of their master.'[4]

This extreme 'gift of love', which is the true price to be paid for existing, can none the less be a deferred moment. How can one be loved by a despot while being ignorant of his wishes, yet certain of responding to those wishes? The despot's subject answers: by giving him the opportunity to love himself through me. In a world where there are those who have nothing and are nothing, while the Other is and possesses everything, after the gift of life the spontaneous form assumed by the gift of love is *flattery*; it is the giving of an image which offers the despot more than he has, but supposes in exchange that he will accept that he is not everything, since you cannot be flattered except by someone who matters in your eyes. A momentary abandonment of power is therefore offset by a gain in *jouissance*. This image must, however, bring the despot some profit – that is to say, he must gain in *jouissance* more than he agrees to lose by transmitting his power for the sake of being flattered. And since there is no common measure between *jouissance* and power, the logic of flattery demands that it be carried always to excess, to inflation, to extravagance. With a populace of mirror-bearers standing before him wherever he goes, the despot is enchanted by the extravagant echoes and reflections of himself.

But 'Whatever good we are told about ourselves, we learn nothing new',[5] and the Oriental despot's insatiable thirst for *jouissance* always demands the new. The descending transmission of power will therefore be answered by a rising flux of presents of every kind – which, however, stand always as gifts of love against gifts of existence, as 'surplus enjoyment' against 'surplus power':

> All those whom the Sultan gratifies with a vice-royalty or an office of consequence are indispensably obliged to give him presents, and not according to their resources, for often these are people elevated from the seraglio, where they have been able to accumulate almost nothing.[6]

And here they are placed under an obligation to give what they do not have, since no one in the despotic state – except the despot – owns anything. Thus the man to whom the despot has just transmitted his power must in his turn transmit it to another, in order to receive presents which will all find their way up to the despot. It is the Grand Vizier who first of all, as Tournefort writes, 'is compelled to give rich presents to his master in order to maintain his position. This means that the Great Lord continually bleeds him of what he has.' And 'the Vizier puts everything up for sale in order to finance such great expense; his Palace is a marketplace where all favours are sold.'[7] He in turn becomes an 'insatiable bloodsucker',[8] compelling those to whom he transmits power to act like him. The despot/vizier relation is reproduced identically at every link in the chain. Whatever level he occupies, the momentary holder of power desires simultaneously like *a* despot and like *the* despot. He is always simultaneously an absolute point of departure and a pure relay, all the way along the chain to its very end, where of course there is only the populace that is endlessly subject to tithes and taxes, with no other care but to stay alive, but in anonymity and nullity.[9]

The transmission of power which is characteristic of the despotic regime thus appears as a *means* to an end, with the name of the master functioning as the efficient cause of an effect which can be summed up in these words: 'Always more *jouissance*'.

The Paradox of the Despot

But there is another way of presenting things: we can say that the Oriental despot, being essentially engaged in his *jouissance*, is incapable of exercising power. He is thus compelled to have it exercised by a surrogate. Instead of being an ultimate goal, the *jouissance* of the despot then becomes the primary cause of the transmission of power, which is its necessary effect. Chardin writes:

> The Mahommedan sovereigns, having been brought up in seraglios with Women and Eunuchs, are so incapable of governing, that for the good of the people and the security of the State, there needs to be set beneath them someone to rule in their stead . . . ; and since these Kings of the Orient have seldom a thought for anything but the pleasures of the senses, it is all the more necessary that there be someone to consider the preservation and the glory of the Empire. These are the principal reasons for the extreme power of the Grand Viziers, and if we go further back in Mahommedanism, as far as its earliest times, we will find that the Kings of the Orient all had their Grand Viziers just as the Kings of Egypt had their Joseph and those of Assyria their Daniel.[10]

Here Chardin is defining a type of power which applied throughout the Orient, where it had long been formed as if by some kind of natural necessity (which Islam would only strengthen). In this Asia, a land of slavery and indolence, which Aristotle had put forward as a fundamental feature of the (domestic) despotic master, the master is truly such only in so far as he abandons himself entirely to *jouissance* – therefore in so far as he gives up the exercise of power (the supervision and administration of the work of the slaves) to his surrogate, the overseer. Like the Aristotelian master, the Oriental despot does not experience the *jouissance of power*. He has *jouissance* only on condition that his power is exercised by someone else, and he hands over this exercise of power only because he gives all his time to his *jouissance*. But while the Greek master can thus fully enjoy the superior faculties of his soul – and, thanks to philosophical leisure, attain true mastery, which is self-restraint (ἐγκράτεια)[11] – the Oriental despot abandons himself instead to a purely sensual *jouissance*. Brought up as uneducated and ignorant, among women and far from matters of state, he has not been educated to prepare for this self-restraint which reproduces the relationship between an individual's body and spirit which that individual maintains with those to whom he gives the task of serving him. Were anyone to attempt to educate him in this way, such efforts would be rendered futile by the exigencies of the climate and Asiatic customs, which exert an unconquerable impulse towards physical voluptuousness and intellectual inertia. Thus the Oriental despot, instead of attaining some kind of higher humanity through the freedom it has been his privilege to enjoy, is obliterated in and through his *jouissance* itself.

Here we are touching on the most disturbing paradox of despotic power, whose scandalous evidence had been denounced by La Boétie, though he was unable to explain it: who is this single individual before whom men willingly debase themselves to the most extreme servitude? Is he a Hercules, a Samson – in other words, a Superman? Not at all; he is, rather, less than a man. He is a

> mannikin, and usually the most cowardly and womanish in the nation; one unaccustomed to the dust of the battlefield, and hardly even to the sand of the jousting lists; not one who can command men by force, but

without the wherewithal to be of useful service to the weakest of women![12]

This extreme power, whose transmission makes all-powerful the man who a moment before was nothing, therefore issues from a being who in himself is nothing. Stupid and ignorant, hidden deep within his apartments, his soft body given up to *jouissance*, the despot, who is made the source and origin of power, is nothing but a totally spent force.[13] We could say that he exists only in the mode of default, in the mode of the negative: 'Such a prince has so many imperfections, that they are afraid to expose his natural stupidity to public view. He is concealed in his palace, and the people are ignorant of his situation.'[14] But far from harming the economy of absolute despotic power, this blankness of the royal person of the despot is, rather, precisely what upholds it and allows its perfect exercise.

And the more the despot's person is obliterated, the more his name seems to become potent and fearsome through its detachment, through its seemingly autonomous blind purpose. It is of little importance whether the despot is drunk, sick or out of his mind, of little importance whether he is dead or alive; the despot is always 'as if dead', and this is how his name is raised to the highest symbolic potency. Chardin, for example, relates how the name of Abbas, an emperor of Persia, continued to reign, while Abbas was long since dead, although no one knew this except two or three of those close to him. The death of Abbas was learned only when his son had been set upon the throne:

> I shall leave you to imagine how much everyone [among the populace] was amazed. I myself found this circumstance to be something so without precedent that I thought what I saw was a dream. To conceal the death of such a mighty Prince for so long a time, and for there to have been no knowledge of it until his son was seen to ascend upon the throne, is something the like of which I have never read.[15]

What is more, this event did not provoke the least commotion;[16] the name of Abbas was obeyed, the name of Safie would be obeyed. And as proof that it was the name alone that governed, when it was realized that this name, Safie, lacked the beneficent effects expected of it, on the advice of astrologers it was decided to change not the person of the Emperor, but his name; hence another coronation, other seals, another currency, and another name, of which wonders were expected: Suleiman.

This is why, paradoxically, it is so easy to become a despot: 'I should never have thought that these things were so easy,' said a pope who 'had started an infinite number of difficulties against his election, from a thorough conviction of his incapacity'.[17] Anyone can do the job, in fact, since, as Montesquieu says, all that is needed to rule is a name: 'When Osman, the Turkish emperor, was deposed, ... a voice which was never identified came by chance from the crowd, the name of Mustapha was uttered, and suddenly Mustapha was emperor.'[18]

If it is easy to occupy the throne, for the same reasons it is difficult to stay on it. The despot's reign is ephemeral, or at any rate aleatory. Since he is nothing in himself, he is not the one who matters to people. Montesquieu explains that this is where despotism differs from monarchy, in which the king is important and exercises power by his actual personal rule, while the Asian princes, by hiding themselves and being invisible, 'inspire respect for royalty, not for the king, and fix their subjects' minds on a particular throne, not on a particular person'.[19] From this comes a fresh paradox: of all regimes, the despotic is probably the one which is most stable, even attaining a kind of immortality, whereas – or rather, *because* – of all monarchs the despot is the most fragile, the most inconsistent and the most constantly threatened.[20] In advance of both Montesquieu and Rousseau, Spinoza wrote that once tyranny is set up: 'it has so commonly happened that peoples have often changed their tyrants, but have never succeeded in getting rid of them altogether'.[21] The despotic state is a theatre stage upon which different actors succeed one another to take always the same walk-on parts in a play which is written once and for all, and re-enacted indefinitely: 'This invisible ruling power always remains identical for the people. Even if a dozen kings, whom they know only by name, were to slaughter each other in turn, they would not be aware of any difference: it would be as if they had been governed by a succession of phantoms.'[22]

Likewise, the histories of monarchies 'are full of civil wars without revolutions, while the histories of despotic governments abound with revolutions without civil wars'.[23] This means that in its division between the rapid but inconsequential cycle of seraglio anecdotes, and the deep immobility of its frozen structure, despotism inhabits a territory which lies either side of what the West will recognize as that of history. In place of history – of which it can have no conception, and which it cannot beget – the Orient substitutes histories, fuelling the Western imagination. Its deep and silent night is peopled with countless dreams which are tireless variations on some major themes. But the Oriental tale, with its magic mirrors and talismans, its words and gestures with the power to transform men and things in an instant, its transportation through space without time, is nothing other than the rhetorical amplification of or free commentary on what the travellers record having seen in the Orient. The insubstantial shadows which move about in the seraglio are of the same stuff as the characters in the *Thousand and One Nights*, and their uncertain fate is the plaything of the same capricious divinities: the despotic Orient delights in *metamorphosis* – a simulacrum and negation of history – and under a perpetual alteration of forms, the identity and permanence of a structure, the repetitive dryness and rigid automaton of a machine, are affirmed.

Perpetual Motion

A machine. This may be only one aspect of the despotic regime, yet it always overlays the comparisons and metaphors used to describe it by the authors of the Classical period.

Let us therefore hypothesize the despotic machine. If we are to understand it, we must answer three kinds of question: by what means, how and why does it function? In other words, we have to locate the nature and source of the energy which drives it; we have to analyse the way in which this energy feeds into the mechanism, and describe the agency of this mechanism; lastly, we have to define what it produces, and for what purpose.

Summarizing the broad outlines of what has been brought out in the preceding pages, we can make the following initial observations:

1. In the despotic state the driving force of energy is, paradoxically, a vacuum. The Prince is nothing, and no positive power issues from his person. Yet because he occupies a place – in the heart of the seraglio – where 'grown every day more infirm, he is the first prisoner of the palace',[24] once he becomes a prince, he is blotted out as a person, while his *name* becomes Master. Within the despotic machine, therefore, the driving agent is a signifier, a name which is also the name of the One; the energy which fuels it is of a *negative* order, and the inability of his subjects to recognize it as other than an arbitrary, absolute and positive *will* is the effect of a necessary illusion with which we will deal further on.

2. Face to face with this unique and heterogeneous element which is the Name of the Master, there is the anonymous, homogeneous crowd, all of them equal: the slaves, those who possess and put into practice a *knowledge* of skills in the service of the Other. They constitute the *mechanism*. Nothing within the apparatus is ordered as a means of transforming, braking or regulating the initial movement. As a result it can connect indiscriminately with any element whatsoever in the mechanism simply by marking (or 'plugging into') the master-signifier. What we call 'education' is merely the operation whereby the parts are standardized so that they are perfectly interchangeable without any risk of the working of the mechanism being modified.

3. What the despotic machine produces is a flux of all kinds of goods which are rechannelled so that they get lost in the central vacuum, in that *hole* which is the habitation and, perhaps, the very definition of the despot.

Within this schema, despotism, the 'personal' regime *par excellence*, emerges in reality as the most *impersonal* of regimes. Power, which seems to reside in the hands of a single man, effectively belongs to no one.

It cannot truly be said that power is possessed by the vizier (or any one of the subordinates in the despotic chain) since, as nothing in himself, he never commands except 'in the name of the despot'. And from where does this name derive its power? Is it from the power the despot possesses? But the despot, likewise, is nothing in himself; he cannot, therefore, as Montesquieu puts it, 'give greatness which he does not own'.[25] It is therefore far from being the case that the person of the despot confers its power on his name, but exactly the opposite takes place: like his vizier, the despot has importance only by virtue of an all-powerful name, for which he is merely the reference point or imaginary support. The despot is nothing without his vizier, who, being effaced in his name, thereby constitutes him as his master. In other words, the vizier creates the despot just as much as the despot creates the vizier.

Absolute power, whose effects are manifest and omnipresent in despotism, is therefore never given *in person*. And this is because it is never simple, but always and necessarily split, riven between its fictive source and the point where it is exercised, between its invisible and secret origin and its manifest but secondary beginning. A despot who erases himself, absents himself in his stupid *jouissance*, and a vizier who merges with the pure signifier which constitutes him (transforms itself into Charles XII's boot) – this is the basic dyad which is constitutive of despotic power. The despot does not transmit to his vizier a power which he would hold as its source and could exercise; but would give up after an interval for the sake of *jouissance*; the despot/vizier split is one which is there from the start, and there is nothing accidental in this division between *jouissance* and the exercise of power. It is unconnected to the spineless personality of this or that despot; it is *essential*, and the roles it allots are defined by the very structure of Oriental despotism. This is probably what Montesquieu means when he writes that in the despotic State, 'The creation of a vizier is a fundamental law'.[26]

This is indeed a fundamental law, since it enables the despotic regime to be upheld – in other words, it enables this machine to go on working indefinitely, continuously reproducing the conditions of its own movement. Until now we have laid stress upon the singular effects of a name, showing how it would be detached from its bearer and circulate all along a chain, giving a fleeting existence to those marked by it. But to these strictly symbolic effects we must add the counterweight of one which depends upon the imagination. For this vacuum, this hole which we said could stand as a definition of the despot, is never perceived as such by those who none the less will lose themselves utterly in it. It is in fact hidden by the *imaginary* figure of the despot, which, fictive though it is, is all the more dazzling and blinding. The grandeur of the Oriental despot is a semblance of grandeur, every part of which is created by those who both command in his name and obey that same name. In short, it is an object of belief, and it is crucial that everyone – including the despot – should believe in it, otherwise the whole system of power collapses. But if people obey only what they believe in, conversely, they believe only because they have already begun to obey. And it is because obedience is given only to a name (and more generally to a signifier stripped of meaning) that an imaginary support is fashioned for it, one endowed with extravagant power, in which one cannot disbelieve. Like the despot and his vizier, obedience and belief are a pairing. The potency of the symbolic and the fascination of the imaginary are mutually formative and inseparable: 'The reason why princes usually have a very false notion of their grandeur is that those who educate them are dazzled by it themselves; they are its first dupes, and the princes are only duped in their wake.'[27] Montesquieu's observation is valid *a fortiori* for the Oriental despot, whose real grandeur is nonexistent. The dazzlement of his subjects is proportionate to this blankness. Here we find again that essential function of the gaze which we referred to earlier, and that characteristic of the kings of the Orient which Chardin described as being 'kings for display' (and through display), idols for seducing the gaze. Obliterated in the real and lost in his own *jouissance*, the despot is resplendent in the imagination, while his name becomes the master-signifier. It is time to measure how much the gaze, the driving element in the imaginary, is linked to the name (whether this is uttered by the voice or inscribed in the letter) – that is to say, to an exercise of power which is acted out in the symbolic. But the two are entwined together in this way only because the real which maintains them can be reduced to a pure vacuum, to a hole.

This interplay of symbolic and imaginary, obedience and belief, fear and love, is repeated at every level of the despotic chain. Once he is marked with the seal, the vizier, who was nothing, brings into being the imaginary person of the despot, and instantly becomes the despot in the dazzled eyes of those to whom he communicates power – who in turn, and so forth. This is why it is essential for despotic power to be transmitted whole, to multiply the stages which are so many transitory supports for the Name. Each symbolic marking is thus answered by a new imaginary creation of the despot, whose fictive grandeur thereby grows, and is confirmed with each instance. It is therefore the strength of the Oriental despotic system that it *induces* a necessary *belief* that the despot is everywhere, when in reality he is nowhere; that he is all-powerful, when in himself he is nothing; that he is unique and singular, when he is both everyone and no one.

We can therefore describe this despotic power – simultaneously and without any contradiction – as functioning according to the strict determinism of a blind mechanism (compare the metaphor of the billiard ball) and also being there 'at first sight', needing only passions to establish and preserve itself. It is what makes this power machine so effective – and so mysterious; it works without anyone knowing how it works, and fully works only if everyone, from the despot down to his lowliest subject, is unaware of what impels their actions: 'Excessive obedience supposes ignorance in the person that obeys: the same it supposes in him that commands.'[28] Camouflaged beneath the externals of a purely passionate relation which is even akin to the seduction of the lover, the despotic machine necessarily produces a misrecognition of its workings in those who are caught up in it. Become cogs in a machine, they are the ones who unknowingly activate and perpetuate its movement. In this they resemble those curious courtesans who, on entering certain grottoes in the royal gardens at Versailles, unwittingly triggered the hidden mechanism of some hydraulic automaton disguised by an illusory fleshly aspect, deliberately placed there by a skilful engineer in order to seduce the imagination and trap desire, thus presenting to the eyes of the Sun King a ludic representation and a scaled-down model of his own power.[29]

5

The Sword and the Book

This, then, if we reduce it to the simple schema which emerges from a reading of the travellers' accounts, is the characteristic structure of power and its mode of functioning in Oriental despotic regimes. It embodies an admirable technical perfection; the travellers observed its effectiveness, an effectiveness all the more surprising for its apparent dependence upon extremely fragile – not to say non-existent foundations. How else could regimes of such manifest absurdity see the light of day and perpetuate themselves, except by a miracle?

Military Discipline

Yet the explanation seems simple: it was through military conquests that the Persian, Turkish and Mogul empires came about, and they explain the vast extent of these empires. The inevitable result of their extent was that they were able to perpetuate themselves only by the same military means through which they were formed. 'We should not be surprised that the government of Persia is despotic and arbitrary,' wrote Chardin, 'since it is in fact a military government.... Everyone knows that military governments are everywhere arbitrary.'[1] According to Ricaut, the same applies to the Turkish government, 'whose early foundations were cast on principles which were best suited to military discipline'.[2] This gives us a better understanding of the source of that 'economy of *jouissance*' which is so utterly centralized. Since the sultan had formerly been the sole leader of the armies, everything the Turks won 'by the blade of the sword and the risk of their lives, was deployed for the use and profit of their master so that . . . all the Provinces now vie with one another in satisfying the wishes of a single person'.[3]

As well as explaining the centripetal movement of goods towards the despot, the military origins of despotic government also explain an institution like that of the vizier. In Persia, every time he left for long-drawn-out wars on the frontiers of the Empire, the emperor, whose primary role was as chief general, would entrust all civil power to a man who was able to represent him while giving every guarantee of loyalty to his master; this man was the vizier, a man plucked from obscurity, with no local family attachments and nothing behind him but the imperial seal. The consequence of this was that when the despot ceased effectively to exercise his power in order to take his pleasure hidden away in the depths of his palace, the relationship was inverted: the vizier became general-in-chief of the armies.

This is why the Turkish army, like all despotic armies, is first and foremost, before being a vast body of men, a treasure house of signifiers, articulated together in a system which combines qualitative differences (standards of every colour but one: green) and quantitative ones (horses' tails, or feathers). Those who command do not do so because, as in Europe, they are scions of some great family or already hold powerful office, but by the sole virtue of an 'additional' signifier, which is transmitted by the despot in the course of a brief and silent ceremony:

> When it is time for the troops to march out, the Great Lord . . . with the vizier by his side, presents him to them as their General. At this point the soldiers say nothing; nor do they give the usual salute, until after the Great Lord has had one of the plumes removed from his turban, setting it on that of the Grand Vizier. It is then that the whole

army salutes him, acknowledging him as its general, and at the same time receiving its wages from him.[4]

The enactment of this symbolism is one of the essential elements of military discipline in a despotic country. But this discipline attains its most perfect form in the militias which are directly attached to the despot's guard, like the Janissary corps, which in the eyes of Europeans has long remained a legendary example. Numbering twenty-five thousand, according to Tavernier:[5]

> Before being enrolled, the Janissaries swear two kinds of oath. The first is to serve the Emperor faithfully; the second is to desire everything that their comrades desire and never to forsake them. This unites them and binds them together so well that there is no power equal to theirs throughout the Ottoman Empire.[6]

These Janissaries are all the children of Christians captured in warfare,[7] orphans cut off from any roots whereby they could be differentiated from one another in reality (and not just numerically), and now all they have is one and the same father. But they are the sons of the same father – in whose name they obey through the mediation of their *Aga* – only because each one of them exists only through and for the others, in whom he recognizes his twin brothers and with whom he identifies body and soul. The two oaths whereby they submit and are joined are mutually strengthening: they come together fraternally because they are children of the same father. But they believe in that father only because they are joined, as brothers, to other brothers. Hence the comparison borrowed from the religious sphere which we find in the writings of the majority of the travellers when they speak about the Janissaries: 'In all things order is so fine and so nicely observed that they live less as soldiers than as monks, and although they are not forbidden to marry, they very rarely do so.'[8] This makes the Janissary corps (or that of the Spahis, which is of the same kind) a double-edged weapon in the hands of the despot. As the object of their exclusive love and their religion, he can hold all sway over

87

them and through them. But they can hold sway over him if they cease to believe in him:

> For fear of being found unarmed, the Sultans have made chains for themselves and their successors, by setting up a formidable militia which exists equally in peacetime as in war. The Janissaries and the Spahis so strongly balance the power of the Prince, however absolute it is, that they sometimes have the impudence to ask for his head.[9]

So we can see that the army is only apparently the source and instrument of despotic power. It merely illustrates and proclaims it, but does not explain it. Even though despotic *government* (as a *political* form) is of military derivation, the structure of despotic *power* itself is always already inscribed in the army, which would disintegrate without it. The army is therefore not a primary force from which despotic power derives, like some abstract form being released from a concrete reality, nor is it a *real* power which is added to an imaginary and symbolic power to render it effective; it is despotic power itself, in operation. The Turkish army is truly strong, and its weapons triumph,[10] because blind obedience is given to the name of the despot, and lives are offered up willingly as proof of love for him. So instead of explaining the structure of despotic power, it redoubles its enigmatic character.

The Masquerade of Religion

We will turn now to religion, to seek the key to this enigma.

And it is not a matter of just any religion. For there is one overriding proof: the countries where despotic power holds purest sway (Turkey, Persia, the Mogul Empire) are those where the Mahommedan religion also holds sway.[11] This cannot be a fortuitous coincidence. 'The flood tide of Mahommedans brought despotism with it', wrote Montesquieu,[12] echoing a view more or less universally acknowledged by the travellers, for whom Mahommedanism and despotism were organically linked. Despotic government 'is most agreeable' to the Mahommedan religion[13], because it is naturally inscribed within it, originates in it, and is both its expression and its guarantee.

The despot and his mufti

In Persia, Turkey and the Mogul Empire, what is the despot if not Mahomet's successor and, like him, an absolute leader, not just in the temporal but the spiritual sense, regarded by his subjects 'as God's vicar and lieutenant on Earth'?[14] This is the foundation of the 'Right of Government' which, in Mahommedan countries, 'belongs only to the Prophets, and to their lieutenants or direct successors'.[15] The criteria whereby one can define who is a true successor are probably open to dispute. In Persia:

> pious men believe that the Royal throne should be occupied by a Mouchtehed Massoum, terms which signify a man whose conduct is pure and who is familiar with every branch of Knowledge to such a perfect degree that he can instantly answer, without prompting, any question put to him on religion and on civil law.[16]

But the majority judge it sufficient that he be a direct descendant of the first imams, and 'that there is no requirement for this descendant to be either pure or scholarly to such a great degree of perfection'. He will not be any the less 'the true lieutenant of God and the true vicar of the Prophet and the Imams'.[17]

Hence the unlimited power of the despot in Mahommedan States; the Ottoman Sultan, Selim I, described himself as 'Master of all the sovereigns in the world'.[18] The Emperor of Persia 'possesses supernatural qualities, like that of curing diseases', and this is only one of his countless titles, a list of which takes up a whole page in Chardin.[19] But this claim by the despot to be the vicar of Mahomet, and thereby 'Master of the world', inevitably provokes that hatred which the emperors of Turkey, Persia and India bear towards one another: 'Each of them claims to be the true successor of that false prophet [and] treats the other two as a

Vely, which means the substitute or lieutenant of a reigning sovereign.'[20] Therefore the despot, in the very religion which gives him his calling to set himself up as the Single Ruler, encounters a first limit to his absolute power. But it imposes another limit upon him – one that is in another respect more severe, at least in appearance.

For the Oriental despot, by definition, is the absolute master of his subjects' lives and chattels: 'One thing, however, may be sometimes opposed to the prince's will, namely, religion . . . . The laws of religion are of a superior nature, because they bind the sovereign as well as the subject.'[21] Here, Montesquieu is referring to a passage in Chardin about the Persians, where he notes that according to 'a singular creed':

> they maintain that the orders of the King are above natural Law, and can decree that the son should be his father's executioner or the father that of his son, whenever the King so commands such a death. But they elsewhere maintain, . . . that his orders are beneath divine Law, and that if it should come about that the King commands something against Religion he should not be obeyed.[22]

Religion's check on the arbitrary will of the despot is all the more important given that religious laws also have validity as civil laws. Both in Persia and Turkey, 'civil Law is one and the same as Canon Law'.[23] Likewise among the Turks, 'who maintain that civil laws are a part of religion and that since they have been handed down by the Prophet, they come from God and demand blind obedience'.[24] Moreover, they are written in a Book, to which, like all his subjects – and even more rigorously, since he is their spiritual leader – the despot must bend. 'The religious code supplies the civil and fixes the extent of arbitrary sway',[25] and has the place of 'fundamental laws'.

Religion therefore functions as a counter-power, which, in Turkey, is embodied in the person of the mufti, who is the supreme custodian and interpreter of the sacred text. At the beginning of the seventeenth century, Gedoyn compared him to the Pope.[26] In fact, his theoretical power is more extensive: 'He is the sovereign Pontiff of their Law, and the first above all Judges', explains Baudier.[27] 'His authority is the greatest there is in the Empire', since – returning to Tavernier's comparison – in him are fused theologian and jurisconsult, and because 'as chief religious leader and interpreter of the Koran, he is at the head of those who hand down the law'.[28] Moreover, the Great Lord shows him an unparalleled respect: 'He frequently consults him upon the most important matters, always follows his counsels, and is the only man on earth whom he receives by rising to his feet.'[29]

All this, therefore, comes about as if religion, by lengthening the despotic chain upwards, became its first link, while simultaneously intimating that despotic power never assumes the pure form in which we have just described it. In fact, the despot, 'God's vicar and lieutenant', is to God – who is invisible and all-powerful, and manifest only through his written Law – what the vizier was to the person and name of the despot. But the Law obeyed by the despot, unlike the ever-changing and contradictory one by which the vizier sought in vain to abide, is a written one, and therefore unchangeable, known and respected by all. It is therefore a good foundation for the power of the despot, who commands in the name of an Other, although it limits this power. So we find ourselves led to this alternative: either one grasps the root of despotic power, with the result that we can no longer represent it in its purely despotic form (which none the less strikes all the travellers) – or we persist in asserting that it is exercised in this pure, absolute, limitless form, with the result that we can no longer establish its source. The outcome is that in both cases pure despotic power remains an enigma.

But this aporia arises from the fact that we have taken seriously what is only a masquerade. Of course, the despot prides himself on his scrupulous obedience to the Law[30] and his respect for his Pontiff. But the Pontiff has no real power; he is utterly dependent upon the whim of the despot. In Turkey, the election of the mufti 'depends absolutely upon the Great Lord'.[31] In Persia, nowadays, 'the spiritual has been altogether subordinate to the temporal', ever since Abbas II decided to leave the post of *Sedre* vacant throughout the last eighteen months of his reign.[32] And when Aurengzeb took power in the Mogul Empire and met with opposition from the State cadi, the chief Lawgiver, he had him deposed with ease.[33] The despot consults his Grand Pontiff 'most often only for appearances' sake'.[34] Whenever he chooses to make use of him, it is to confirm his own arbitrariness. In other words, the man of law has a role which consists in affirming that the only law is the will of the despot: 'Their cadis and their legislators say that he is above the laws, which is to say that he explains, amends and cancels them out whenever he pleases, that his words are law itself; and that his explanations of them are infallible.'[35] The paradox, therefore, is that the Law gives the force of law to that which exceeds or violates it:

> For, while he [the despot] is obliged to carry out Mahomet's law, that same law says unfailingly that the Emperor is its infallible oracle and interpreter, investing him with the power to change and annul its most established rules, or at least to dispense with them and overlook them whenever they are set against the manner of his rule, or of the Empire's grand designs.[36]

If this is the case, what is the point of being burdened with a Grand Mufti or any others who claim to stand for the Law, and making a pretence of bending to their commandments? The point is that by affecting to respect the Law through them, the despot endows this Law with a transcendence and an omnipotence which are invested in him in exchange, endowing his speech and his name (and similarly all those who command in his name, across the chain of despotism) with their absolute symbolic power. Or – to be more precise – *the despot, too*, by submitting to it like everyone else, endows the Law with its *universal* character, while he *alone* receives from it the power to speak *imperatively*. This universal imperative through which the Law is defined exists within despotism only as something split and sundered: on the one hand the universal, on the other the imperative. To such an extent that it can equally be said that the despot creates the Law, and the Law creates the despot. The one does not exist without the other, as Sade, a great reader of travellers' accounts, was to say at the end of the eighteenth century, through the mouthpiece of Prince Chigi. Answering Olympe, who still believes that the despot arises out of anarchy and the absence of laws, he says: 'the despot is he who creates the law [who bids it speak or be still], who uses it to serve his own interests'. But it is also the Law which begets despots, he adds, since '[Never are tyrants born of anarchy,] you see them flourish only behind the screen of the law',[37] and arrayed in their false light. Every despot, however autocratic, produces 'Laws' that are above him, even if they are reduced to the pure form of a regular sequence like that of day and night, fostered by the Oriental despots with their habit 'of showing themselves to their subjects only in accordance with fixed hours, days and the ordered passage of time'.[38]

In reality, therefore, the arbitrary will of the despot is indeed the one and only power, but this is thanks to an interplay of mutual illumination and eclipse between the exception and the rule, the imperative and the universal, the person of the despot and the impersonality of the Law.

Mektoub

None the less, for the whims of the despot to 'stand as law' it is necessary that the Law which endows them with their power itself has power already invested in it, and that it is obeyed. How the problem of the combined origins of Law and despotic power is posed and resolved is something that could be demonstrated, from Spinoza to Boulanger. If we keep within the bounds of Islamic regimes such as those described by the travellers, we can affirm that obedience to the orders of the despot appears essentially as obedience 'to the letter'.

We already know how much respect and reverence are attached to the letter *per se* in Persia or in Turkey. This respect extends to whatever gives it a material basis or delineation; all the authors observe that the Mahommedans do not use paper after completing their natural bodily functions,[39] and whenever they sharpen a quill to write with, they take great care to pick up all the shavings. But the reason for their granting this awesome value to the letter is its status as the very form and substance of their Law, inscribed for all time in one book, the Koran, to which every Mahommedan must offer blind obedience.

The content of the Law – the message – seems precisely to be nothing other than the graphic and linguistic code in which it is pronounced. The Koran is written 'not in the Turkish language, nor the Persian, but in Arabic, which is the only tongue in which its adherents read it, even though it has been embraced by several nations with quite different tongues'.[40] No doubt these letters always carry a meaning. But while 'It might seem at first sight as if a book written under inspiration should contain the ideas of God conveyed in human language,' observes the Persian Usbek, 'in our Koran, on the other hand, you often find the language of God and the ideas of men, as if by a remarkable act of caprice, God had dictated the words, while mankind provided the thoughts.'[41] Here, therefore, in its very materiality, the Book is a direct emanation of God and, as such, is immutable, 'eternal, existing in the Essence of God, without any capacity for separation or division from God'.[42] Moreover, it is not in adherence to its meaning that obedience is given to the letter. On the contrary, it is through obedience to the letter that one is regarded as a true believer. This is the source of the conviction that it is necessary to imbue oneself with the letter, through a scrupulous and indefinitely repeated reading of the Book,[43] in order to be a good Mahommedan. To make an error of reading is to transgress the Law; P.M. Nau writes:

> when they read their Koran, the Turks continually shake all over, as if they worshipped every single word, and it is like a sin of infidelity for them to make an error in reading it. They use it to teach children to read, and when they stumble and make a mistake they are rebuked with having sinned against the Law.[44]

This being so, it will be no surprise to observe the Persians –
'the most superstitious people in the world', according to Chardin
– wearing on their bodies or sewn into their garments a great
number of amulets and talismans made up of fragments of the
Koran, the names of saints or a 'collection of gods' Names, which
reach one thousand and one. They call this collection *Giauchen*,
which means "coat of mail"',[45] and cover their bodies with it as
protection. In Turkey, they even go so far as to ingest the signifier.
Once a year, the Great Lord imprints the seal of Mahomet (a few
intertwined letters) on squares of paper, which he folds and sends,
along with a phial of water in which the Prophet's robe has been
dampened, to those chosen for his favour; this (folded) paper is
then plunged into the bottle, and all of its contents are drunk.[46]

The Mahommedan religion is therefore reduced to a cult made
up entirely of externals, in which the signifier is law. In order to
become a Muslim, all that is needed is to utter once or to write
down a standard formula – whether or not one understands its
meaning.[47] As for the rituals of washing, prayers, Ramadan, alms
and pilgrimage, the travellers readily condemn their hypocrisy and
absurdity. What impresses them most of all is that the commandments and prohibitions seem to be most scrupulously observed
with reference to matters which have no importance in their eyes.
The more 'philosophical' among them see in this one of the major
reasons for the Mahommedans' attachment to their religion, as if
the power of the signifier, which is for them its epitome, were
elevated to the point where it regulated even what is insignificant.
The less logical it is to obey, the more reasons one has in that part
of the world for obeying. The more numerous the derisory rules
and pointless prohibitions, the less one transgresses against them:
'A religion burdened with many ceremonies attaches us to it more
strongly than that which has a fewer number. We have an extreme
propensity to things in which we are continually employed.'[48]

This is why the Mahommedan religion is so well suited to
despotic regimes. It effectively teaches one thing only: obedience
to the letter, with neither understanding nor demur. If, within
despotism, education is reduced to mere training,[49] then the

Mahommedan religion is the school of despotism. Trained to follow what the Book decrees, the subjects will be the docile instruments of their master's capricious will, and he will know very well how to exploit them:

> Those who command them open at random a book of their Law, to take from therein the resolution to their journey, and to follow what advice a reading will give them; this they call 'using the book'. But, before they open it, the foremost leaders have decided what they must do, since they open it at the place where they know are contained the things relating to their plan, thus deceiving and abusing their soldiers.[50]

But above all, by accustoming its subjects to strict obedience over small things that are not important, the Mahommedan religion gives free rein to the arbitrary rule of the despot alone in those things which are:[51] 'Laws which render that necessary which is only indifferent have this inconvenience, that they make those things indifferent which are absolutely necessary.'[52] An inconvenience which is turned to the despot's advantage. For since his subjects are accustomed to obey *to the letter*, they do not even imagine that their lives and human relationships as a whole can be governed by anything other than the letter. Nor do they have any notion of the universal laws of natural rights, with their recognition of a free human will which is able to say yes or no to another will. Within despotism, human conduct, outside the domain openly coded by the Koran, assumes no free arbiter; it is prescribed already and for always, and recorded in writing, just as the Koran itself teaches. For it is in the Book itself that it is written that 'everything is written', and nothing escapes the Letter of a text which is transcendent and indecipherable, overriding its subjects and constituting them, all the way through from birth until death, as subjects of the signifier. This, at any rate, is how the Turks and the Persians understand predestination:

> in which they believe without the least reserve and in the most emphatic manner . . . . They believe that the destiny of each individual is written

on his brow, which they call *Narsip* or *Tactir*, which is the book of good or bad luck for each person written in heaven, which they can never circumvent, neither by precautions, nor by any efforts they might make to oppose it.[53]

Each individual, convinced of his preordained fate, will from that moment be the willing plaything of the despot's whim, which he will accept as a sovereign command. The written order for his death carried by the messenger is only the key, now at last revealed to him, to the destiny he carries inscribed on his brow and which he can now decipher.

The shadow of God

On this basis, we can therefore say that the Mahommedan religion – through its very literalness – is the cardinal support of the despotic regime. It is 'fear added to fear. In Mahommedan countries, it is partly from their religion that the people derive the surprising veneration they have for their prince.'[54] But it remains fear *added* to fear, reinforcing a respect which is already there. If indeed, by entailing a belief in predestination, religion does reinforce the power of the despot, the very arbitrariness of this power is constant in its fostering of this belief: 'The Mahommedans have daily before their eyes examples of events so unexpected, happenings so extraordinary, consequences of arbitrary power, that they must be naturally inclined to believe in the doctrine of a rigid Destiny controlling everything.'[55] Belief in Destiny therefore brings about blind obedience to the despot, and vice versa; obedience to the despot binds his subjects more strongly to a religion of submission to the letter (does not the word 'Islam', Chardin points out, mean 'submission to the commandments of God' which are written in the Book?[56]).

'In a despotic government the power is communicated entire to the person entrusted with it. The vizier himself is the despotic prince; and each particular officer is the vizier.'[57] We can see that this principle is now rooted at a superior level. The despot is God himself. Allah transmits his power to him, since the despot commands in his Name. But we have to go further: just as the 'symbolic' power of the vizier brought about the subjects' belief in the being of the despot, as (imaginary) support for his name, so the power of the despot brings about belief in God as the author and support of the Law. It is not surprising, therefore, that the God of the Mahommedans and the Oriental despot should have the same attributes: God is '*Unique*, without any peer, *Singular*, without having any like, *Distinct*, without having any opposite', omnipotent, like the despot. He is invisible; the despot is hidden. 'God sees without pupils and without eyelids', and hears 'without ears and without orifices';[58] the despot's gaze is everywhere, and he knows everything. In short, the (imaginary) being of the despot in itself leads to imagining that of God. Moreover, the Mahommedan religion, whose essential dogmas come close to those of the 'true religion', is in reality the most false and most dangerous of religions, because it is only a simulacrum of the true one. The Turks say that the Great Lord is 'the shadow of God'.[59] But their God is himself only the shadow of the despot and his alibi. Do not Muslims speak out against the cult of idols? But who can fail to see that this condemnation of idolatry, instead of preventing it, makes possible and even inevitable a still more grievous and raging form of idolatry? For 'the Great Lord is adored by his subjects',[60] and is the object of a 'species of idolatry which means that he is looked upon as a God'.[61] In Mahommedan despotism, monotheism and idolatry are not mutually exclusive; they enfold one another,[62] as did the rule and the exception earlier. To such an extent that political relationships can be described in religious terms, and religion can be analysed as a despotic system.

The despotic regime and the Mahommedan religion therefore form a circle, without it being possible to determine which is the cause and which the effect, which the principle and which the consequence. They initiate a structure of power which is one and the same, with an internal coherence and a surprising solidity which can be explained only by a return to the joint origins of despotism and religion, and through the person of the founder of the Law, the false prophet Mahomet. How, then, did Mahomet manage to reach the point where he himself was able 'soon to enjoy that vain happiness of finding himself the General ruler of an army, the Lord of a great land, and deemed to be a prophet sent from God',[63] and to maintain and communicate the triple military, political and religious power now held by that vain phantom – the Oriental despot?

6

Mahomet Beside Himself

Tradition

The legend of Mahomet, elaborated in Muslim countries and embellished – the better to ridicule it – by Christians in the Orient (Byzantines, Egyptians, Syrians and Armenians) between the seventh and the eleventh centuries, was taken up again by the West in medieval times, for the purpose of proselytizing against the Turks, from the First Crusade onwards, and was handed down from book to book until the eighteenth century, when many authors still recorded it without reservation.

The body of the legend

Already circumcised and marked from birth by a sign from God between his shoulders, his face illuminated in the cradle by a light which designated him clearly as the Messenger, surrounded by angels who spoke into his ear and opened his belly to remove from it that drop of black liquid which leads common mortals to sin, then taken one night to the Seventh Heaven, where he came face to face with a God whose face was covered with seventy thousand veils, and so on,[1] the Mahomet of legend appears first as a glorious *body*. Two features above all are exceptional: first his waste products are perfumed:

The sweat of his body flowed like liquid coral; his sweat was even used to confect exquisite perfumes and spices; and when he went by in public places, after him there remained for several minutes a very pleasant fragrance of musk. . . . When he wished to fulfil his bodily functions, the ground would open up and promptly swallow his urine and his excrement; and it would emit a very sweet odour . . . .[2]

Moreover, he was endowed with an incomparable sexual prowess. The precise number of his wives, those in law and others, is not known. It does not matter, since God had given him that unique privilege of having as many of them as he desired. He always had the means to satisfy them: 'It is written in an Arab book whose title is *On the Good Ways of Mahomet*, that he boasted of exercising his eleven wives in a single hour, one after the other.'[3] We know besides that 'God had given him the grace to equal in the lustful power of his loins the strength of forty lubricious fellows who are the sturdiest in all the world'.[4] Others maintained, however, that this strength did not come to him directly from God, but that 'the Angel Gabriel taught him how to make a stew which gave him great strength to enjoy women'.[5]

In contrast with this idealized body of the golden legend of Mahomet, there is the abject body of opposing Christian legend: Mahomet was a frenzied lover of women, but was not above consorting with his she-ass; he drank wine to the point where he fell into a drunken stupor; his body was devoured by dogs, or swine, and so forth. This systematic discrediting of the false prophet is the basis of the early formal refutations of the Koran which were elaborated by the Byzantines (Theophanes, Nicetas . . .) at the beginning of the ninth century. No holds are barred; Mahomet is variously regarded as 'a treacherous rogue, a barbarian, an enemy of God, a man possessed by the devil, an atheist, a blasphemer, a looter, a fool, a man who is debauched, bestial, arrogant, etc.'.[6] Sometimes he is seen as an incarnation of Satan, the Antichrist; sometimes as a fanatical ranter or a crass imbecile. As for his book, unread, it emerges equally as a fearsome scourge and a pack of nonsense and obscenities.

The Middle Ages welcomed uncritically this simultaneously fantastical and insulting body of literature which spread throughout lay society by means of the epic cycles of the Crusade, enriched by the addition of new elements.[7] In the world of scholarship there were stirrings of interest in the Koran, but this was always in order to refute it. Until the sixteenth century (when chairs of Arabic were established in the great European universities), moreover, only two Latin translations of the Koran were available (or rather, versions of the Vulgate which were very far from the original text): one was that of the Englishman Robert de Ketton, undertaken at the request of the Venerable Peter and completed in 1143. It is accompanied by a collection of edifying 'documents' (an *Arab Chronicle*, a *Life of Mahomet*, the anti-Islamic *Polemical Tract* of the bogus Al Kindi) and a prefatory letter by the Venerable Peter offering a *Complete Summary of the Heresy and the Diabolical Sect of the Saracens*.[8] The other translation – more faithful but less widely disseminated – had been done by Marcus of Toledo around 1210. But until the Classical age, despite the enlightened sympathies of men such as Jean Bodin or Guillaume Postel, and the fairly well-documented studies by Arrivabeni,[9] in the view of the West, Islam and its founder remained not so much objects of knowledge as of opprobrium or, at best, of jokes.

The impostor and his Law

While it echoed this rich and contradictory tradition to which it was heir, the seventeenth century set about rectifying it, albeit in continuance with its own ends. In France – but most of all in Holland and in Britain – new tools were rapidly acquired to enable critical work: Arab lexicons and grammars appeared (Erpenius, Du Ryer,[10] Hottinger, etc.), which made it possible to publish accounts of the Islamic religion that were easily accessible to a wide audience. The first of these – which was without doubt to be the principal work of reference throughout more than a century, and would serve as a *vade mecum* for many travellers in the Orient – was Michel Baudier's *Histoire générale de la religion des Turcs*, published in 1626.[11] Baudier was only a scholarly popularizer, but he took it upon himself to establish the 'truth' about the false prophet, and to shed light on the true origin of his power: Mahomet was neither Satan nor an inspired fanatic, merely a coarse, unschooled man who managed to set himself above others only through fraudulence. Instead of being blessed at birth, Baudier declared, Mahomet was in fact born from 'the lowest dregs of the common people'.[12] Orphaned at a very early age, he was sold as a slave, and would have remained one had he not been taken in hand by a heretic of the Nestorian persuasion who had come from Constantinople; this was the famous monk Sergius,[13] who was able to turn the unlettered but ambitious man into a prophet. He counselled him first of all to feign sainthood by withdrawing from the world for two years. When God had punished this hypocrisy by making him epileptic, Mahomet had the skill to turn 'this warning from Heaven into an evil from Earth', and to make good use of the sickness with which he was stricken by passing off his fits as moments of ecstasy during which he received the revelation of the precepts of the Koran from the mouth of an angel. But this alleged angel was nothing other than a pigeon trained to peck a few grains of rice out of his ear. The anecdote had long-established veracity,[14] which made it an admirable example of the kind of 'claptrap and fanciful tales' which would feed the appetites of a 'people as coarse and ignorant as the Arabs'.[15] To this it is added that the first sermon given by Mahomet, that former slave, was an announcement to an audience of slaves that 'the will of God was that all men should be free, and he came down from his throne and gave freedom to his slave Zeidimi. Then the slaves ran to him from all around and believed and did unquestioningly what he commanded.'[16]

This, then, says Baudier, was the origin of Mahomet's power: to slaves bereft of a master, this former slave proposed only another master, with the requirement of total submission from them to his decrees. He makes of this God a material being: 'he gives him movement from place to place, in the manner of a body of perishable substance and weight',[17] which satisfied the idolators, but he also declared that he was unique, in order to win the adherence of the monotheists. In short, this 'ape of Judaism and Christianity'[18] gathered into his Koran all 'the most monstrous heresies', 'like a collection of impurities in a sewer'.[19]

But in fact, Baudier continues, when we read the one hundred and twenty-four chapters of the 'complete' version of the Koran,[20] we realize that it

> contains two principal things: these are *Laws* and *Privileges*; laws for those who would follow his doctrine . . ., privileges only for Mahomet, but of such a strange nature that they allow him to exercise the most untrammelled vices, with as much merit and reward for his salvation as though he were zealously practising the most sublime and elevated virtues.[21]

From Baudier to Prideaux, at the end of the century, lists would abound with all the privileges accorded to Mahomet by God in the revelation of the Law, and duly for the satisfaction of his two dominant passions, 'ambition and the love of women, which he expressed in every part of his Koran, having in it scarcely a single chapter free of bloodthirsty laws, or of thorough abandonment to a licentious life with women'.[22] Thus, regarding his ambition, we read that he 'would be in the future the most perfect of beings created', that 'on judgement day, he would enjoy a higher glory than any other', that 'he would be the redeemer of those who believed in him, . . . no language, living or dead, would be unknown to him . . . no spoils of vanquished enemies would need to be shared, since henceforth the right to them would be his'.[23] As for lust, while establishing for others rules that were severe, albeit 'licentious' within marriage (the number of wives and degrees of consanguinity), for himself he assumed the right to violate his own law. He even went so far as to make God the accomplice and support for his lubricious passions, and to bring about his intervention 'in procuring his shameless actions'.[24] Does he not introduce God: 'in the twenty-third chapter of the Koran, which exempts him from this law; and which gives him the right to marry the sisters of his brother, his nieces, daughters either of his brother or of his sister, and in fact any Muslim woman'?[25]

Here, therefore, is a Law which has no purpose other than to establish and confirm the arbitrary and lawless power of its author. Moreover, the Koran is less 'a sustained doctrinal system than an ill-made tissue of things created to suit a circumstance, and in accordance with what he deemed favourable for himself'. Hence those continual additions, which provoke 'enormous contradictions', 'because with every alteration in the Impostor's view, he was obliged to forge or to change the new revelations'.[26]

We can see (and this is precisely what these authors wish to show) that Mahommedanism, from its beginnings, embraced every characteristic of despotic power such as it is found now in the States of Persia, Turkey and the Mogul Empire. Since the Koran was only an incoherent register of the false prophet's desires from moment to moment, concerned with his *jouissance* alone, none of its articles is logically deducible from any other; the contingency of their formulation from one occasion to the next is expressed in the permanent contradiction of a book which, according to Baudier, means nothing more in Arabic than a 'heap of precepts'.[27] This, therefore, is what stands as a model of the Law for the Mahommedans. We can see that it has been nothing more for them thereafter than the unpredictable written expression of a passing desire.

Total submission to such a legalized exception to the rule could be so easily and so widely accepted only by

coarse minds, like the herdsmen of Arabia, who were the first sectarians, or men who [had] entirely extinguished the torch of reason in the mire of the foulest and most obscene abandonment to the senses, for which the soul is but a manner of salt to prevent the corruption of the body, as one of the ancients said of the swine.[28]

For contrary to Christian law, which promises the salvation of the eternal soul of those who are able to renounce the temptations of the flesh, Mahommedan law balances the deadening of souls and the enslavement of hearts through the licence given to the pleasures of the body on earth, and the prospect of pleasures that are even more intense in the life hereafter. To those who have observed his Law to the letter, Mahomet offers a carnal paradise, filled with everything that can gratify every one of the five senses, but above all peopled with objects of love that are infinitely superior, in quality and in quantity, to those that are found on earth, and enabling the attainment of unalloyed sexual *jouissance.* For it will not be their wives that true believers will enjoy in the hereafter (these are excluded from paradise, approaching it only 'as much as is necessary in order to discover what is done within it through its enclosure') but virgins

> of ravishing beauty, created by God in heaven and destined for them from all eternity . . . . There will be a greater number of them than the men, so that each man can have two or three of them, or more, in proportion to his merit. They will be given only for pleasure and not to bear children. They will always be in a state of readiness to satisfy their husbands, since they will never be subject to menstrual flux, as physicians call it.[29]

The Truths of the False Prophet

This, approximately, is the image of the Muslim religion and its founder which circulated widely throughout the whole of the seventeenth century. All accounts still vied to discredit it as a religion and to set it in opposition to the 'true religion'. But anathema and insult were replaced by arguments and explanatory accounts of a historical, geographical, climactic, sociological or political nature. If Mahomet was able to install this power wherein he alone enjoyed everything when an entire people were enslaved to the letter of his Law, it was because he was able to turn skilfully to his own advantage a situation of division,[30] and exploit the character and natural inclinations of those who heard him: a burning-hot climate, making them tend towards a laziness of mind

and a lasciviousness of body, had ever prepared them to accept
the doctrine of predestination, and to propel them fiercely towards
a belief in a purely carnal paradise, to the point where they wished
to die for their religion in order to reach it all the more quickly.
Sex in preference to life – that is the secret of the Mahommedans'
blind obedience to their Law, and the explanation for their famed
courage! We can also invert the adage and say that Mahomet was
a prophet in his own land: 'Could the Arabs have a prophet any
more to their liking?',[31] asks P. Nau ironically, seeing in this utter
conformity the greatest proof of Mahomet's fraudulence.

This figure of Mahomet – serving as a foil the better to enhance
the divinity of the Christian religion – is to be found in the middle
of the eighteenth century, dramatized by Voltaire. At a point when
the studies of the Orientalists endow the person, the life and the
teachings of Mahomet with an image increasingly in keeping with
historical truth, it is surprising to see Voltaire still treating him as
'a rogue, a rascal, and a fool',[32] and – after the first performance
of his tragedy *Mahomet*, in Lille in 1741 – congratulating himself
on the acting of Lanoue, who 'with his monkey's face played the
role of Mahomet' to perfection.[33] His impostor proclaims unceasingly, in verse, what his seventeenth-century biographers had made
him brood upon in the depths of his unlettered, unrefined heart:
his imperialist ambitions, his great historic plan:

> I am ambitious, for sure every man is,
> But no king nor pope, no citizen nor chief,
> Did conceive a design so great as this.
> Each nation on earth has had its shining past,
> Through its laws and its arts, and supremely in war;
> Arabia's moment has come now at last . . . .
> I cast out false gods; my religion is new
> Cleansed and paving the way for my greatness to grow;
> Do not hold me to blame for deceiving my country;
> I'll destroy its weakness, its idolatry,
> Thus with one king and one God its unity is saved,
> For the sake of renown, it must be enslaved.[34]

He does not hide the instruments of his absolute power:

> Threaten and promise, that the truth might hold sway;
> Let my God be adored, but be feared most of all!
> You must obey me, like the God I obey.[35]

A power, of course, which rests upon a dumb obedience to the letter,[36] and the belief in an imaginary being – a phantom. For this self-proclaimed messenger from God is only a contemptible man, as was understood by Zopire, one of his few opponents, one capable of using the faculty of reason:

> Look on this prophet and the way you adore him;
> See the man in Mahomet, and consider how high
> You raise a phantom to heaven by bowing before him.[37]

But Omar, to whom this warning is addressed, is the prototype of future grand viziers, and exists only through and for his master; he will remain true to the idol who, after confessing his secret weakness to him (love is my only god, 'the idol of my adulations'[38]), will entrust him with maintaining the future illusion:

> You are the one; purge this memory of shame;
> Hide my frailty and save my glorious name;
> I must rule as a god the world that I plan,
> I'll lose my whole empire if unmasked as a man.[39]

However, how could any member of the audience, on hearing these declarations, have mistaken the true intentions of the tragedy, and failed to take its point? One would have to have been Pope Benedict XIV, to whom Voltaire ironically dedicated his play, to be taken in and proclaim it 'an admirable tragedy', and to imagine that Voltaire, too, by blackening the false prophet and his doctrine, had wanted to highlight the contrasting benefits of Catholicism. The story of Mahomet and of Islam serve instead at this point to illustrate – for Voltaire, at any rate[40] – the ravages of religious revelation and the fanaticism which it necessarily brings about, along with their complicity with arbitrary power. Yet – and this is the paradox – it is not the most vehement critics of Mahommedanism, like Baudier, Nau, Gagnier, and others, but those who have sought to restore its true faith who have allowed this paradigm of imposture to be made of it.

In fact, at the end of the seventeenth century the fundamentally pejorative view of the false prophet and his religion that was held by the West was somewhat suddenly called into question. Now it is striking that this calling into question should have been done first by authors who belonged to the reformed religion. On the basis of authorities like Hottinger and R. Simon,[41] P. Bayle states, in the article on Mahomet in his *Dictionary*, that nothing in what this false prophet preaches is derogatory to the teachings of the Gospel; and that, rather than being complicit in the corruption of the heart, it articulates precepts which are sometimes more severe than those of Christianity. In the writings of certain anti-Catholic authors – or those variously opposed to the politics of Louis XIV – the Muslim religion is no longer the butt that it was (and, for many, remains), and almost becomes a standard of reference. In a work that is both erudite and polemical, published in London in 1705, Adrian Reeland accuses the papists of having sought to compare the Lutherans to the Muslims. But this analogy, with which they tried to discredit the reformers, was offensive only because they had fashioned a totally distorted image of Mahommedanism: 'Only anti-Mahommedan writers wheel out their guns with a great deal of care and energy, not against real enemies, but against chimerical adversaries with whom their victory is guaranteed since nobody opposes it.'[42] And Reeland, who has a perfect knowledge of Arabic, offers his *Of the Mahometan Religion* followed by *Some Things Falsely Charged upon the Mahometans*, which make quite plain everything about the alleged idolatory of the Muslims, their materialism, not to say – the supreme insult – their 'Spinozism'. Reeland's translator-adaptor into French (himself a Protestant) in 1720 is in complete agreement with his author: 'The sects that differ from the dominant sect have always been spoken of badly', he writes, and what the travellers record (with the exception of Chardin, Sandys, Tournefort) of the religion of the Turks and the Persians is only an ignorant replication of what has been written by 'all the little Greek liars of recent centuries, along with all the copyists who came after them up until ourselves'. He adds that it was Tournefort who showed plainly, in letter 14 of his *Relation d'un voyage*, everything positive about the Mahommedan cult.[44] The truth is that this is a 'simple' religion, founded by a man with superior qualities of intellect, one which was perfectly in keeping with the customs of the herdsmen to whom he spoke. Even Abbé Maracci, the Italian translator of the Koran and the author of a *Refutatio alcorani*,[45] was obliged to acknowledge, Reeland notes, that the Koran 'preserved what was essential in Christian law, eliminating what was too difficult to be understood'.[46] As for Boulainvilliers, he goes even further in his unfinished *Vie de Mahomet*, published in 1731, maintaining:

> Mahomet established a System of Religion which was not only in keeping with the ideas of his compatriots, with their feelings and with the dominant customs of the country, but also of such measure with the common outlook of the human race, that he brought more than half of mankind to his opinions in less than 40 years; so much that it seems that his teaching only had to be heard for minds to fall under its sway.[47]

Far from being the Devil or the Antichrist, Mahomet was the one chosen by God to announce his oneness all over the earth: 'and all he said is true, in relation to the essential dogmas of Religion; but he did not say *all* of what is *true*, and it is in this alone that our religion differs from his'.[48]

Without going so far as this extreme thesis, at the beginning of the eighteenth century a fairly broad current acknowledged the existence of a basis of belief and common morality between the Christian and Mahommedan religions. The objection might be raised that Mahomet's carnal paradise explains the latter's success. But, as Bayle answers, what notion are we given by Holy Scripture

itself – in the Apocalypse, for example – of the happiness promised
to those who are called in the next life? 'It speaks of it as a state
whose delights surpass all that the eyes have seen, all that the ears
have heard and all that can spring into the hearts of men.'[49] No
doubt the reference here is not to pleasures of the flesh but to
those of the spirit, presented in the form of images. But even if we
allow that the idolators addressed by Mahomet could not see
beyond these images, what remains is that both religions make
their paradise a place of supreme *pleasure*. The Scripture's
superiority lies only in conjuring a pleasure greater than sexual
pleasure. In promising less, how could Mahommedanism have
seduced the Christians of the Orient, debauched as they might
have been, to the extent of mass conversion, as it did? A Christian,
even one whose morals are corrupt, would have thought: 'What
does it matter to me . . . that the Christian Paradise does not offer
the pleasures of good cheer, or enjoyment of beautiful women,
[etc.], for it offers other pleasures which infinitely surpass all that
the senses find most voluptuous on Earth?'[50] In other words, it was
not through the promise of its paradise that Mahommedanism
spread throughout Asia: 'For those who did not believe him
[Mahomet] to be sent by God took no reckoning of his promises;
and those who believed him to be a true prophet would not have
ceased to follow him even had he promised them only a spiritual
happiness in the next World.'[51]

Must we then admit that the reason for the Mahommedan
religion's conquest of Asia was its closeness to the truth? But
Christians, enlightened by the true religion, would not have
embraced it. For Bayle, only one explanation remains: armed
conquest. The main reason for the advance of the Mahommedans
was that they took the path

of forcing submission to [their] religion from those who were unwilling . . . . How can conquering armies demanding signatures be resisted?
Ask those French Dragoons who undertook this task against the
Huguenots in 1685; they will tell you that they would have had no
trouble making everyone under the sun sign to the Koran, provided

they were given the time to put into practice the Maxim: *compelle entrare*, force them to enter.[52]

This argument is clearly polemical, and – coming as it does from the author of a *Commentaire philosophique* on the same maxim – not surprising.[53] Its effect is to undermine the Christian religion's claim to prove its truthfulness on the basis of its spread, the sign that God would uphold it by enriching it with temporal blessings. It is not the spread of a religion which demonstrates its truthfulness, nor its military successes. Or we must acknowledge that Mahommedanism, which has so widely triumphed by force of arms, is the true religion! It is a fine advantage for a religion 'to understand better [than anyone else] the art of killing, bombarding and exterminating the Human Race!'[54]

Indeed, Mahommedanism did not convert, it compelled. It did not make *believers*, but new slaves. What does it mean, strictly speaking, to become a 'Muslim'? Chardin – who had himself been exposed to religious intolerance, and whom Bayle had read closely[55] – gives his readers a warning: the Muslim religion is certainly a religion of salvation, since 'Muslim' means 'he who has arrived at salvation, from *Salem*, a term which in almost all Oriental languages signifies peace and salvation, in the sense of "saved"'. But we are to understand this 'salvation' not as the eternal salvation of the immortal soul, which Christ promises to those who follow him, but as the salvation of the body – life saved:

> In the beginning of Mahommedanism, when this religion was even crueller and more bloodthirsty than it has been since, no quarter was given in war to any but those who embraced it with a habitual Profession of Faith .... And whenever someone made this profession of faith in order to avoid death, the cry was raised: *Muselmoon est!* 'He has reached salvation.' This shows us that the term does not mean a true believer, as the majority of the Accounts testify.[56]

Thus Mahommedanism appears less like a religion of the debauched and wholly false, than a religion which, though not

112

necessarily bad, becomes so only through the means used to impose it. Precisely the same comparison had been made with the Christian religion in the conception of it held by the papists (and still held, ever since the Revocation of the Edict of Nantes). Admittedly, it can be said that this use of violence is written into the very teachings of Mahomet, while it is only a perversion of Christianity. This is all the more reason to condemn the Catholics, since their actions contradict their faith. There is even this paradoxical outcome:

> according to the principles of their faith the Mahommedans are obliged to use violence in order to destroy other Religions; none the less they have tolerated them for several centuries. The Christians were commanded only to preach and educate; none the less they have been exterminating by fire and by sword those who are not of their religion.[57]

So if the attacks against Mahommedanism and its false prophet seemed to be pursued, even redoubled, in the course of the eighteenth century, this is not because the early-seventeenth-century positions remain unchanged. On the contrary: the rehabilitation of its teachings and the superior knowledge of the conditions of its emergence and spread allow comparison with the 'true religion', giving a bias for attacking the latter. What is condemned in Mahommedanism is the perversion to which a religion of revelation is always liable to succumb when it lays sole claim to possessing the truth.

Hence that emphasis on setting the two religions fundamentally in opposition after comparing them to one another, and stressing the points on which they cannot be compared. Montesquieu's case is exemplary in this respect: the ironic scepticism of the *Persian Letters* – which was expressed through the device of Usbek's deism, and played on the comparison between Parisian Catholicism and Persian Mahommedanism in order to highlight their common failings – is replaced twenty years later by his peremptory statements in *The Spirit of Laws*: 'From the characters of the Christian and Mahommedan religions, we ought, without any further examination, to embrace the one and reject the other.'[58] What is the source of such an apparently abrupt shift in a reader of Boulainvilliers, like him suspected of Spinozism,[59] and disinclined to espouse the theses of official Christian apologetics? It is because the question of despotism is on the agenda for Montesquieu. And just as he strives at all costs to maintain an essential difference between monarchy and despotism, so he cannot fail to insist on what separates the two religions which effectively go hand in hand with these respective regimes. It is no longer a matter, then, of giving a verdict on their truthfulness, but on their temporal effects, be they domestic, civil or political.[60] From this point of view, 'it is much easier to prove that religion ought to humanize the manners of men than that any particular religion is true'.[61] Now, here, Christianity and Mahommedanism are radically opposed: 'The Christian religion is a stranger to mere despotic power. The mildness so frequently recommended in the Gospel is incompatible with the despotic rage with which a prince punishes his subjects, and exercises himself in cruelty.'[62] This is as much a clarion warning as it is a statement: take away the mildness, and by being corrupted the Christian religion is at risk of dragging along with it the corruption of the monarchy, since the arbitrary violence of the monarch is henceforth unbridled.

The history – both ancient and recent – of the Catholic Church (whose structure has long been a model for despotic power) always provokes the suspicion of such a perversion, as the *philosophes* endlessly remind us throughout the whole of the eighteenth century. This question of recourse to violence or not is therefore far from being an adequate basis for settling the division between the two religions, as it was in the past,[63] and consequently of confirming that a 'pure despotism' is impossible in a Christian country.

'Polygamia Triomphatrix'

There remains a second point on which the two religions essentially differ: it is the status they give to the relation between the sexes. Together with its bloodthirsty violence – and in certain periods even more so – the sexual licence of the Mahommedans has always been considered by the Christian West as a sufficient indication of the falsity of their religion. On this point there is unanimity among the writers – even those who acknowledge its positive aspects. The toleration of 'polygamy, divorce and even enjoyment of the slaves that they own', 'a man's highest happiness set upon the satisfaction of these shameful desires', 'this alone must render that religion suspect and detestable to any man of sense', declared Reeland, for example.[64] This is where the false prophet's fraudulence is blatant; on this subject Bayle writes:

> Let us admire human weakness here. Practising and teaching the most excessive licence, Mahomet none the less made a great many people believe that God had established him as founder of the true Religion. Did his life not strongly refute this imposture? For according to the words of Maimonides, the principal quality of a true Prophet is to scorn the pleasures of the senses, above all the one we call venery.[65]

What is more or less exclusively condemned right up to the end of the seventeenth century, however is the moral scandal and religious deceit of such a conception of relations between the sexes. Similarly, when, in 1674, the German pastor Johann Leyser ventured to publish a pamphlet which was a justification of polygamy (under the pseudonym Theophilus Aletheus), he drew down upon himself such disapproval from Freiburg circles that he had to flee to Denmark, and from there to Sweden, since Christian V had also expelled him from bringing out, in 1682, his imposing *Polygamia Triomphatrix*, whose essential thesis Bayle sums up in these words:

> The reasons put forward with regard to the Law of Nature are that man is so constituted that he is able to make several children in a year; but nature does nothing in vain, and he would be unable to exercise this potential with only one woman. It is said furthermore that since nature has given the gift of continence to all females after conception, but not to their husbands, it is plain that nature intended men to have several

wives, and with all the more reason, since continence is very useful to women with child, so as not to disturb nature in the formation of the *foetus*.[66]

Bayle adds: 'All these reasons assume falsely or prove overmuch.' None the less, Leyser's publication continued to reprint, right up until 1703.[67] This was because, in raising the issue of polygamy in new terms, it fuelled a much wider debate which had been opened in 1685 by Isaac Vossius, whose thesis it was that the Earth had been undergoing depopulation ever since Antiquity.[68] The whole of the eighteenth century became persuaded of the truth of this, and there was much searching for the causes. Now, Muslim polygamy did indeed seem to be one of the main causes; this was Montesquieu's view in the *Persian Letters*,[69] based on the observations of Ricaut or Chardin. In authorizing polygamy, Mahomet tends, therefore, to be disputed no longer as a false prophet whose incontinence betrays his fraudulence, but as a bad legislator. This is not because he has violated nature, but because he has allowed the imposition of his own law. For it is possible – albeit certainly without justifying its practice – to explain the institution of polygamy in Asia by physical causality alone; this is what Montesquieu proposes to show in Book XVI of *The Spirit of Laws*: 'In the countries of the South there is a natural Inequality between the two sexes.'[70] There women are nubile from childhood, and since they age very early – and, moreover, lack any intellectual education which might allow their minds to compensate for the decrepitude of their bodies (unlike European women) – they soon lose the interest of their husbands, whom the hot climate makes sexually demanding. The latter, therefore, turns to other, younger objects. One could add – although the evidence is not entirely clear – that more girls than boys are born in Asia.[71] Polygamy, therefore, seems to be an institution in keeping with the natural givens of the climate of Asia, even contributing to the re-establishment of a certain balance in relations between the sexes. It is this conformity of the laws of the Muslim religion with the necessities of the climate which explains for the most part how this religion

116

was so easily established in Asia, and with such difficulty extended in Europe; why Christianity is maintained in Europe, and has been destroyed in Asia; and, in fine, why the Mahommedans have made such progress in China and the Christians so little. Human reasons, however, are subordinate to that Supreme Cause who does whatever He pleases, and renders everything subservient to His will.[72]

Yet these considerations do not in any way prevent Montesquieu from condemning polygamy, not just in general – for the sake of the demands of human nature recognized by the true religion – but even in the specific case of Asia, where it none the less seems unavoidable. For its consequences are disastrous, in that – as we saw above – in the end they contradict the very reasons which explain its institution.[73] It must now be added that it is inseparable from despotic power; first at the domestic level, since the extreme natural inequality between the sexes entails total servitude for women and outright domination by men. But this form of 'domestic government' is itself compatible with any form of political government other than despotism:

The slavery of women is perfectly conformable to the genius of a despotic government, which delights in treating all with severity. Thus at all times have we seen in Asia domestic slavery and domestic government walk hand in hand with an equal pace. In a government which requires, above all things, that a particular regard be paid to its tranquillity, and where the extreme subordination calls for peace, it is absolutely necessary to shut up the women; for their intrigues would prove fatal to their husbands. A government which has not time to examine into the conduct of its subjects views them with a suspicious eye, only because they appear and suffer themselves to be known.[74]

Everything, then, happens as if the servitude of women – as the *condition* of tranquillity (that is to say, of the subject's blind obedience) in a despotic regime – also became the general *model* for subjection to the despot. Indeed, on the one hand, despotic society presents itself as a chain of domestic despots (men) all ruling absolutely over their underclass of slaves (women). But on the other, these men themselves, faced with the One, are nothing; they erase themselves before his law, and worship his person, which their lively imagination invests with every kind of prestige. In this respect they behave exactly like women; this, moreover, is what the climate of Asia destines them for, giving the men there all the features which in Europe characterize femininity.[75]

As a consequence, it must be acknowledged that Oriental despotism is essentially bound up with a certain kind of relation between the sexes, with a certain sexual economy which roots the power whose exercise it enables in a natural, incontrovertible necessity. This is more fundamental than despotism's military origins, or even its complicity with the Mahommedan religion, which is only the expression of that very necessity, and is perhaps the ultimate explanation of that power which the Oriental despot wields, a source of both passionate fear and passionate love. In their way, the *Persian Letters* already intimated this; upon the explosion of the dramatic events in the seraglio with which the work ends, Usbek is compelled to assume his role as despot, a role which his long exile and new customs had made him momentarily forget, but which he realizes was the basis of his being and his reason for existence:

> I am living in a barbarous region, in the presence of everything that I find oppressive, and absent from everything I care about. I am prey to sombre melancholy and fall into dreadful despair; I seem not to exist any more, and I become aware of myself again only when lurking jealousy flares up in my heart and there breeds alarm, suspicion, hatred and regret.[76]

Oriental despotism, which rests on the passions alone, is there at first sight, is directed always to what is simplest, and pays no heed to temperaments. This is why within it the domestic, the civil and the political tend to merge together, uniformly repeating the order induced by a relation between the sexes deriving from natural necessity, which the Muslim religion only reinforces. It is not surprising, then, to see all power concentrated in the person of a man who, in the eyes of those who serve him, is endowed with a sexual prowess beyond compare since Mahomet. The sexual *jouissance* without limits which is allowed him as an exclusive right is also the means of his absolute power and the fundamental explanation of the form this power takes. In Europe – where the Christian religion holds sway, forbidding more than one wife – princes are 'less confined, less concealed from their subjects, and consequently have more humanity: they are more disposed to be directed by laws, and more capable of perceiving that they cannot do whatever they please'.[77] In order to grasp its true nature and measure the force of its fascination, we must situate Oriental despotism in terms of the sexuality in which it is rooted. Likewise the heart of despotic power in the Orient, extending over vast empires, is hidden in that very place where the despot exercises his *domestic* power: in that walled space, forbidden to the gaze, saturated by sex and structured by it – the seraglio.

At the beginning of his *Histoire générale du sérail du Grand Seigneur*, Michel Baudier wrote:

> I thought that having given the history of the Turkish Empire, from its origins until our day, it would not be in vain to show the customs and manner of living, the preservation and order of ruling employed by such powerful and such fearsome conquerors. To do this with more certainty we must enter into the Seraglio, where the secret of all these things is carefully locked.

PART III
The Shadow of the Seraglio

7

The Anatomy of the Seraglio

Raising the Curtain

Acomat
Viens, suis-moi. La Sultane en ce lieu doit se rendre.
Je pourrai cependant te parler et t'entendre.

Osmin
Et depuis quand, Seigneur, entre-t-on dans ces lieux,
Dont l'accès était même interdit à nos yeux?
Jadis une mort prompte eût suivi cette audace . . . .*

With *Bajazet*, the seraglio becomes a 'site' of tragedy.[1] Racine justified his dramatization of 'such modern events' by saying that for a French audience there is:

> scarcely any difference between what is, dare I say, a thousand years away and what is a thousand leagues away. This, for example, gives to the Turkish characters, however modern they be, a dignified presence on our stage. They are regarded as ancients before their time. Theirs are ways and customs that are altogether different. We have so little

---

* 'Come with me. The Sultana will be in this place,/For now I can speak to you and listen to you.'
'And since when, my Lord, might one enter these places,/Always barred and forbidden even to look upon?/Death would have swiftly followed such daring as this.'

commerce with the princes and those others who live in the seraglio, that we regard them, so to speak, as people who live in a different century from our own.[2]

But it is not just because those who live and die there are suddenly raised, through distance, to the dignity of archetypes, nor even because the passions there are more violent, that the seraglio can now serve as the setting for a tragedy. The seraglio is more than a setting or a scene; it is the supreme tragic site. Shutting out all strangers' eyes by definition, the exclusive realm of a single being, it is the paradise of pleasure only because prohibition surrounds it everywhere. Merely raising the curtain is already a transgression, therefore, and makes the spectator an accomplice, even before he becomes a witness to the inevitable drama triggered by the vizier Acomat, when, accompanied by Osmin, he enters this place and speaks within it. Regardless of what will be said or done thereafter, regardless of the motive for an action or the meaning of a word, it is enough to have dared to cross a threshold, to be present and to venture speech, for the crime to be perpetrated and the tragedy to culminate, ending only in bloodshed. This is why, of all Racine's tragedies, *Bajazet* is probably the most violently, intensely and continuously tragic; every single word and gesture transgresses against the first prohibition, repeats the crime and merits death. Admittedly, Amurat, the Sultan, is absent, kept away by a war in which he, too, stakes his future. But it is precisely Racine's genius that he has excluded from the scene the man who is its absolute master, while at every moment letting the threat of his sudden appearance hover over the action. Amurat the despot shows himself only through mute slaves bearing letters, and exists only as an imaginary figure in the manner of a spectre unceasingly conjured up by words charged with hatred and desire, the words of those who fear him because he has been their idol, and themselves exist only through his passing whim. 'Rentre dans le néant d'où je t'ai fait sortir,'*

* 'Return to the obscurity whence I plucked you'

124

Roxane tells Bajazet peremptorily. But what is she herself, like all those who move to and fro before our eyes, but one of those ephemeral creatures who are 'elevated in the morning like rising vapours, to the highest degree of honour, by the Sultan's favour alone, and vanish into the air before nightfall', in Ricaut's words[3] – in short, a being whose lifespan is measured in the unity of a tragedy's time: a single day?

'I made it my goal to give clear expression in my tragedy to what we know of the customs and maxims of the Turks',[4] Racine declared. But what do we know about the seraglio, and what is known by those who are trustworthy sources for Racine, except what is spawned by their own Western imagination,[5] based merely on what is told to them by some old Jewish woman briefly allowed inside the apartment of some sultana's servant, or embroidering on the memories of some eunuch met by chance outside the walls of the seraglio?

Now it is striking to observe just how much the descriptions of the seraglio of the Grand Turk – the obligatory *topos* of all the accounts of travel in the Orient – are alike, to the point often of repetition in the very same words. This is not to be taken as evidence of corroborative information, nor as proof of their accuracy. Quite the contrary: there is repetition, there is copying (each time with the pretence of contributing something new, something never heard before), because the stereotyped image of the seraglio which was produced at the beginning of the seventeenth century, probably coincides exactly with what is expected. If those who live in the seraglio and what takes place in it could, for an entire century, be so easily transposed to tragic drama and furnish material for fiction, it is because they were already representations. So we must also analyse them as such. In this stereotyped image of a site of absolute power which is so thoroughly invested with sexuality, what is repeated and stressed is a different reality from the one the historian vainly seeks to rediscover. Beyond the anecdote in which it is dressed up, the 'Seraglio tale' betrays its rootedness in a West which is beginning to question the principles of its political institutions, the goals of education, the role of the family, and the enigma of relations between the sexes – all questions in which its essential metaphysics is engaged, more deeply than it appears to be.

The Divided Body of the Despot

'The Seraglio of the Great Lord is like a Republic separated from the rest of the city. It has its laws and its ways of living quite unto itself.'[6] It is a mysterious centre shut in upon itself, windowless and almost without doors, but for all that, it is the microcosm reflecting the despotic State in its entirety; the secret order of its labyrinth and the figures haunting it yield up its truth with the clarity of a blueprint.

Certainly, as Guer acknowledges, everyone can pass through the first enclosure of the seraglio, through the 'One and Only Door' (or 'refuge of the afflicted', 'unshakeable foundation of might and power'), and, even, reaching the council chamber, through the second (along the 'corridor of justice', or over the 'threshold of obedience and martyrdom'), but the seraglio strictly speaking begins behind the third door, through which no one can pass: 'the threshold of happiness'.[7]

There is no ease of movement in the heart of the seraglio. There is a boxing in of courtyards, of gardens and rooms, each hermetically closed to the rest, each wall standing as a prohibition, each place defining one function only. Every time a threshold is crossed, a new and uncertain fate is embarked upon, but always leading from one prison to another. The captive and functional structure of this space effectively corresponds to the status of those who occupy it. All are slaves: 'The seraglio can be seen as a fortress filled with Slaves, each of them employed in guarding the others.'[8] Its distinctions are not those of greater or lesser freedom, but those of diverse specialties of servitude. Aristotle made the point that in the barbaric Asiatic regimes (unlike Greek regimes), only one kind of power is known: that over children, over women and over servants; that of the master over slaves, which has no other end but the pleasure of the master alone. For the European traveller in the seventeenth century, the seraglio confirms – at the very least – the accuracy of Aristotle's observation.

The order of the seraglio is organized for the purpose and the practice of the despot's *jouissance*, above all his sexual *jouissance*, starting with the scopic privilege: 'Of several thousand men who are there as if in prison, and who are answerable to one another, only the Prince has the sight of the women.'[9] The seraglio is also 'altogether a delicious and solitary residence; but in the manner that I have observed things, it is solitary for everyone and delicious only for one'.[10] Solitary for everyone, since no relation – no coitus – is allowed between the sexes, apart from the endless and perfect one of the One and Only with the countless multiplicity of his wives. The discipline and unfailing order of the life of the seraglio, the seclusion of its spaces, the scrupulous specialization of its activities, and the constant mutual surveillance of its occupants – all of this has its only end and *raison d'être* to let *jouissance* be concentrated in a central place, where it can attain the absolute. Everything converges on this blind point, this imaginary focus of *jouissance*, which is the *harem* (Chardin remarks that the word evokes both the idea of something sacred, and that of something 'illicit, forbidden, prohibited and abominable', designating the object of 'execration' and 'excommunication'[11]). By its structure and its way of life, the seraglio thus appears as a complex apparatus, built from start to finish in order to suck from outside it and everywhere beyond it all that has worth as an object of *jouissance*, in order to purify it, load it to its greatest potency and stockpile it in order to prevent even the smallest particle being lost or diverted to other paths besides those that lead to the despot, whose glorious body alone can make credible this dream of an unalloyed sexual happiness.

The body of the despot must be the absolutely Other, and the seraglio, too, seems to be conceived in order to appear so. In all the despotic regimes of Asia, the despot is to his people what the stars, in Aristotelian cosmology, are to the sublunary world. Although he is not always of godly origin, the despot – usually the descendant of a conqueror – comes *from elsewhere*. In Turkey (or in Persia) the same difference is established, but in reverse. The master is separated from his people by an uncrossable frontier, of which the walls of the seraglio are merely the visible form. The reality is that the inhabitants of the seraglio themselves are responsible for creating the despot's transcendence, for instituting and maintaining his radical otherness. All of them, in fact, come from another world. None of them – children, wives, or eunuchs – is a native of the country. As a result, the despot's difference from those who serve him is not merely that of the One to the many, but of the Other to the same. The lower orders of the seraglio, made up of a multiplicity of solitudes, stand therefore, in the eyes of the real people of the Empire, as a paradigm of the subject-people, and above all its primary function is to bring about the radical division which establishes and confirms the obedience of an entire people, endlessly producing the despot as the incomparable and absolute Other, as the Man who bears no more comparison with other men than the celestial constellation of the Dog bears with the barking animal called dog.

Better still: if the seraglio in its totality is the living and unceasing reminder of the despot's transcendence, every person in it has the role of conferring on this transcendent being his essential attributes. In the seraglio, every individual effectively belongs to a class which is defined by a specific *lack* which, like the hollow of a relief, exhibits a quality of the despot. If, indeed, the power which a man recognizes in his master rests always upon an identification, it is in some sense identifications, albeit *negative* ones, with which we are dealing here. Each individual seems to identify with *a feature* of the master, but makes himself the visible and tangible emblem of its absence. The blind, the mute, the dwarves, the buffoons, the eunuchs, the women and children, and so on, all stand negatively for the fragmented body of the despot. They are the living analysis of his Unity, the active affirmation that he alone has eyes and speech, the cosmological proof of his omnipotence and uniqueness. In short, through them, through the composition of their defects reproduced in multiple examples, the infinite positivity of the essence of the despot is there *at first sight*. Here negative theology (or anthropology) speaks for itself. Delivering the figure of the *ens quo nihil majus imaginari potest*, a baroque zoo spells it out in silence. Let us now examine the principal species it contains.

Children

Princes of the blood

There are many children in the seraglio. But those who are encountered, and who matter, are not the ones whom nature has given to the despot.

Of course, the despot does beget children, and in quantity. Amurat III had 102, by all accounts.[12] But such prolific fathering, which was regularly offset by efficient massacres, became increasingly rare, and derives more from legend than from reality – the reason will become clearer further on. Moreover, for reasons connected to their status, favourites for a single night were quite adept at 'cheating nature' (even better than French women, who at that time were beginning to worry the early demographers[13]). When these methods failed them, they did not hesitate to use more brutal practices to prevent the fruit they carried from reaching maturity.[14] Some of these children of pleasure survived, and were strangled soon after birth.[15] They might even have been the sons of the official wife, but that would not get them very far: since the despotic regime was such that there was little probability of them succeeding their father (even if the law, which was made to be violated, prescribed it) and too much likelihood of their conspiring against him should they be allowed any hope, it was as if they did not exist. They were imprisoned, they were blinded, they were driven mad. At best, after a sumptuous circumcision ceremony, they were exiled to a seraglio in Magnesia. There, all they had to worry about – because it was their only salvation – was to try to retain the body of a child indefinitely, or at least to display symbolically that they were not men: 'This is the reason that when

129

these young Princes are at Magnesia they are accustomed to have themselves frequently shaved, and to send their hair to the Great Lord their father, in order to show him that they are still children and not fit to rule.'[16] Let us make it clear, however, that in proclaiming their childhood state in this way, they do not lie; for theirs is a state of mind with all the features of that *puer robustus* whereby Hobbes defined the wicked man, or the features of a polymorphously perverse Freudian child, if we are to rely on the descriptions of the 'despotic character' given by the majority of the authors. This is hardly surprising, anyway, in children brought up in indolence, as objects of love and desire in a seraglio where they are forever handed back and forth between women who have been completely abandoned by a man and eunuchs who are subject to all manner of aberrant desires.[17]

There is really nothing in their upbringing which prepares them to occupy the throne: 'The elder son of the King [of Persia] is never told that he is the heir presumptive to the throne . . . we can tell from this whether the upbringing he is given is worthy of his destiny.'[18] This is also the view taken by Bernier, who stresses the outstanding exception to this: Aurengzeb, the new despot of the Mogul Empire, who is concerned about the upbringing of his sons. But these observations assume their full resonance if we bear in mind that in Europe this is a time when the issue of the Prince's upbringing (that is to say, the way he embodies the relation between knowledge and power) is being posed in new terms which, a century later, will lead to debate on 'enlightened despotism'. What does it mean to learn to be master – how, for example, should one teach *majesty*, that concept which is fundamental to Bossuet, who analyses it at length?[19] Against this royal majesty is set the eternal *minority* of the despot. The education of a future king assumes identification with heroic models (father, forebears); it requires lessons from history and always tends towards the outcome that the young prince bends very early to the harsh reality of the Law, starting with the first of all laws, grammar, which, in governing his tongue, will later enable him to govern the world;[20] in short, the education of a king who must be worthy

130

of the name hastens to install an exemplary man within the child. But being a despot is not something that is learned, and this is probably the only necessary condition for becoming one eventually. By contrast with the education of the French Dauphin, the pseudo-education of the son of the Oriental despot cuts him off from the world and from history, shuts him away in a cave where the only examples he has are castrated and servile shadow-men, and thrusts him into the arms of a mother who, having made him her plaything, will turn him into the tool of her passions and ambition. If one day the sceptre should unexpectedly be placed in his hands, this sceptre will not be the sign of his power (like that of a king) but will remain, as it was for his father before him, a signifier which refers only to itself, and is stranded in a vacuum which is masked by the imaginary brilliance invested in his person.

Furthermore, while it is of the essence of the monarchy that the reigning king always encompasses a *future king* – his son – and that a king is not fully a king until he has fathered and educated a son called to be his successor,[21] the expression *future despot* (be it a sultan, as in Turkey, or an emperor, as in Persia) has no meaning. Without either reference to the past or project for the future, despotism is a regime that neither repairs nor prepares, and where the idea of *inheritance* is unknown. Even if it is pronounced hereditary from father to son, the despotic regime seems by nature to repudiate continuity, succession and that reassuring difference-within-repetition which a dynasty expresses as a regular sequence of numbers bracketed with the name of the founding Father, which means that each monarch is simultaneously the same and other than his father, and gives him in everyone's eyes that tranquil prestige of being the 'next in line', the true legitimation of his power. By contrast, the despotic regime, outside history, endlessly collapses and is born, in an impossible time which is conceived not as 'the number of the movement according to what comes before and after' (if we follow the formulation which Aristotle gives in his *Physics*) but as the juxtaposition of discrete moments without any relation to one another, each marked by the Name of the master of the day, whose backdrop is a dismal and empty eternity. Between

131

one despot and another, as between Achilles and Zeno's Tortoise, there always remains a space, a blank, a nothingness: the place of the arbitrary. And it is to preserve this arbitrariness (is not the 'idea' of despotism a *cutting off* in every area?[22]) that the offspring have their 'education' in the seraglio. The only education (whatever Chardin may say) truly worthy of their destiny.

No man's son

If, by abandoning his sons to women and eunuchs, the Oriental despot abdicates from his functions as *natural* father, it is doubtless all the better to assume his role as *symbolic* (and imaginary) father in the eyes of all other children. We have just seen that he annuls those whom he does father. But it could be said that he *creates* the ones who matter. The true creatures of the despot are in fact those children who come, every one of them, from the *other world* (the Christian world) – either paid in tribute or carried off in war, orphans with no natural or cultural roots, no memory.[23] All of them are brothers, since, after a solemn circumcision ceremony in the course of which they have uttered the ritual formula, they have all become the utterly devoted sons of the same father who is undifferentiated from his name. They are so many blank pages whose unsullied virginity is the ideal raw material for a model education.[24] Being nothing to start with, they can become the neutral – but technically qualified – supports of the signifier which will later make them agas, pashas and viziers. In them and through them will function, without any subjective flaw, that economy of power and *jouissance* referred to above which is the characteristic of Oriental despotic regimes, where the order which comes down from the master and constitutes the subject as such reaches him as a tide of 'surplus enjoyment', if we can make so bold as to use here the term forged by Lacan on the model of Marx's 'surplus-value'. For this is more or less what is involved:

> In his Ministers, the Great Lord takes no account of birth or property. He prefers to be served by those who are utterly his, and who, being

indebted to him for the education and the food they have received, are obliged to employ in his service all the skills and virtues that they have; and to give back to him, *in a form of repayment with interest*, what he has spent in order to form them in mind or body. Thus he can bring them up without jealousy, and destroy them without danger.[25]

These children of the seraglio are divided into two groups: the *azamoglans* and the *ichoglans*. The former are trained for tasks which require only physical aptitude, and will later become artisans or sailors in the service of the Sultan.[26] The education of the latter, by contrast, will qualify them for higher functions, not the least of which is the immediate service of the despot.

The image that this always prompts in writers, in order to bring to mind the disciplinarian regime which the ichoglans must undergo from the start, is that of the monastic life. Mortification of the flesh, vigils and fasts; the ichoglans must demonstrate more submission and observance than do the Capuchins or other religious orders in their novitiate.[27] Tournefort writes that the four hundred children of the first rank hear only exhortations of 'civility, modesty, courtesy, punctuality, honesty; they are taught above all to remain silent, to keep their eyes lowered and their hands folded over their stomachs'.[28] However, an extremely strict course of studies is instituted, with four levels separated by tough selection: six years for learning to read and write, and study the law of Mahomet. Then four years of physical exercise and practice in Turkish, Arabic and Persian; four more years when they are initiated into the service of the Great Lord, and finally, the paradise of servitude – the chamber of forty pages [*hazoda*], where they are at the total beck and call of the master. Ricaut stresses that there is no element of initiation into the sciences – no logic, no physics, no metaphysics, no mathematics – nothing that may be likely to 'introduce any subtlety of understanding that might be harmful to government,'[29] or anything resembling a solitary intellectual pleasure which would distract from the service of the despot. 'The Prince is their idol', writes Tournefort of those who attain the completion of the course.[30] Baudier's comment is: 'They never speak, nor ever look their master in the face'.[31] The ultimate goal of the novitiate is, in fact, to magnify the Body of the despot by being turned into a kind of detached organ, 'created for one single function', in accordance with the Aristotelian conception of the natural organ which has the function of the slave:

> Twelve of them are chosen to be given the greatest duties of the Court; each has his Office. One of them carries the Great Lord's sword, another his cloak, a third his stirrup, yet another presents water for drinking or washing. There is one to arrange his Turban, one to take care of his wardrobe ... ; one whose duty it is to cut his nails and another to take care of his Beard [etc.].[32]

There is a room [*oda*] corresponding to each level of study. No communication is allowed between one room and another, and each room is under the constant surveillance of a white eunuch, as are all the places (baths, latrines, bedchambers) where the children must go. All the observers are struck by the extreme attention given to the discipline of the body. First and foremost a scrupulous cleanliness, which is, moreover, widespread among all Asiatics, 'who cannot tolerate the least dirtiness, neither on themselves nor on those who come near them'.[33] Then a ritual around the act of excretion, confirming the sacred character of the written signifier, or even its support:

> Each seat has a small tap from where they draw water to wash. They would judge that they had committed a great sin by using paper for this purpose, and give as their reason that if by chance the name of God were written upon it, or else a text from the Law, this would be a profanity which must be avoided.[34]

But above all the rigorous prohibition of contact or communication from 'body to body'. Gerson or J. B. de La Salle might well have signed the following ruling:

> At whatever time, there cannot be between them any familiarity except the most modest, and marking the respect they have for those in whose

presence they are. When they go into these places whose purpose is to satisfy the call of nature, or to the bath, a Eunuch follows them and never loses sight of them, and never allows any of their fellows or their friends to speak to them . . . . The chambers where they sleep are great long rooms, in which there are lamps lit all through the night, and their beds are arranged side by side . . . . Between every five or six beds, a Eunuch sleeps, situated in such a manner that he can very easily see and hear whether anything is said or done between them which is not honest, or which injures modesty.[35]

The dirty-minded obsessions of the eunuch are comparable to those of a saint.[36] The one channels all pleasure into the service of the despot, the other into that of God. But both, as anxious observers of the slightest signs of what they have renounced, by necessity or by vocation, offer the same figure of the exemplary educator as generally conceived in the Europe of the Reformation and Counter-Reformation. Likewise the education of the ichoglans can be seen as a model education.

This is the view taken by Baudier, for example, in 1623, pronouncing himself favourably impressed by the educational institution he has just described, since it enables attainment to the highest offices by persons who are fit and well prepared, and not:

unfit persons who in the course of their lives have learned nothing except the game of *paume*, or the skill of throwing dice, or speaking bluntly and exercising every manner of vice. Thus one should not be amazed if the Turkish State should prosper, since ways are known of making from a great number of young men the finest minds to be nurtured with care under a good discipline which makes them honest people, adding the perfections of art to the endowments of a happy birth.[37]

The same commendation, penned by Tournefort, can be read at the beginning of the next century, albeit accompanied by a criticism:

Nothing seems more fitting for turning out clever people than the education given to the pages in the seraglio; they are made, so to speak, to undergo all the virtues; none the less, despite these attentions, when they are advanced into great offices, they are still truly only school-boys; they ought to be taught to command, after having learned to obey.[38]

The prosperity of the Turkish State has now given way to decad-ence, and there is an awareness that such an education is complicit with a regime which by now represents political evil in its pure state. It is precisely because, like their master, they have never learned to command that the children of the seraglio will one day be able to command despotically, as he does; they will be the ideal props and carriers of this blind power. Hence Montesquieu's view of education in the despotic regime:

It must necessarily be servile; even in power such an education will be an advantage, because every tyrant is at the same time a slave . . . . Here, therefore, education is in some measure needless: to give something, one must take away everything, and begin with making a bad subject in order to make a good slave.[39]

'Learning to command' was the aim set by Bossuet in the education of a young prince. But ever since Locke (if we take him as a convenient marker) it has also been the aim of any 'liberal education', which must enable the child to become a good citizen – that is to say, a subject capable of assuming his responsibilities within a political society founded upon the new principles of the Contract. Both the eunuch and pedagogical saint, once symbols and models of the educator, are now subjected to the same criticism; both of them are in the service of an arbitrary, tyrannical power, and play their baleful role as well as they do only because they have given up being men in order the better to serve their Master. From this comes their cruel zeal, which is only the outlet for frustrated desire. In 1670, Ricaut wrote of the eunuchs attached to the education of the pages in the seraglio that they were 'naturally cruel, whether because of the envy they bore other men who were whole and undamaged; or because their nature was that of women, who are usually more cruel and vindictive than men'.[40] Less than a century later, it is the symbolic castration of the pious educators of youth that will be the target. 'Experience proves', wrote Helvetius:

> that in general characters suited to self-denial of certain pleasures and who take upon themselves the maxims and austere practices of a certain kind of devotion, are usually unhappy characters. This is the only way of explaining how so many religious sectarians have been able to combine sanctity and the mildness of the principles of religion with so much wickedness and intolerance.[41]

It will doubtless be said that the despotic education, whose exclusive goal was blind obedience and the production of *jouissance* for the master, could only be condemned by the period's nascent 'spirit of capitalism', which thought in terms of utilitarianism and 'surplus-value'. But if we have only to substitute God for the Great Lord, and the Christian Brothers (or the Jesuit or Oratorian Director of Studies) for the eunuchs, to find the school and its disciplines in the terms instituted by the Classical age, then need we not only replace God or the Great Lord with the State itself (or the Motherland) in order then to see – in its essential means and ends – the school in the terms conceived by the reformers of the late eighteenth century, and above all the secularizing bourgeois of the nineteenth? Admittedly, there are marked differences. But in the end, the State, too, proclaims that it takes 'neither birth nor property' into account in its servants, and that in return for the (free) education it gives its children (who are wrested from their natural parents for a time) it expects only a tribute of love which will prompt them to give their lives for it, or for those who speak in its name, without a murmur, not even a murmur of joy. The eunuch, the saint, and the secular teacher use the same methods with the same zeal, even if they do not serve the same master. This means that there are not two economies (on the one hand the despotic and totalitarian, on the other the bourgeois and liberal) but, rather, two interchangeable languages to describe the same deception, off which every variety of political power lives.[42] Every extortion of surplus-value, every tribute of surplus labour, goes hand in hand with the subtle extortion of 'surplus enjoyment', and a forced offer of love. And these two sides of the economy serve mutually to mask one another as circumstances demand. It is our view that the myth of Oriental despotism allowed the reformist theoreticians of the eigthteenth century to elaborate this dual language; through it, with the scope furnished by a fiction that is believed in, they test modern ways of eliciting obedience; this is the usefulness of this exotic despotism, which operates only in the register of *jouissance*, in order to establish the 'despotism of the useful',[43] which professes not to want *jouissance* unless it is reinvested in the service of the State.

Dwarves and Mutes

As sons of this symbolic Father who is reduced to his Name, all the ichoglans magnify each part of the despot's body by extending it through their own bodies, which are monofunctional but whole.

However, the sham majesty of the despot is also made brilliant by being the negation of three negative figures who, multiply replicated, are its living reminder at every moment and for all those in the seraglio.

Dwarves, deaf-mutes and eunuchs are monsters. And it is as such that they have their place in the seraglio. But unlike those who were once exhibited in funfairs, their function is not to give reassurances of their own normality to those who point at them. The seraglio is the opposite of the funfair, for here the norm is monstrosity. What they show you is an ideal which you attain only metaphorically, while they have the good fortune to realize it fully and fittingly. All must be lowered before the despot. But dwarves are so, literally. Silent and attentive to any gesture, any blinking of an eye by their master – so the mutes are. Impotent – so the eunuchs are. Despotism likes to take everything literally and in its strict meaning, as is illustrated by the blinding of the royal children in the Ispahan seraglio.

The Great Lord always eats alone, Tavernier notes. This solitude must be understood as that of the One and Only, of the Peerless One, for it is in fact diverted by a numerous company: 'At meals, the mutes and dwarves perform countless antics to entertain the Emperor, who throws them scraps that he might have the pleasure of seeing them tussle over them.' Enjoying the spectacle of division and rivalry between his subjects is one of the despot's favourite amusements. Like Nero in earlier times, the Great Mogul organized combats setting the palace slaves against the wild beasts of the menagerie. And in Sade's *Juliette*, it is Ferdinand of Naples's cornucopia that fulfils this same pleasure – the One and Only's pleasure in seeing a great crowd of small men tear one another apart for the sake of a crumb given by the master.

The dwarves seem to have no other function than to be the grotesque counterpoints of 'His Highness'. The mutes have a different, more serious part to play: they are the stranglers. In the words of P. de La Porte, this is how justice is meted out on those days when the Divan is held: 'The Great Lord is hidden at the end of a low room, accompanied by the chief of the white eunuchs, along with his Great Chamberlain and three mutes.' The Aga of the Janissaries, for example, might come in to report on his duties: 'If the Great Lord finds that he has done something at odds with how he should serve, he strikes his foot against the ground, and the three mutes throw themselves upon the poor Aga and strangle him without there being any other kind of trial.'[44] Moreover, the Great Lord is usually accompanied by a gang of 'mutilated mutes' [*diltsis*] whenever he visits the different apartments of the seraglio. They are the ones who have:

the honour of being the privileged executors of his policies, his vengeance, his anger or his jealousy. They herald their execution with hooting sounds akin to those of an owl, immediately advancing on the wretched man or woman who is condemned, carrying their silken cords,[45] the lethal signs of a quick and certain death. The simplicity of this device, which makes it all the more sinister; the ensuing sudden mortal attack; nightfall, the time usually prescribed for execution; the silence of these demi-monsters who can give voice only with a sharp, doom-laden yelping which they wrench from their gullets as they seize the victim – all this, I say, makes the hair stand on end and the blood run cold even in those who know these horrors only by hearsay.[46]

These sinister executioners hold the interest of the travellers for another reason:

The mutes of the seraglio are a strange species of thinking animal. In order not to disturb the prince as he rests, among themselves they have invented a language whose characters are expressed only by signs; and these traces are as intelligible by night as by day, by the touching of certain parts of their bodies.[47]

This language which the forty deaf-and-dumb inhabitants of the seraglio learned to perfect every day before the Mosque of the pages was apt to become the official language in use at the Ottoman court, since 'there are scarcely any who do not study it, and who are not able to employ it to convey what they are thinking; but above all, those who are obliged to be frequently close to the Great Lord, in whose presence it is a lack of respect even to whisper in someone's ear'.[48]

Although it is very superficially described and analysed by the travellers, this language of sight and touch could not but interest a century of empiricists and sensualists. In it Lamy saw proof that 'men could have noted what they thought by gestures',[49] without ever having recourse to the voice – which, conversely, prompts reflection on the art of speech and, more broadly, on the origin and nature of speech and languages, like those of – among others – Rousseau, in his *Essay on the Origin of Languages*, or Diderot, in his *Letter on the Deaf and Dumb*, which mention the mutes of the seraglio. But these loose-tongued monsters also stand as models of reference for all those who followed the early attempts of R. de Cortone, P. de Castro and P. Ponce to educate deaf-mutes – like

140

Amman in Holland or Wallis in England, and later, Péreire and the Abbé de l'Épée in France.[50] In other words, these Samsons of the Orient are doubly dedicated to the norm, as the Vaugelas of silence.[51]

Along with the dwarves and the mutes, the eunuchs form the third species of monster who people the seraglio. All the same, since their function can be understood only in terms of their relation to the seraglio as a whole – and especially to the women – let us postpone our study of their situation for a moment.

The Women

'This would be the place to speak about the Ladies of the seraglio, but we are dispensed from doing so, since they are not in evidence, no more than are pure spirits', states Tournefort in his account of the seraglio at Constantinople.[52] This was also the view of Tavernier. Yet according to Chardin, 'the seraglios of the Turks, and that of the Great Lord like any other, are public places' in comparison with a Persian seraglio – and, *a fortiori*, with the harem of the great seraglio at Ispahan: 'which can be described as an unknown world' where, it is said, 'the order, the silence and the obedience . . . are incomprehensible'.[53]

What is known, however, is that the harem, at Constantinople and Ispahan alike, immures (usually for life) a vast number of women, young virgins of unimaginable beauty, all of foreign origin,[54] given to the despot as gifts by his high-ranking slaves (pashas, viziers, agas . . .) who have often bought them with payment of gold to Jews. It is also known that they live, two by two, in bedchambers which resemble nuns' cells, with the exception that each bed is separated from the other by the couch of a black eunuch. But the most harsh surveillance is undertaken by an old woman ('*boula*' in Turkey), who is under the command of an *odabachi*, carrying three daggers at her side, which distinguish and mark out her authority. These old women 'punish these girls severely for the smallest failing, and are no more indulgent towards

141

the fair sex than the white Eunuchs are towards the pages'.[55] Their lives are spent reading, writing and embroidering, while waiting for the moment, both desired and feared, when the sultan will drop a white handkerchief upon the one he has chosen for the night.

It is said, furthermore, that this rigorous discipline, which turns the harem into a prison, is justified by the hot-blooded temperament of these women, for one never knows into what aberrations it might lead them. The prolixity of racy novels and tales for which Galland's translation of the *Thousand and One Nights* supplied both the model and the inexhaustible subject matter makes up, in this case, for the relative discretion of the travellers who, for their part, had no occasion to hear talk of indiscreet jewels. But it is rumoured that at the impenetrable heart of the seraglio burns a fettered and frustrated lust, and that the piercing eyes of the old women, alert to every vestige of *jouissance* kept hidden from the master, might at every moment be deceived, for all their precautions.

> Strict orders are observed for guarding these women; searches are made not only of the women who arrive, and of the Eunuchs on their return from the city; but animals are also suspect: it would not be allowed for the Sultanas to own monkeys, or male dogs of a certain size. Circumspection is employed whenever fruits are sent in to them; if they should express an appetite for gourds of extended shape, or cucumbers and like fruits, these are cut for them in round slices at the door, so as not to admit among them this flimsy opportunity for wrongdoing, so low is the opinion of their continence. This is doubtless an indication of the violent jealousy of the Turks; for who in such a case could prevent an unvirtuous woman from doing wrong? . . .[56]

A thousand and one wooden arms

But what strikes the travellers perhaps as much as this exacerbated femininity which is greedy for the phallus in every guise and form – that is to say, quite literally, hysterical – is that it is manifest as an innumerable multiplicity of almost interchangeable examples.

Take this 'story' by Tournefort – which, oddly enough, can be found already in Baudier, who has perhaps himself borrowed it from Courmenin.[57] He tells of his indignation that a doctor called to the bedside of one of these women was not given permission either to see or be seen by her, and was allowed only to touch her pulse through a piece of gauze, being therefore unable to 'perceive whether the movement was in her artery or her tendons' (if he 'asked to see the tip of her tongue or to touch any part of her, he could be stabbed upon the instant'). Tournefort adds that he himself was summoned to the harem for a consultation:

> These apartments are made like the dormitories of our nuns and I found at each door a gauze-covered arm extended through a hole made for this purpose. On going round at first I thought these were arms made of wood or copper meant to hold lights in the darkness; but I was very surprised when I was told that the persons to whom these arms belonged were in need of cure.[58]

Everything occurs as if the primary object of the despot's gratification were not so much woman as *women*. Of course, in the seraglio it is only the despot who can enjoy the other sex. But it is less the *other* sex that he enjoys than its multiplicity which, beside his own singularity, marks out the inferior. Women in the harem are without number – on a scale with the *jouissance* of an all-powerful master, it will be thought. Not so. There is precisely no corresponding scale, as if their number, however high it be, could reach this One-All which is their master only asymptotically. It is here that we need to stop regarding the harem as an exotic curiosity and recognize it as a phantasmic place, whose power to fascinate (the endless amount that is said about it is a mark of this) can be grasped only by reconnecting it to its deep roots, which are metaphysical. Let us elaborate:

The Christian West has long debated polygamy, eventually condemning it irrevocably. But the question underlying this debate – the question of woman's very being – has never been clearly resolved. As if there were no concept of woman. Furthermore, as

143

we have seen, Muslim polygamy was shocking to the Classical age. But it was also disturbing, for ultimately, maybe, the Mahommedans were really the only ones to act coherently on the metaphysical principles they shared with the West on this matter. Whether they were philosophers, jurists or doctors, the Europeans did nothing other than define woman's 'being', after Aristotle, as a 'lesser being' in relation to man. Metaphysically, she is an existence without essence, or a (male) essence whose actualization is hindered. It is something which exists 'in otherness', not 'in itself'. A woman, therefore, can 'be or be thought' only 'in man and through man' – as, for example, Spinoza's finite mode can be and be thought only by the attribute of the substance it expresses. And just as the difference in ontological status between substance and mode means that between substances there is a *real* distinction, while between the finite modes of the same substance there is only a *numerical* distinction, so – *mutatis mutandis* – between man and woman the distinction is real, while between women there can be only numerical distinctions; man is to woman what substance is to mode, and the *one* which makes a man is of a quite different order from the *one* which makes a woman – just as the *one* of the substance is not like the *one* of a finite mode. Finally, just as Spinoza's substance can have several attributes, or express itself in an infinity of finite modes, while a mode, conversely, cannot express two or more substances, so a man can have two – indeed, an infinity of wives, but a woman can have only one husband.

This metaphysical excursion is in no way gratuitous; for some time now (ever since Jacques Lacan) people have been fond of saying that 'woman does not ek-sist', that she is 'not-all', that women are not totalized within a concept which subsumes them, that they can only ever be 'one by one', in an always incomplete catalogue, like Leporello's in *Don Giovanni*. But it is clear that such pronouncements, relaunching the old debate on femininity in analytic circles, were already implicitly contained within the categories and the conceptual apparatus of Classical metaphysics – which, says Lacan, with justifiable irreverence, has been talking about sexual relations unremittingly ever since Aristotle. And what it says about them, in its fundamentals and principles, comes down only to this: the concept of a male-sexed being, since it is only in the male that the possibility of realizing all the potentialities of human essence is recognized. A woman, therefore, can be conceived only as falling short in relation to this essence. She is thereby ontologically devalued, and therefore inferior. Since the relation of superior to inferior tends to be expressed always as the relation of the One to the multiple, if Man exists (if we can form the concept of him), *then he must be polygamous*, just as there must be only one God who stands above a number of souls, or only one master above a number of slaves, and so on.

Should there be any doubt of this, a text by Saint Augustine, who became very fashionable again at the end of the seventeenth century, should persuade us. These are the metaphysical foundations on which he bases the core of his evidence to justify polygamous marriage among the ancient Patriarchs:

Therefore, while it was permitted for one husband to have several wives, it was not permitted for one woman to have several husbands, not even for the sake of offspring, if, perhaps, she was able to bear while her husband was not able to beget. For, by a hidden law of nature, *things that rule love singularity*; things that are ruled, indeed, are subjected not only each one to an individual master, but also, if natural or social conditions allow, *many of them are not unfittingly subjected to one master*. Neither does *one servant have many masters, as many servants have one master*. And so we read that not one of the holy women served two or more loving husbands; we do read, however, that one man had several wives when the customs of that people permitted it and the nature of the time encouraged it, for it is not against the nature of marriage. Many women can conceive children by one man, but one woman cannot do so by many men – *this is the nature of principles* – just as many souls are properly subjected to the one God. Therefore, there is only the one true God of souls; one soul through many false gods can commit fornication, but not be made fruitful.[59]

It is therefore 'the nature of principles' (metaphysics) which requires and justifies polygamy. Of course, Saint Augustine will

145

add that in our day, a 'new natural and social order', and above all a new law, go against these principles: Earth is sufficiently peopled for Christians, now exempt from the reproductive mission so piously fulfilled by the Patriarchs, to turn towards the heavenly wedding of their souls with the One God. And for them, continence and celibacy are the better choice. If, however, they cannot avoid the enticements of the flesh, they will find a pleasure that is permitted in monogamous marriage, on condition of its chastity and of there being no other purpose than begetting new Christians. The metaphysical principles and the hidden law of nature, whereby the only conceivable *sexual* relation between men and women is polygamous, are no less enduring. (Even in monogamous marriage, the man/woman couple is not a unit made up of two 'ones' of the same kind, except when they renounce the illusory and deceptive union of bodies, and the man and woman are united soul to soul.) Well, it is these very principles and this very law that can be seen in practice in the Muslim Orient.

If power is expressed in the relation of the Other to those who are alike and of the One to the multiple, we can understand why the harem is essential to despotic power. Impenetrably closed off to curious eyes, inhabited by women who – as Tournefort puts it so well – 'are not in evidence, any more than are pure spirits', the harem prompts an imagined plurality that has no limit (the Greeks' ἄπειρον) which accordingly enhances the singularity, uniqueness and transcendence of Him for whom and through whom these women are. In this sense, the journey to the Orient is perhaps metaphysics in Épinal images. But did not the greatest metaphysicians dream, like Kant, of humble toilers who would illustrate their teachings?

This system of ontological cuts and metaphysical distinctions which is the seraglio – and its harem – is maintained in reality, however, only thanks to the presence of an indispensable character who, having himself been 'cut' or 'clipped' (in the words of the period), carries out cuts in his turn, keeps guard over thresholds, and assigns roles: the eunuch.

8

The Guardian of
the Thresholds

'The impure fire of nature corrupted is so common a disease, and so ancient a sin among the Turks, that the Ottoman Princes believed, as did the other Princes of the Orient, that it was not fitting ... to entrust the great offices of their household to any other but eunuchs.'[1] This is the reason usually acknowledged for the presence of eunuchs in the seraglio. We shall see that it is not the only one.

Black and White

Like the ichoglans, the azamoglans, and the harem girls, the eunuchs always come from elsewhere. Whether they are natives of Africa or Asia (India, the Malabar Coast, and Bengal supplied the greatest number, and there were certain countries which specialized in their fabrication and exportation[2]), they were always prized objects. In Persia, moreover, only three or four of them would be found in the households of the rich. But the emperor had three thousand in his service.[3] Chardin explains that they were bought at an age varying between eight and sixteen, and:

> they are scarcely wanted above this age, because they are cut when young, which is to say between seven and ten years, after which they are sold at once, and they scarcely ever change their Master, because

once they have entered a household, they are set to their duties with punishments that are severe if need be, whereby they are formed to the humour of those whom they serve.[4]

Cut off from everything ('since they are all born of people who are lost to them, the majority of them know not from which country they come', writes Chardin), they are also, so to speak, cut off from themselves: 'With neither household, nor wives, nor children, nor parents', 'far less subject to the passions of love and ambition', without even bonds of friendship, they are unattached to that by which and for which a man who is worthy of the name might live. It is understandable that they will be 'tied to their duties more strongly than other men'.[5] Their total blankness makes them ideal slaves, which means that the ultimate reality of their impotence becomes omnipotence, by that same logic of despotic power which we saw earlier to be at work in the pairing of despot and vizier:

> Since they see plainly on the one hand that their well-being depends on their Master, for they are his slaves and he is the arbiter of their fate; and on the other that they can lay no claim to his trust and goodwill except by serving him well, they make themselves fit to do so with all their might and they generally succeed so well that they manage and govern everything.[6]

Yet within the corps of eunuchs, there is one fundamental distinction: a eunuch is either black or white. White eunuchs are the officers of the seraglio, which they command and administer in accordance with a very strict hierarchical order, or they serve as tutors or supervisors of the children in the seraglio. In Turkey the chief of the white eunuchs (the *Capi-Aga*), Grand Master of the seraglio, stands permanently by the side of the Great Lord, accompanying him like his shadow. No one, not even the vizier, can enter the apartment of the Great Lord, nor leave it without his order. The black eunuchs, on the other hand, are specialists in guarding the harem, whose entrances and exits they survey. The white eunuchs stand by the despot's side, doubling as his shadow. The black ones are beside the women, and their eyes never leave them.

The difference in skin colour is only the external indication of this division of labour. For the white eunuchs are men 'who have merely been clipped'. As for the black ones, 'they have been completely sheared down to the skin of the belly'.[7] On this point, too (something already observed in relation to blinding or the bath), we should note a recent move towards radical actions; total eunuchs have been used to guard the harem only since Suleiman the Second 'who, one day seeing a gelded stallion covering a mare, concluded that the eunuchs guarding his wives could equally entertain their passions'.[8] The mortality rate entailed in this operation makes them very highly prized, but their true value does not reside in this.

One might believe that the white eunuch has more value than the black, since he still has something of a man in him. By the logic of the seraglio, this is far from being the case. For the black eunuch's perfection lies precisely in his degree of distance from the ideal type imagined to be embodied in the despot: 'I do not regard as men the black eunuchs, who by their deformities of face and body have been made monsters', wrote Tavernier. Their blackness of skin is already a precious blemish. But it would be best of all to attain the furthest limits of ugliness: 'The most deformed are those who cost the most, their extreme ugliness standing for beauty in their kind. A flattened nose, a fearsome gaze, a large mouth with thick lips, black teeth separated by gaps between them . . . these are advantages for the merchants who sell them.'[9]

As a totally negative figure made up of multiple variations which comment in every possible way on the theme of the central lack, like all the principal characters in the seraglio, the black eunuch has a value in relation not to an economy of need, but to one of desire and *jouissance*. There is no doubt that his usefulness within the harem is irreplaceable, since there is nothing – in principle – he can do to the women. But from another point of view, he can do everything, since he prompts them to imagine the despot, and in some way, therefore, gives him life in their desire. The black eunuchs are in the women's bedchambers, P. de La Porte explains, 'so that having such monsters always before their eyes, they will thereby see the Great Lord to be finer and more worthy of love'.[10] In those days when doctors themselves credited the mother's imagination with an enormous influence on the physical development or malformation of the unborn child, the traveller experienced amazement that mothers-to-be might have such sights before them without risk. Baudier writes:

> Elsewhere, there would be an outcry about giving Moors as servants to queens, even to women of lesser estate, for fear, lest conceiving children, their imagination might imprint upon them either the complexion or the form of such lackeys; but this does not deter the Turks. And I have never heard it said that any Sultana gave birth to a Moor, although I know that this can take place; history provides us with examples of such accidents, where we see that women have been delivered of children resembling the paintings that were in their bedchamber.[11]

Is it to ward off this risk, or because through them they can glimpse the object of their love, that 'the Ladies give them names that are more in keeping with their own dainty affectations than with Moorish ugliness', and 'give such names as Hyacinth, Narcissus, Rose and Carnation' to 'those withered and faded flowers that can never blossom'?[12]

Thus the eunuch matters only in terms of what he lacks. He makes absence positive. Whether black or white, he is there to 'be seen', and to offer to the eyes of both men and women the negative image of him who must not be looked upon directly, and can only be imagined as omnipotent.

The 'Treatise on the Eunuchs'

That such human wreckage might be invested with such power is clearly a matter for reflection:

> Date operam, cum silentio animum attendite
> Ut pernoscatis quid sibi Eunuchus velit,[13]

pronounces Terence at the beginning of his play. Striving to the utmost, racking his brains to understand the meaning of the eunuch, was in any case what Charles Ancillon was engaged upon as he made the most of the leisure afforded him by an exile in Berlin to which his Reformed faith had sentenced him. In his very scholarly *Traité des eunuques*, published in 1707, Ancillon expressed amazement that Theodor, tutor to the emperor Constantine, took it into his head one day, 'by a strange and singularly formed plan, to write an Apologia *"pro Eunuchismo et Eunuchis"*',[14] seeing therein a sophisticated rhetorical game of the kind to be found in Isocrates' *In Praise of Busiris*, Favorinus' *On Ugliness*, Cardan's *On Gout*, or Schuppius' *On Vermin*. In his view (though he is wrong) there is nothing to be learned from these eulogies of the Negative, from these philosophical crumbs dropped by a few great men,[15] from these brief eulogies to Nothing and Nothingness[16] – in short, from these nothings bearing on nothings.

Yet Ancillon knows very well that in speaking of eunuchs he is taking on a subject which is as difficult and disconcerting, but also as worthy of interest, as that of Plato's *Parmenides* or *The Sophist*, whose subtle dialectic could alone give order to and breathe life into that terrain of Eleatic ruins represented by the vast documentation with which he presents us.

As announced in his 'Dedicatory Epistle to M. Bayle', he writes to warn women against seduction by eunuchs. Once, this would not have been necessary: the voices of Italian castrati could charm, and they prided themselves on their great and illustrious conquests, but our ladies did not let themselves be dazzled. Alas, here is one who now pays heed to the marriage proposal made by one of these eunuchs. How can someone let herself be thus deceived? What manner of being is the eunuch then (and likewise the woman who promises herself to him), in the eyes of nature and the law? What becomes of the institution and the sacrament of marriage, if the eunuch is one fit to contract it? And finally, what of man himself, if the eunuch is a being worthy of desire?

It is important to point out here that Ancillon was writing at a period when an old debate about the purpose of marriage was being reanimated. This debate would soon be fuelled by the warnings of 'demographers', who saw the depopulation of France as the outcome of sundry causes, all of them directly linked in some way or another to the topic of despotism (the impoverishment of the countryside and the luxury of the cities are two opposing but complementary causes of the low birth rate). Would all the French gradually turn into eunuchs? Ancillon presents a portrait of eunuchs, after Lucien – 'those who, through weakness, coldness or amputation, cannot father children, those with a shrill, languid voice, a womanly complexion, with naught but down on their chins, in a word those whose ways and manners are very effeminate' – in which we can easily recognize those self-important little men from Paris salons who are ridiculed by Duclos or Rousseau. But there is more to it than ridicule; there is an unvoiced anxiety (as borne out in Rousseau's case), as if despotism would win and thrive only in a world where the difference between the sexes was effaced.

The jurisconsults classified the eunuchs into four groups: 'Those born as such, those with everything cut off, those who have only been made sterile and those among men who are so badly formed or so frigid that they are unequipped to play a part in begetting children.' Whatever their group, it is generally agreed – whether by pagans like Seneca, or Christians like Saint Basil – that 'they are as contemptible in mind as in body', for which reason 'the overall name, whereby it is claimed they are all designated, is *Bagoas.* This name is that of the character representing the Eunuch whom, in Lucien's dialogue, Diocles wishes to exclude from the profession of philosopher'.[17]

Let us confine ourselves to the eunuchs who have been made so by an operation.

The loser wins

Why are eunuchs made? asks Ancillon. To begin with, he answers, for 'legitimate' reasons. It is said that Semiramide, queen of the Assyrians, was the first to make them, and one can understand that a woman might use this means to maintain her power (I, 1). Likewise, one can imagine that it would have been deemed useful to deploy castrated custodians to guard girls and women (I, 5). In short, the eunuch was in the first place a necessary instrument for the holder of power, be they man or woman.

It can also be understood, as a result, that castration, which weakens, would have been used as a mode of vengeance and punishment, and regarded as a mark of ignominy. It is thus the penalty inflicted on adulterers, and even, among the Gauls, on slaves guilty of theft.

But what cannot be explained – except in terms of a deep perversion of desire – is the fact that the eunuch, the tool of power and bearer of ignominy, could have become at the same time a holder of power and an object of desire. Before the Italians of our own day, according to Macrobius, the Romans in decline took pleasure in the voices of castrati, the delicate fruit of a criminal pruning.[18] And:

> men, who had them only for legitimate use, abused them and made them in order to serve foul and criminal purposes. With these in mind they chose the handsomest boys that they found between the age of fourteen and seventeen years. Saint Gregory bitterly lamented this in his Life of Saint Basil and in his Prayer XXXI. But this infamous custom must be a lot older, for Juvenal pronounces against these abuses in one of his satires.[19]

Instead of being a means to protect the natural object of desire (woman), the eunuch himself becomes an end and, although totally contemptible, is supremely desirable. In the Orient, women have been seen and are seen to marry eunuchs.[20] There is such firm belief in their value that – as Saint Augustine observes[21] – they have been made to furnish offerings to divinities.

Successive laws forbidding castration ever since Domitian bear out this dual character of the eunuch. The eunuch is a *fake*, and he who makes him must be punished as a forger. But this fake – is he man or woman? – is simultaneously worth more than the genuine article.[22]

But there is more: some make eunuchs of themselves, like those priests of Cybele in Phrygia or Diana at Ephesus, and above all like Origen, who castrated himself, in the belief that he was pleasing God by following the literal sense of the Apostle's words 'make oneself a eunuch for the kingdom of heaven',[23] or like Valesius and his followers who saw in castration a necessary condition for being raised to the dignity of the priesthood.[24]

There is something here which eighteenth-century rationalism fails to understand: that in the same period, and in the same nation, both the presence and the absence of an organ can be endowed with a similar effect, and that power accrues equally to those who have it and those who do not: 'What a wondrous thing! The Syrians revered the figure of what we call Priapus, and the priests despoiled themselves of their virility!', observes Voltaire.[25] Why? Purely utilitarian explanations are untenable, in his view. What we must see instead is 'the effect of the ancient custom of sacrificing to the gods what one held most dear, and of not exposing oneself to accidents of what one imagined as impurity before those beings who one imagined to be pure'.[26] But Voltaire explains nothing, and goes no further than projecting his militant anticlericalism – for which the celibacy of priests and monastic asceticism are prime targets – on to the origins of things, the cradle of prejudices.

None the less, he senses that what is played out in the darkness of origins, where castration is so patently bound up with the question of power, arises from a 'symbolic' order which enlarges and outstrips reality – as when he interprets circumcision as a form of symbolic castration, refusing to allow that its origins are 'a principle of health'. Castration can indeed only be the symbolic progression of an original castration: 'After such sacrifices, can we be amazed at what was done with the foreskin among other peoples, and the amputation of a testicle among the African nations?'[27]

It is therefore always something more and something other than a real organ which is sacrificed and worshipped, Voltaire argues. Idolatry, *in the literal sense*, does not exist, and has never been able to exist:

> It is not possible for a statue really to be worshipped.... One commentator, Dacier, came to the conclusion that the statue of Priapus was really being worshipped, because Horace gives the power of speech to this ghastly thing, having it say 'I was once a tree trunk; the woodman, uncertain whether to fashion me into a god or a stool, settled for making me a god [etc.]'. The commentator ... fails to see that Horace is poking fun both at the alleged god, and at his statue.[28]

But while refusing to acknowledge that one can believe in the power of a thing, Voltaire cannot but say: what one believes in is the idea represented by that thing, which is only a *sign*, representing a different thing to someone. The theory of the sign – as it was elaborated at Port-Royal, organizing the 'episteme' of the Classical period – is thus a weapon against superstition and prejudice, but it simultaneously prohibits any understanding of the thing whose effects are none the less experienced continuously: the power of the signifier as such.

Medical literature did, however, give reason for reflection. In the period when Voltaire was writing the *Essai sur les mœurs*, the medical journals recorded numerous cases of self-castration. Thus, in 1758 the *Journal de médecine* published two case studies.[29] Although one of these cases can be compared to the action of Origen, the other seems to make no sense and can be explained only by a profound mental derangement. The only firm conclusions reached are strictly surgical. None the less, these convey a sense of the extraordinary nature of this operation, since 'in man it results in fearsome accidents, while with animals it is always successful'.[30]

It is from Ancillon's bemused investigations, in Chapter 12 of his *Traité*, that we see how – albeit obscurely – the case of the eunuchs illuminates the essential connection between castration and mastery, and the paradoxical nature of what we must call the phallic signifier. For example, of the two princesses of Borneo, one wants all her ministers to be castrated, the other does not. Or again, on the one hand we see Nero having Sporus castrated and disguised as a woman so that he can marry him, while the kings of Persia, on the other hand, let themselves be complete dominated by the eunuchs. His contradictory status illustrates the fact that the eunuch is always much more or less than a eunuch, which means that he is a eunuch only through and for beings dedicated to language, and in a universe ruled by the symbolic order, whose operation indeed 'results in fearsome accidents in men'. Ancillon recognizes this implicitly, for he writes that the term eunuch designates both a certain *real* living person and a *function* within a hierarchical order which can only be symbolic: 'Those who filled offices which had originally been occupied by eunuchs were themselves called eunuchs', just as the name 'senators' is given to 'people who are not necessarily aged' (I, 7).[31] Someone is a 'eunuch' just as he is a senator, or a father, or whatever: just as he is a man.[32] But it must also be said that the 'real' eunuch who is replaced by the one who is so only in name – like Potiphar, Pharaoh's eunuch – was also simultaneously the thing and the title, and how else could the title have originated and stood as a mark of honour? Every man – every 'speaking being', we should say, using Lacan's term – is thus simultaneously more than he *is* and less than he is *said* to be, compelled always to *act*: to act a part, on the stage of human history, in the sense meant by the Stoics, but also to act, in the way that is said of a machine part's *action*.

An ambiguous husband

This is why the second part of the *Traité des eunuques* – 'in which the right of eunuchs in relation to marriage is discussed and in which the question of whether they should be allowed to marry is considered' – is both crucial and derisory.

Crucial: Ancillon is surprised that eunuchs have been talked about by everyone, but that one finds 'almost nothing about any jurisprudence or casuistic theology on the marriage of eunuchs which is universal and conclusive' (II, 8). From our point of view this almost total silence is an index of what La Rochefoucauld turned into a maxim, and Rousseau, with his procession of lofty souls, would strive to make us forget: 'There are good marriages, but none is delightful.' Ancillon does not stop at this subtle *distinguo*. For him things are clear-cut: the 'marriage' of the eunuch goes against all received definitions of marriage, be it in Canon Law or Roman Law. The *conjunctio* of the two spouses assumes coitus, and its purpose is to engender children. *Falsum quod est, nihili est*, says the maxim of the Law. Now the eunuch is *false*, he promises what he cannot hold to; he gives what he does not have. For marriage 'is a kind of contract of purchase and sale, in which each partner acquires the potency of the other's body'. To be more accurate: of a part – to be thought of as *pars totalis* – of that body of the other. This is borne out by the speech of those women whose husbands, captured in war, were going to be castrated by the enemy general: 'When you make eunuchs, they told him, it is not they, but us whom you mutilate . . . . My husband has eyes, a nose, hands, feet, and these are his property, which you can take away from him if he deserves so, but my plea is that you leave him what belongs to me' (I, 4). After such pleading, how can it be maintained that the marriage of the eunuch is a formal contract, since one party knowingly deceives the other about the merchandise, offering no more than a specious packaging?

But people will say that if the wife who marries him 'knows that he is a eunuch and is not ignorant of the consequences of his condition, it should be allowed that she marry him if she wishes, since the Law affirms that: *volenti non fit injuria*'.

No, answers Ancillon. The wife *believes* that she knows, 'but what does she know of her future desires'?[33]

But there are eunuchs who are perfectly capable of satisfying the desires of a woman!

What? How can they do so? Ancillon protests. 'Of what nature are these desires, are they *permitted*? Which means: are they inseparable from the desire to procreate, the true purpose of

157

marriage? For after all, 'what is this pleasure of marriage given to women without them running its risks'?[34]

Thus, not only does the eunuch nullify the marriage, since he cannot beget children, but most of all he renders it unnatural, since he takes and gives in it a pleasure sought out for itself. Having seduced the woman and deceived her, he perverts her. We can see how the issue of the eunuch's marriage, and the way in which it is put on trial, interrogates the whole essence of marriage, and exposes the sexual norm which is to hold sway within it.

But the wavering of the jurists and the casuists shows that Ancillon's proclaimed certainties are derisory. For who can really say with certainty where the line is that marks off the eunuch from the man who is not a eunuch? The pre-pubescent child, the old man, a husband who is frigid, sick or fickle, or even – an increasingly frequent case at the beginning of the eighteenth century – the one who makes use of himself to 'cheat nature' by abandoning himself to the sin of Onan – are not these, each in his own way, eunuchs? Yet they are allowed to marry. Moreover, these deceiving husbands are eunuchs only after having been (or before being) good husbands, or by accident, circumspection or boredom. But there are husbands who are eunuchs by vocation, and who, if everything was as it should be, ought to represent the majority of cases. For what is most disturbing is that they are perhaps the ones who most scrupulously fulfil a certain Christian ideal defined by the Fathers of the Church. Is it not indeed the eunuch whom the Christian woman must learn to desire and cherish in the man whom she marries? Making love with a eunuch – is this not the very acme of Christian marriage, the holiest of conjugal duties as well as the only path to unalloyed bliss, since it offers the only relationship which makes it possible to *make One* out of two? There is no *sexual* relation. This is something affirmed by Saint Augustine before Jacques Lacan. Out of two bodies, two fleshes which are in such a close embrace, such a deep interpenetration as one can imagine, a single body, a single flesh, can never be made, for concupiscence can lead only to *conjunction*, which is a caricature of *union*. Whereas two souls vivified by love have perfect union. This is what married couples must seek: 'The chastity of souls rightly joined together continues the purer, the more it has been proved, and the more secure, the more it has been calmed.'[35] This is why 'now, since the opportunity for spiritual relationship abounds on all sides and for all peoples for entering into a holy and pure association, even they who wish to contract marriage only to have children are to be admonished that they practise the greater good of continence'.[36]

Thus the eunuch simultaneously stands for two types of husbands who are extreme opposites: he is the worst that can be imagined as a perverse husband, and the best that can be dreamt of as a Christian husband. But let us not be misled by his ambiguity. If he can navigate between these extremes in this way, being simultaneously a subhuman man and a superman the most abject of slaves and the most prestigious of masters, it is because, as naive women or ignorant peoples, we let ourselves be seduced despite ourselves by this semblance of being. Furthermore, with a little more audacity or liking for dialectic, Ancillon could have made of his *Traité des eunuques* a modern version of Plato's *Sophist*.

'A New Harmony'

Hunting the eunuch

For Theaetetus, a boy who is well born but too readily dazzled, Plato set about hunting the sophist, the ever-fleeting productive appearance of appearances. If he did in the end capture him, it took a harrying pursuit on which the antique gardens of knowledge were looted, their fixed order was overturned and Parmenides, the venerable Father, was ridiculed. For the sophist lays ambush in argument, deceiving as he speaks. And how could he do so, if there is no reality in error – that is to say, if non-being does not exist? In order to avoid Parmenides' paralysing assertion – being is, non-being is not – it must therefore be acknowledged that non-being exists in some way, and recognized that non-being

159

is the *other*. The other: this is the mode which makes it possible to flush out the sophist, to separate him from that which his art of camouflage lets him be mistaken for, down to the very name: the 'sage', the αόψοζ. So what is the sophist, Theaetetus? the Stranger can then ask at the end of the hunt; what is the secret of his art? It is this:

> The mimetic kind that the art of making contradictory speeches characterizes (it's the ironical part of the opinionative art), the proper part of the phantastic genus (it descends from the art of making images) that conjures in speeches, which distinctively set itself apart as not a divine but a human part of making – whoever says that the sophist in his being is 'of this generation and blood', will say, it seems, what is the truest.[37]

It is for a woman, one who is oversusceptible to the specious charms of a eunuch, that Ancillon, for his part, embarks on a similar hunt, vainly interrogating on the way, one by one, all those (philosophers, jurists, Fathers of the Church) who are imagined to know. Did he feel his male certainties to be threatened – as Plato was threatened in his mission as philosopher by the sophist – and put on his mettle in front of a woman by a rival just as fearsome and elusive as Plato's? What is a eunuch, Madame, if not also a specialist in the mimetic and a producer of simulacra, a being who comes from the phantastic genus and produces before you phantasms that leave you open-mouthed, γένοζ ψανταστικόν καὶ θαυματοποιικόν? In other words, of the same blood and stock as the sophists? Does not he, too, hide inside words, to start with in the equivocal nature of his name, which can be a title of glory as much as a mark of infamy? But this equivocal nature even covers a deeper, more secret and more essential ambiguity in that it concerns us all, an ambiguity whose root cannot be grasped without violating a thesis as venerable as that of Parmenides. This thesis (like that of those ancient Ionians according to whom the Whole 'is, or it has become, or it is becoming many, one, or two, and hot in turn is mixing with cold'[38]) describes the Whole (of

160

human nature) as composed of two sexes, whose existence and complementarity is a fact of nature, and says, that in between man and woman, as in between being and non-being, there is nothing. Now, where are we to seek the eunuch, if not precisely *in between* the one sex and the other? If we say, as asserted by many, that he is neither man nor woman, how are we to grasp him? He evaporates, he does not exist. Yet this eunuch whom you, Madame, desire, like this castrato with whom you depraved Neapolitan men are in love, is certainly something too. It will be said that the lady desires in him the appearance of a man, the others the appearance of a woman. But how can it be that a real woman should thus prefer – even to the point of proposing marriage – the appearance of a man to a man who is complete and authentic, and that a real man should seek in an appearance of a woman what real women eagerly offer him, just as they are meant to do? Would this, then, mean that men or women who desire a eunuch are not real men and women? But how can we support this, if our only criterion of sex is the blinding obviousness of anatomical reality?

The second birth

And what if, precisely, this anatomical reality misled us? What if, instead of vainly seeking the eunuch in between these two sexes existing naturally for all eternity, we were to make the eunuch primary, so that each of the two sexes would then be defined in relation to him? What if the eunuch, like the sophist, came under that gender of the *other*, through which the genders communicate? What if the difference between the sexes came second, and castration came first, and one became a man or a woman only in relation to it? It should not then be said that the eunuch is *neither* man *nor* woman. Nor that he is *simultaneously* man *and* woman. Within this logic of sexuality, he is neither the non-being as nothing, nor being as Everything. But he is the picture of alterity itself, the Other who arouses all the others, the educator of their desire, the stroke or the cut which connects the sexes and makes their connection both necessary and impossible, since the eunuch is always (is this not his function?) in between the two of them, and, so to speak, in the middle of the bed – even, and perhaps most of all, when his not being there is certain.

Of course, Ancillon does not come to these conclusions. They are none the less imposed upon us by our visit to the seraglio, in which the eunuch now appears as the master component. Castration, wrenching him for ever into natural servitude, makes him, by 'a second birth',[39] the commander and arbiter of that symbolic game of which we spoke earlier. It is through him that roles are assigned; it is he who creates, in their reciprocity, the husband and his wives, the master and his subjects. But what is fascinating in the seraglio eunuch is that the equivocal nature of his being, which so tormented Ancillon, is resolved by its manifestation in the two opposing 'colours' which clothe this double-faced monster: on the one hand white, resplendent and venerable, in the eyes of the despot's subjects he has all the outward show of the sanctity of the Roman pontiff, of him who, renouncing his own desire, commands that of others.[40] On the other hand black, repugnant and abject, for the mass of women he is the petrifying Medusa-head buckle which protects its wearer while making him resplendent in the eyes of their imagination. Whether luminous aura or sinister shadow, he is always the inseparable double of the master, preceding and heralding him, making him feared or desired.

We can also say that this cut-up body, for its own part, cuts and divides human beings. It inhabits the between-two (between two women's beds or the beds of ichoglans), becoming the means of every relationship as well as the guarantor of its impossibility. Its place is on *thresholds* (that of the harem, that of the Great Lord's apartment). 'Riveted forever to the door that he is tied to, harder than the bolts and hinges which hold it',[41] it is as if he were the door itself.

Nature seems to have placed women in a state of dependence, and to have removed them from it again. Between the two sexes disorder arose, because their rights were reciprocal. But we form part of a new and harmonious scheme: between women and us we create hatred, and between women and men, love.[42]

Thus speaks Jahrum, Usbek's black eunuch. Within these few lines we can see the stages of a mythic 'history, rather like the condensation of a 'Treatise on the Origin and Foundations of Inequality Between the Sexes': a state of nature, a golden age when the natural order of men's domination ruled; then the revolt of women, a state of rivalry and war; finally there is the appearance of the eunuch, who, by leading the sexes to become totally *denatured*, restores the lost harmony on different principles. But what the black eunuch says about this new (inegalitarian) alliance between the sexes, the white eunuch could also say: he in fact is the one who, by making himself hated and feared by all (he is cruel, he does not even know what friendship is, etc.), sets up between the subjects and their master a relation of love, which we can imagine he substitutes for an original relation of natural dependence.

The palace Phoenix

From Aristotle to Montesquieu, the West gave itself confirmation by relating the political monstrosity of Oriental despotism to natural determinants alone. 'Setting all the facts aside for a moment' and entering the seraglio in imagination, we see that the system of Oriental despotism, far from resting on natural determinants,[43] instead assumes a radical denaturation, in the sense that would be understood by Rousseau. If this denaturation does not appear as such, and manifests itself instead in the outward appearance of the most brutal and direct natural relations, it is precisely because all the symbolic functions which are at stake within this system of power, and enable its effectiveness, are in some way *naturalized* inside the seraglio, and subjectivized in the personages whom we have just reviewed. All of them (the blind, the children, the mutes, dwarves, women and eunuchs) matter only inasmuch as they exhibit in the negative what the despot does and has.

Therein they contribute in their turn to naturalizing power itself, by subjectivizing it in that imaginary central figure who hangs over them and around whom they revolve, mesmerized. The eunuch is one of them, without a doubt. But simultaneously he represents them all; he is the motive for their series, the theme whose motley variations they develop. By corollary, that omnipresent gaze, that Name of the Father, that domination of the signifier, whether uttered or written, that factitious majesty and that uniqueness which are the qualities of the despot, appear as so many metonymic equivalents of what gives him his essence, and which the eunuch dedicates himself to offering: the phallus.

Moreover:

> when a dwarf is found born deaf and in consequence dumb, he is looked upon as the palace Phoenix; he is admired more than the handsomest man in the world, above all if this monkeyish creature is a eunuch; but these three defects which would make a man very much to be scorned, create the most perfect of all creatures, in the eyes of the Turks.[44]

'He is infinitely more esteemed than if Nature and art had together conspired to make him the most perfect creature in the world', says Ricaut, going even further,[45] likewise struck by this paradox. As expected of a species rich in so many perfections, it does not take long to acquire its status: 'A Pasha presented one of these [a deaf-mute eunuch dwarf] to the Great Lord, with which he was so pleased that he thereupon had him dressed in golden draperies and gave him permission to enter all the apartments of the seraglio.'[46] This grotesque harlequin of the negative enjoyed that unique privilege – which belonged only to the master – of free movement everywhere – in other words, of crossing the classifications without belonging to any. What an extraordinary exaltation of such abjectness personified! As if, by attaining the perfection of the negative, one found oneself closer to what gathers every perfection in itself. To the point where we can ask: what if this deaf-mute-eunuch-dwarf, this *nothing of nothing*, were the despot himself, merged with his double? For is this absolute master, who 'spends his life in continuous solitude with children, women, eunuchs, mutes and dwarves who revere him like a god, and tremble when they see his mere shadow',[47] anything other than that shadow itself, that phantom – that phantasm – conjured before them by these subjects who all have something lacking? What each of them finds and fears in him – that gaze, that voice, that phallus: everything, in short, which makes him great – is that lost part of themselves for which his slight being is the fragile support.

A paltry conclusion – let us be honest – and one which, further-more, we discovered long ago. The seraglio only confirms what philosophers ever since Plato have never stopped saying: that the worst tyrant is only ever the slave of his slaves, and that there is no better slave than the one who forges his own chains. But we can also see that the seraglio gives this classic thesis an unprecedented illustration, whose exoticism is only a mask. Behind this exoticism it is the roots of power – and of its representation of power – with which the West in the Classical age is confronted.

Let us therefore linger a little longer in the seraglio, so that we can discover under what forms there appears the final 'stage' of this dialectic, which is perhaps too crude and infantile to take its place within the Hegelian conceptualization, but is childlike enough to deserve elucidation by the author of the *Interpretation of Dreams*.

9

The Other Scene

The World Turned Upside-Down

The very writers who describe the power of the despot as personal, arbitrary and absolute therefore always go on to show that it seems what it is not, and that in reality, everything in the seraglio takes place as the opposite of what its order and discipline would have us believe.

Viragos

The harem is a prison; the women in it are slaves, desperately in love with their Man, and guarded by eunuchs whom they hate; so much for appearances. But who holds the reality of power? Chardin writes that in Persia it is 'a *Privy Council* which usually prevails above everything, and which lays down the law for everything. It is held between the mother of the King, the Grand Eunuchs and the mistresses who are the most adept and the most in favour.'[1] In Turkey, likewise, power is in the hands of women. In the first place because it is passed on through them; this, for example, is the case with the daughters or sisters of the Sultan. By marrying them to pashas or other 'grandees', he keeps the latter at his mercy, because the women emasculate them almost totally; you have only to read the accounts of the marriage and the wedding night of a sultana to be convinced of this. In public, moreover: 'the sultana continually makes distinctions between herself and him (her husband) and carries . . . her dagger by her side, as a mark of superiority'. But these phallophoric women are the tools of the Sultan only in appearance, since he himself is reduced to nothing by a phallic woman, his mother, the *Valide*, surrounded by 'eight ichoglans dressed as men', the queen mother is the object of a kind of cult on the part of her son; he visits her in the morning, and: 'she affects such gravity, and the Sultan such great respect, that he does not sit unless his Mother has asked him three times. . . . He rests on his knees and on his heels without any cushion, with his tunic tight closed, which is a mark of the greatest submission'.[2]

This man, therefore, who is supposed to be the only one to hold power, is only the instrument of the one who, as a woman, is supposed to be deprived of it. In this universe saturated by sex, let us not hesitate to write that he who, to all appearances, *has* the phallus, *is* the phallus for his mother. That, as we have seen, is what his entire upbringing necessarily leads to. We can even say that it is because he has let himself become, so docilely and so totally, the object of his mother's desire that, since he remains incorrigibly a child, the exercise of his appearance of power takes the form of a masquerade. Hence the despot's fragility, and his sudden reduction to nothing once he ceases to maintain the illusion; Macrobius recounted that Hermias, the eunuch prince, 'could never tolerate anyone speaking in his presence of knives, or of cutting, because he imagined that since he was a eunuch, these words were addressed to him'.[3] But is not every despot a Hermias who is cheating his world, and seeking reassurance by refusing to hear the lesson which all those around him – like King Midas's reeds – are teaching him?

The mannikin

Faced with such a contradiction between appearances and reality, and such a total reversal of roles, should we be surprised that these Oriental despots produced so few children, for all the numerous wives at their disposal and the effective means to elicit their desire?

La Boétie used the word 'mannikin' to describe the tyrant, 'often the most cowardly and womanish in the land'; he had no idea how true this was! For the aggressively heterosexual and phallocentric order of the seraglio is also mere appearance. It hides – and engenders – passionate desires that make nature tremble: 'It is not', writes Ricaut,

> that there were never Turks who fathered more than a hundred children, but since they gave themselves up to the abominable sin of sodomy, which is now the public shame of this nation . . ., there are very few large families among them, and especially among persons of quality, who have it in their power to pursue these impure practices where they let themselves go to excess.

So that: 'since men burn with illicit love for one another, as Saint Paul has said in earlier times, among them the natural use of women declines'.[4] Ricaut goes on to say that this barrenness explains why so many young children are brought into Turkey from foreign countries. This is the case with the ichoglans, those model pupils. But what is their real purpose, if not to feed criminal passions? Galland bears this out, confirming what Baudier had noted at the beginning of the seventeenth century: 'Requiring of nature what she does not even possess', the grandees of the Porte:

> abandon their affections to the young boys and are besotted by the charms of their tender beauty; they caress them, using them instead of women. This abominable vice is so commonplace at the Court of the Turk, that one will find scarcely a single Pasha who is not wretchedly in its grip; it is a common topic in the conversations of the Highest, whenever they are gathered they talk only of the perfect attributes of their Ganymedes. [There follows a reconstruction of one of these conversations.] What virtue, what wisdom, what piety can be found at a Court made up of such men? He who is their Leader, commanding them, gives them this pernicious example; for the Sultan's seraglio is full of these little boys chosen from among the most beautiful in the Levant, and meant wholly for his unnatural pleasures; it is this that authorizes such disorder and corruption at the Ottoman Court; as are the Courtiers as a rule, so is the Prince that they follow.[5]

Is Baudier thinking of Louis XIII and his court when he continues:

> The misfortunes and disasters which happen every day in Turkey are too great in number to be set down in this story. The Highest kill one another, or take poison for such reasons, families are beset with troubles, wives have their husbands slain, husbands their wives . . . and if some wretch among them seems monstrous, this vice which is monstrous has begot him; well-born men abhor it, heaven detests it, when it was born in this land, idolatory was its twin sister . . .⁶?

One could go on for ever quoting texts by the travellers who dwell on the abominable vice of the despot, though always to vent indignation. The clever ichoglans, who are the victims of this unnatural father, themselves – despite the prohibition upon all *jouissance* which eludes the master – know no other love but the Platonic: 'They execute these gallantries of love with all the civility and courtesies one might ever imagine.'⁷ It is this same passion which impels them to run the risk of death, and to climb over the wall disguised as pastrycooks or confectioners. The eunuchs themselves, it is whispered, 'can still go on being able to give and receive pleasure without congress with women' . . . . But let us move on: 'Embarrassment does not allow us to recall merely what we have heard said about a certain subject.'⁸

Can it be imagined that the women of the harem will be satisfied with such disdain? No, and it is not just out of spite but from a perverse inclination that they seek out one another, despite the surveillance of their duennas. Chardin, a reliable witness, states: 'Oriental women have always been thought of as *Tribadists*. I have heard it insisted upon so often, and by so many people, that they are, and that they have ways of mutually satisfying their passions, that I regard it as something quite certain.'⁹ According to La Boullaye le Gouz, what goes on in the old seraglio at Constantinople (where the wives of the dead sultan were transferred) is sufficient proof that 'perfect men' are superfluous to these ladies, who pervert 'the order of nature by crimes the knowledge of which would do no service to the reader'.¹⁰ Baudier devotes an entire chapter, entitled 'Of the Loves of the Great Ladies of the Turkish Court, and the Ardent Affections Between Them', to describing the effects of 'this depraved appetite' which 'dominates them so tyrannically that it stifles in them the desire for a natural and legitimate love', and imagining the talk he will provoke by referring to the crazed lover who, 'burning with a flame which she cannot extinguish, embraces her lover, kisses her, and does with her, albeit to no avail, what here we must not speak of'. Baudier adds that this vice is so widespread among women in Turkey that 'whenever a Turk wishes to marry a Turkish woman, he begins by finding out whether she is in the thrall of some other woman'.[11]

The Salaams

Although these passions are universal among the inhabitants of the seraglio (who merely imitate their master), they must none the less remain secret. Not because they are severely condemned by divine law. On the contrary, this prohibition favours them: while 'the Laws sacredly established in the Roman Empire arm the avenging hand of justice against such lost souls who remove sex from its rightful place', the Turks, for their part (and the Mahommedans in general), judging that 'divine justice reserves its own punishment for this crime, refer the guilty to God's tribunal, and allow the free exercise of this infamy to those who wish to commit it'.[12] In the seraglio, this vice is hidden because it transgresses against a different prohibition which is infinitely more severe, concealing a *jouissance* which is reserved exclusively for the master. Able only to proceed in disguise, it will therefore invent for itself the coded language which allows its fulfilment.

We have seen that in this universe of silence and observance which is the seraglio, communication takes place in a language that is both universal and precise, made up of signs – looks and touches – which are codified and taught by the mutes. Since everyone is able to understand and speak it, it is dangerous for lovers. So they must modify the code, like those ichoglans who, 'to communicate their thoughts to one another in their bedroom, and to cheat the attention of the eunuchs who guard them, have invented a mute language and with the movement of their eyes, through certain actions made with the whole body and with the fingers, they tell one another everything that they have in their hearts'.[13] The fact remains that this is still a very poor language for such passionate lovers as the Asiatics are. This explains how they sometimes reach the point of proclaiming with their whole body that passion which burns and tears them apart, by cutting themselves with a dagger and igniting liquid sulphur in their wounds.[14] Here, too, is the tyranny of 'literal meaning' which, rather than the mediation of the sign, prefers the clear confession of the symptom written into the body itself.

But there is another means of expression and communication for desire. The travellers allude to it only rarely. One alone, Du Vignau, formerly secretary to a French ambassador to the Sublime Porte, describes in detail this 'art of expressing one's thoughts without being seen, without speech and without writing' which is the *Salaam*. An art taught by the love which, lacking even the natural means of expression available to animals, invents unusual ones:

> This wise Master, whose Empire, by its sway over all creatures, shows it-self by this maxim to give wit to those who lack it, and to suggest inventions to go beyond the plans it inspires, does not fail to exercise its power when lovers in Turkey have need of it . . . . Flowers, fruits, woods, herbs, silks, gold, silver, colours, fabrics, in all, nearly everything which is of use in the commerce of life, for the Turks enters into the commerce of Love.[15]

Things turned to advantage

Almost everything which is of use in the commerce of life is therefore of use to desire as a means of expression: little folded sheets of paper are exchanged, enclosing different objects, or fragments of objects, which together constitute a 'highly expressive language'. The Turks even believe that these salaams 'have more power, and impress more upon the mind, than the characters which would be formed in a letter'.[16]

Du Vignau explains that these salaams are comparable to 'the ancient mode of explaining things by ciphers and figures, as did the Hieroglyphics among the Egyptians before letters were invented'. We know of the still prevailing fashion at the time for allegorical or cryptographic languages, running from the charade and the rebus to cabalistic speculations. Ever since Horapollon's *Hieroglypha*, the manuscript of which, found in Greece, was published in 1420, by way of Francesco Colonna, author of *Hypnerotomachia Poliphili* (1449), Andrea Alciato, in his *Emblemata* (1522), Pierius Valerianus, in his *Hyroglyphae* (1556), Pierre Langlois, in his *Discours des hiéroglyphes des Égyptiens*, 'where it is shown how one can express all conceptions in the manner of the Egyptians, through figures and images of things' (1593), up to Father Athanase Kircher's *Oedipus egyptianus* (1652–54), the crowning work of Egyptology, the fantastic Egyptian writing – which, without doubt, contains profound knowledge in its mystery – appeared to Western eyes as a model of expression which was simultaneously more powerful and more condensed than alphabetic writing allowed.[17] Warburton, a portion of whose *Divine Legation of Moses* was translated and published in Paris, in 1744, with the title *Essai sur les hiéroglyphes*, identified in this writing – which represented not sounds, like alphabetic writing, but 'things themselves' – three states, each of increasing complexity. Besides simple pictography (the writing of the ancient Mexicans, for example) there is what is called the *curiologic* hieroglyph, which employs 'the principal attribute of a subject to stand for the whole' (for example, two hands, one holding a shield and the other a bow, will represent two armies in battle); the *tropic* hieroglyph, which is more complex, 'substituting the real or metaphorical instrument of the thing for the thing itself' (an eye and a sceptre, for example, will represent a monarch); and finally the *symbolic hieroglyph*, which is subtler still, using one thing to represent another 'where some resemblance or analogy is visible (thus a coiled serpent will represent the universe, and its markings the stars and the sun)'.[18] However far removed it is from simple pictography, the hieroglyph 'bears no relation to actual writing', so that the invention of alphabetic writing has to

172

be regarded as something which suddenly came into being, by a stroke of genius which legend traditionally attributes to King Thot. The language of salaams is commonly confused with this hieroglyphic language. Rousseau wrote: 'Salaams are any number of the most common objects, such as an orange, a ribbon, a piece of coal, etc., the sending of which conveys a meaning known to all lovers in the country where this language has currency.'[19] He views the instruments of this epistolary language – 'which, without fear of the jealous, conveys the secrets of Oriental courtship through the best-guarded harems' – as identical to those which were said to be used by the king of the Scythians, in order to discourage Darius from attacking him: by sending him a frog, a bird, a mouse and some arrows, he made him understand, much better than through a letter, that if Darius did not flee as fast as a bird, or hide in the water like a frog, or in the ground like a mouse, he would perish by his arrow. Now, when we read Du Vignau we realize that the language of the salaams, despite appearances, is not so assimilable to this simple and transparent language of signs to which Rousseau seems to reduce it. The example of the cucumber, an object which is particularly overdetermined in the seraglio – and could be the subject of a rather well-turned racy tale – is sufficiently persuasive.

The cucumber signifier

A custom which has its roots, it is said, in the sacred text would have the sultan at Constantinople employ himself in some useful labour. He therefore tends a vegetable garden. In this vegetable garden he grows splendid cucumbers, of which the travellers record that he is at least as jealous as he is of his wives: no one, writes Tournefort, would dare 'to enter the places where he cultivates them, ever since Mahomet II had seven [of his pages] eviscerated in order to discover who had eaten one of his cucumbers'.[20] Here, therefore, a real object, which is 'useful in life', is promoted to the rank of a metonymic equivalent of what the despot alone possesses, what he alone can enjoy: women.

But in the imagination of these same women, the cucumber is

173

touched by a different allegorical meaning. Whether this meaning implies the use which they can make of it or that which ensues from it does not matter; the eunuchs, just like the duennas, are not easily taken in. If women like cucumbers so much, let them have them, but cut up in slices.

Now this is where the censors are mistaken; the cucumber – up to now oscillating between its (imaginary) meaning and its (real) use – is also an element in a symbolic system, where it now counts only as a signifier. Cut it up in slices, in the belief that you are doing a good turn to the odalisque while diminishing the ambiguity of her appetite; but she is the one who has duped you.

Certainly, one can always interpret the sending of a cucumber as self-evident proof of a lover's desire. But the manifest content of the message, which invites an easy interpretation, works all the better to mislead the interpreter; salaams, like dreams today, have plenty of Jungians with something to say about them. In reality, Du Vignau explains, if you send a cucumber to your correspondent, you are not offering him (or her) the proud symbol of your desire, and the proof of your ability to satisfy his (or hers); what you are saying is: 'I fear very much that the suspicion there may be of our affairs might bring them to light.' Are you answered with a vine leaf? It is not the mute cry of offended modesty, but this confession: 'My face is like the ground beneath your feet; I submit wholly to you.' Do you want to say that you are faithful? Above all, do not send ivy, for instead it will be understood as: 'Remove yourself from my presence, betrayer.'[21]

These semantic surprises, these contradictions between a 'manifest' but deceptive meaning and a true but hidden meaning, arise from the fact that in the language of the salaams the objects which are used do not refer – even through some subtle symbolism like that of the tropic or symbolic hieroglyph – to subjects, events or feelings, but *to their names* (or fragments of names). The salaam is therefore much closer to the rebus than to the hieroglyph, which at this time is exclusively a matter of pure imitation (unlike the ideogram, of which Chinese writing is the best example, and which is a matter of pure convention). But the salaam is also more than a simple rebus, to the extent that the name (or fragment of name) of the object used has itself the purpose of bringing to mind an element of the sender's message, according to a somewhat free association which plays on homophonies. Du Vignau writes that the salaam 'is understood by the interpretation of the name of each thing', which assumes a perfect knowledge of the Turkish language on the part of those who use it. It can proceed in the manner of rhymed endings: 'For example, a lump of sugar, which in Turkish is called *cheker*, would signify *seni madem tcheker*, which means: "Within me I entice you, my heart desires you passionately."' A stone, which in Turkish is called *tach*, will be interpreted as *koyalum biryastuga bach*, which is to say: 'Let us lay our heads by the same bedside', and so on.[22] Things can be done the other way round, with:

> a word or a phrase whose first syllable resembles the first syllable of the name of the thing which one is sending . . . . A plum, which in Turkish is called *erik*, will give to understand *eridik*, which means: 'We have melted together in grief', and likewise with others, allowed more by usage than any clear rule; for the Turks do not only take the right explanation literally; but also metaphorically, and by helping a little to make the connection of meaning.[23]

Thus, by assembling several objects, an entire message can be composed; Du Vignau supplies a model, in the form of the following table.

Salaam (thing)	Name (in Turkish)	Signifying	Value
a grape	*uzum*	*iki giaizum*	my eyes
a piece of blue silk	*mavi*	*mail oldum*	I have fallen in love
a plum	*erik*	*eridik*	we have melted
a pea	*noboud*	*derdounden o dum beihoud*	my grief has made me lose my mind
sugar	*checker*	*seni madem tcheker*	within me I entice you
aloe wood	*eud agadgi*	*bachimung iladgi*	medicine to cure my head

This is what the message would produce, when elucidated: 'Dear heart, I am in love with you, and the sorrow that my love causes me has made me dissolve and almost lose my mind; my heart desires you with passion to bring it the necessary remedy.'[24]

This representation, however, oversimplifies things. For the salaams often have several 'significations', the choice of which can be settled by the context alone (which is to say the sequence of other salaams). Each message therefore assumes an interpretation, on the part of the recipient, which is not 'symbolic' (since it is not a matter of regarding the thing as the symbol or allegory of another thing) but located on a different level, in a different register: that of the signifying chain itself, which allows homophonies. It is therefore not possible, as Du Vignau himself acknowledges, to give a satisfying lexicon of the language of salaams for an uninitiated public. But this is precisely the interest and purpose of this language of desire: it is intelligible only for and through the desire which, unable to write or read itself, makes a pretence of playing with things in order the better to play on words. Eliminating 'circumlocutions and ambiguities', it goes straight to the point, so that 'the least witty of women can say as many fine things as the most enlightened man in the world'.[25] Moreover:

> This manner of expressing a passion, for all its apparent extravagance, is not lacking in charms, and although it derives only from a great absence of freedom, and from an ignorance of the most common of skills, that of reading and writing, it is none the less so courtly and so witty that those who can read and write do not scorn to use it.[26]

But it must be observed, adds Du Vignau, that this language of desire knows no difference between the sexes: 'Since the Turks have no gender, and they say indiscriminately "un bel homme" and "un beau femme", the same terms and the same phrases are used for the Lover and for the Mistress.'[27] It is not, therefore, possible for correspondents who cannot see one another (which is precisely the case in this cloistered space of the seraglio) to determine whether the message reaching them is from a man or a woman. The desire expressed in it so strongly is a desire 'outside sex', a kind of pure desire for the Other. In defining the object which supports it, everyone is free to give body to his or her dreams. But if we are to believe what the travellers tell us about object choices within the seraglio, it can be concluded that rather than holding unpleasant surprises, the sexual uncertainty of the language of the salaams corresponds perfectly to the inclinations of those who use it.

This, of course, is what Du Vignau chooses not to see, although elsewhere he vigorously stigmatizes[28] 'that abominable vice which prevents the birth of future generations' to which the Turks (male and female) abandon themselves. Strangely, in fact, while the testimonies of the travellers converge to present the Oriental seraglio as a hell of perversion, the image of it preserved and diffused by literature or drama is that of a world severely subjected to the norm of a heterosexuality which is jealous of its hierarchy (women are subjugated to the male by means of eunuchs), merging the structure of despotic power in which it is inscribed. This is the image, it seems, in which people wish to believe. It will perhaps be said that if male and female readers up until the middle of the eighteenth century delighted in the courtly or tragic – though always passionate – love affairs produced by this imprisoning world, it was because, in these girls locked away in harems where they waited to be taken by a husband they had never seen, and in these men whose fleeting glory is only worth the price a sovereign master sets upon it,[29] they find – but even worse – what makes up the daily lot of the subjects of an over-Christian king. But this representation of the seraglio is more than a caricature; the naturalizing and subjectivizing of its elements reveals the very structure of Oriental despotic power, but also, more deeply, the archaeological foundation upon which, in its own eyes, Western civil and political society rests. Everything happens as if, at the very moment when some of its certainties were being dislodged, the Western audience discovered in the Orient the principles of an order which it is in the process of losing; this leads some (for example, the Rousseau of the *Letter to d'Alembert*) to refer to the Turkish woman locked up in her household as a model of feminine conduct, as perfectly in keeping with order. This world of order and discipline, this 'new harmony' established and maintained by the eunuchs, are, however, only a surface mechanism, hiding a hell of debauchery and perversion wherein burns an indomitable desire which speaks all alone in the coded language of the rebus – a desert of barrenness, where the difference between the sexes evaporates, where the hierarchical relations between them even go so far as to be inverted, and where the master, far from being the all-powerful male that he seems, is only a name masking a contemptible effeminate creature reduced to nothing at the bosom of his mother, who alone – a dagger at her belt, surrounded by her female janissaries and her eunuchs – holds in her hands all the threads of the Empire.

It is also not surprising that the phenomenon of despotism should appear simultaneously, for the eighteenth century, as a primordial, archaic and 'natural' form of power, which a society made up of men and women freed from their prejudices must set themselves to outstrip by setting up new interpersonal relations – and as the inevitable outcome of a decline which finds expression in the relaxation of morals, the shipwreck of the family, and sexual disorder, which, in the eyes of many, are characteristic of contemporary society.

The Invention of the Couple

How do we avert this future, which comes to us from the Orient as if from the deepest recesses of our past, defining 'the ultimate point which closes the Circle and meets the point from which we set out'?[30] This would be the theme of Rousseau's entire *œuvre*, the principal goal of his *Émile*, but also the torment of his life, his innermost torture and ultimately his madness. For Rousseau was no doubt the one who – in the light of his insanity, with the exalted

178

confidence of paranoia – perceived and formulated the connection which everyone suspected between the rise of despotism and the decay of a particular sexual order. This is what we refuse to see, what we do not wish to know about, he cries, yet this is what our diseased society has in store for us. Paris, with its women who look like grenadiers, and prancing around them, like puppets, the powdered and painted shadows of men, 'phantoms and deathly shades who strike the eye for a moment then disappear as soon as one might touch them'[31] – Paris is the new Constantinople: 'I enter this vast desert of the world with a secret horror. This chaos offers me only a terrible solitude in which a baleful silence rules....'[32] What Saint-Preux finds here, and expresses in terms that echo the last words of Roxane ('Horror, darkness, and dread rule the seraglio; it is filled with terrible lamentation'[33]), is the very thing that Émile will find intolerable. For he is made for his Sophie, just as she is made for him. *Émile* is much more than a treatise on education. In it we must read the invention and construction of an object which is unprecedented: *the couple*, the illustration and idea of the possible sexual relationship, happy and all of a piece, because it is founded in nature. In Rousseau's eyes this is the only imaginable revolution, the only serious alternative to despotism. Reinventing man and woman, offering a formula for their relationship, finally showing that this relationship quite plainly produces all others (parents–children, State–citizen, etc.), means a foundation for the double-sided unity which will be *the* political subject as the guarantee of a State preserved, if not from injustice, at least from the risks of despotism.

The Rousseauist ideal embodied in the couple, then, appears as a way of bypassing the intolerable dilemma which is phantasmically uncovered by the seraglio, wherein an absurd point is reached by the consequences of the truth that there is no sexual *relationship*. The 'new harmony', which is set up by the eunuch, is order re-established between the sexes, but at the cost of a unilateral renunciation of *jouissance*, at the cost of misery and servitude; it is not tenable. But it can be contested only at the level of debauchery, perversion and crime. The vacuum of a natural sexual relationship

179

inevitably produces increasingly sharper contradiction, between two figures of extremes against nature. Moreover, in order to give Rousseau's dream all the due force of its conviction (for *Émile* will apply a theoretical balm to those hearts broken by the tragic drama of *Julie*), we can situate it alongside two others, which heighten or comment upon it in a different tone, but also reply, each in its different way, to the 'dilemma of the seraglio'.

Cyclophile's island

We made our way through the crowd with difficulty, and reached the sanctuary, where the only altars were two damask beds, uncurtained. The priests and priestesses stood around them silently, holding thermometers which had been entrusted to them like the sacred fire to the vestal virgins. At the sound of oboes and pipes, two pairs of lovers approached, led by their parents. They were naked, and I saw that one of the girls had a circular 'jewel', and her lover a cylindrical 'jewel'.

'That is nothing out of the ordinary,' I said to Cyclophile.

'Look at the other two,' he answered.

I turned to see. The young man had a parallelepiped-shaped 'jewel', and the girl a square 'jewel'.

'Pay attention to the holy operation,' Cyclophile added.

Then two priests stretched out one of the girls on the altar; a third applied the sacred thermometer to her; and the great pontiff carefully watched the degree to which the liquid rose in six minutes. At the same time, the young man had been stretched out on the other bed by two priestesses; and a third had fitted a thermometer to him. When the high priest had watched the liquid rise in the same given time, he pronounced upon the validity of the marriage, and sent the spouses to be joined at the paternal house. The square female 'jewel' and the parallelepiped-shaped male 'jewel' were inspected with the same rigour and tested with the same precision; but since, after studying the progress of the liquids, the high priest had observed some degrees less in the boy than in the girl, according to the relation marked by the ritual (for there were certain limits), he went up into the pulpit and declared the parties unfit to be joined. Union was forbidden to them, under the penalties wielded by ecclesiastical and civil laws against incest. Incest on this island was therefore not something quite devoid of meaning. It was also a real sin against nature; it was the conjunction of two 'jewels' of different sexes, with forms that could not be joined through insertion or circumscription . . . .

From the little one knows of geometry, one can easily see that anything concerning the measurement of surfaces and solids on the island was very highly perfected in its execution, and that everything which had been written about isoperimetric forms was very necessary there; whereas among us these discoveries still await their use. Girls and boys with circular and cylindrical 'jewels' were regarded as having been fortunate at birth, because of all forms, the circle is the one which encloses most space within the same contour.

Meanwhile the sacrificers waited to go on with their rites. Their leader picked me out from the crowd and waved me to go to him. I obeyed. 'Oh stranger!', he said, 'You have been a witness to our august mysteries; and you see how among us religion has very close ties with the good of society. If your sojourn were longer, no doubt rarer and more singular cases would arise; but perhaps your homeland calls you back for pressing reasons. Go, and teach our wisdom to your fellow citizens.'[34]

The fiction of a world where marriages are happy, because sexual relationships can be strictly calculated and matched up to the closest millimetre. *Inserting* one jewel into another while avoiding hot and cold, fitting form to form: a game, a child's dream, yet here is the secret of conjugal happiness along with peace in the State. No more cuckolds, no more unpartnered rejects, no more nuns and monks, cohorts of hysterical women, Don Juans with their endless lists of conquests. No more of being ruled by blind love and dictating fathers, both with their despotically imposed desire to square the circle. No more eunuch priests in the service of injustice, perpetuating misery, but priests who are geometers, blessing solved equations, with nothing left over, nothing irrational. Happy Pythagorases everywhere. Everywhere parallel-epipeds inserting themselves into their squares, circles marrying their cylinders, everywhere delighted nuts and bolts telling one another: 'I will always be screw to you.' To say nothing of the fact that since this pre-established harmony could still be perfected with the invention of new forms, we would witness a continual progressing of technical knowledge and skills, which are useful for a free and thriving State.

But what are we to do in our world where nature has created female jewels with no precise form, their temperature fluctuating – in other words, liable to discourage any attempt at measurement? Deprived of those eyes of the soul, arithmetic and geometry (which would make the blind Saunderson the ideal go-between on Cyclophile's island), we let ourselves be led by the eyes of the body and their fraudulent glamour; we fall in love, which means that since we are incapable of finding the complementary body, in a desperate search for our twin soul, we bind ourselves to the futile supplementary object. This relation between sexes which neither fill out nor circumscribe one another is one we rush to write into our registers, believing that thereby we make it exist: 'For in our world nothing is more in keeping with the laws than a marriage; and nothing is often more contrary to happiness and reason.'[35]

The boudoir

Sade was to proceed from the same observation, in which the same problem is cast: how to eliminate what is always not quite right in the relation between the sexes? We know how this problem is concretely solved within the Sadeian boudoir. It is no longer a matter of reducing to the ideal order of geometry and arithmetic what is vague and undefined in the relation between the sexes as it is pictured by the approximate formality of our anatomies. What Eugénie learns is that there is no harmony pre-existing this relation, but that instead it is the relation itself which forces forms into birth, the contact of bodies which unceasingly invents its own geometry. Once *broken*, through practice, into this new geometry, the pupil will grasp its scope and theoretical foundations. In this practice she will be able to see the highest practice of politics, since what is at stake is the definitive eradication of the despotic monster. 'Français, encore un effort!' – your jewels are shapeless and misshapen, and you agonize over finding them illusory natural terrains. Your sexuality has no laws, and you bend it to the cretinous law of monogamous marriage. Tell yourselves instead that between your bodies, if everything is possible, then everything is permitted, therefore everything should be desired. Transform the undefined that is your lot into a potential infinity, an ever-gushing spring of brand-new pleasures! Create and re-create a thousand non-Euclidian geometries, and you will be republicans! You have cut off the despot's head, now cut the heads off those ghosts who tyrannize you, cut off the head of Leibniz's God who, you foolishly believe, has worked out this world with precision! It is always in the shadow of laws that despotism is born. Learn how to get rid of it for ever by getting rid of them, and start with the first one, which prohibits incest and patricide!

Diderot, Sade: two 'utopian' solutions to the impossibility of the sexual relation (but is not this impossibility the original burning flame of all utopias?). On the one hand, the happy harmony of a sexuality that is geometrized and mathematicized, which would have no need of eunuchs to uphold it; on the other the unbridled freedom of a desire which would not even be transgression of the law any more. In short, of the two inseparable sides of the seraglio, the choice of one *or* other, whereby each of them, as a consequence, can be taken to the purity of the ideal. Between these two utopias, and against them, Rousseau forged his illusion, the one which people were eager to believe. What we now have to do is take these three versions of the same rejection and through them measure, in contrast, the phantasmic knot which, for a whole century, the despotic seraglio was able to represent.

Wo es war

'My longing for Rome is, by the way, deeply neurotic.'[1] It was Rome that Freud dreamt of visiting in the closing years of the nineteenth century, at the point when he sensed that he was about to discover 'the key that would have opened the "doors to the Mothers"',[2] the Oedipus complex. It was a journey endlessly planned and endlessly postponed. While he was waiting he studied the topography of the Eternal City, the outline of its triple-walled defences, with the same ardour which made him seek to read in the speech of his hysterics what was written in the unconscious.

Could one say that Ispahan or Constantinople, with their seraglio whose triple wall raises the beings who live in it to the tragic dignity of heroes of Antiquity, were, for a subject of the king of France, the object of a similar nostalgia, and, like Freud's Rome, places invested with the power of revealing their own truth to their visitors?

In the course of this bookish sojourn, all we have wished to do with those phantasmic places, the capitals of Oriental despotism, is to revisit them. Here, therefore, the material accuracy of what the travellers record was of little importance. What matters is that they believed it – or at least, that their readers, in believing them, believed it. This belief, which is not necessarily erroneous, is of the kind that Freud called *illusions*: 'Thus we call a belief an illusion when wish-fulfilment is a prominent factor in its motivation, while disregarding its relation to reality, just as the illusion itself does.'[3]

Setting out from the Freudian principle that in this case it is by 'believing the believer' that we have the best chance of coming close to the truth, we have aimed to strip this illusion bare, lay out its anatomy, and draw up a thorough inventory of it. Having chosen to be the dupes of this phantasmic representation of power, we have sought to preserve its *signification*, knowing full well that we would thereby let its *meaning* escape us. If we have sometimes yielded to the temptation to interpret the travellers' story through a secondary discourse, this has always been by way of oblique elucidation, only in order to draw out the meaning that could be released without difficulty by the reader enamoured of hermeneutics. For here, everything assumes meaning, is amenable to translation into the language and concepts of analytic theory, and – once articulated in its terms – can be co-ordinated into a system.

Here, then, laid out and explored, is this phantasm of power, which inhabits the 'theoretical' discourse on Oriental despotism according to the model articulated by Montesquieu in the *Spirit of Laws*. I have said that the *Spirit of Laws* was an extension in a different version of what was already conveyed in the *Persian Letters*. But by aiming to offer a means of understanding, the vast theoretical edifice actually obscures what the 'seraglio novel' offered as a means of imagining: the hidden heart of despotic power, the simultaneous reason for its permanence and its fragility. Hence, in the *Spirit of Laws*, those gaps and contradictions whenever it is a matter of explaining the insolent and provocative existence of a form of government which becomes, however, manifestly incomprehensible if one aims to reconcile the demands of its nature and those of its principle. We have also seen that Montesquieu in order to explain the existence of such a monster, ascribes it to the laws of a nature which is in opposition to the goals of human nature, and can produce men not worthy of the name, who relish their state of most shameful servitude. But this essential natural rooting of Oriental despotism, meant to reassure the West, is not enough to ward it off; despotism re-emerges as the internal threat of monarchic European societies. This threat, which becomes daily more defined, receives its ambiguous aspect – both strange and familiar, repugnant and seductive – from the seraglio, an enclosed world thoroughly permeated with sex. The seraglio is the heart of the despotic machine, which now appears as a 'celibate' machine or – in more Classical terms – as a perpetual motion, an unrealizable dream of that mechanistic century which manufactured automata. What it produces is the very thing it consumes: *jouissance*. It is because of his *jouissance* that the despot effaces himself and communicates his power (his name); but it is because he communicates this power that he has *jouissance*, and effaces himself a little more in his *jouissance*. The communication of power always produces surplus enjoyment which, rechannelled into the motor (the person of the despot), produces surplus power; the name flies a little faster, strikes a little sooner.[4] But also, the more this power is reduced to the efficient symbolism of a name, the more the real person of the despot is effaced, and the more it is resplendent in the imagination of its subjects, whom it dazzles. In short, the more mechanically the name is obeyed, the more passionate is the belief in the Idol. The more one fears the arbitrary authority of the letter, the more proof of love one gives to him who is its supposed author. And vice versa. Perpetual motion of this kind is maintained – keeps turning, we should say – only thanks to the specific structure of the seraglio and to the function of every one of its elements, whose effect is to produce the necessary illusion of the despot, whose kernel is belief in a sole and absolute holder of power, a power which is manifest here not through its metonymic or metaphorical equivalents, but in person: the phallus. This is an awesome masquerade, for which the eunuch is the stage director (the one who allocates the parts) as well as the leading actor (once in costume, is he not able to play all the parts, from the wretched slave to the *ingénu* seducer?). But this living incarnation of otherness, without whom neither the One nor the others would exist, this caster of human lots, this guarantor of hierarchies, this educator of the sexual relation, this tireless go-between, can set up his new harmony only by immediately bringing about, as a consequence, the conditions for its

187

failure. Under the hard Law laid down by the eunuch, an irreducible and perverse desire unceasingly wells up. Throughout the seraglio, pleasures whose enjoyment is forbidden are enjoyed, and enjoyed because they are forbidden. But this indomitable effect is all the more reason for the Law's preservation and its unceasing reinforcement. The imaginary body of the despot shines out ever more in its inaccessible transcendence; his name makes and unmakes viziers . . . .

In the shadow of the harem, as custodian of the seal, the Mother is triumphant.

Epilogue

This is not a Story

– So what do you think? – *I think that a subject as interesting as that ought to have been made thrilling; ought to be enough to keep the town amused for a month; ought to call for endless chewing over; ought to provoke a thousand disputes, twenty pamphlets at least, and several hundred verse-plays, on one side or the other. So, seeing that, with all the author's subtlety and learning and wit, his work did not stir us particularly, it must have been second-rate, terribly second-rate.* – Still, it seems to me to have given us a pleasant evening; and the reading has left us with . . . – *With what? A litany of shopworn anecdotes, telling us what everyone has known since the day of creation: that man and woman are two very mischievous creatures.*[1]

– Well then, what else did you expect?

– Not so many anecdotes, and a little more meaning. What! the author makes us scale walls as impregnable as the amnesia which protects the adult from the child surviving inside him, he leads us to the very heart of the seraglio, presents it to us as the site of a timeless drama in which each element, each character and each gesture are rich in lessons on the secret springs of power. And just at the very moment when we expect him to give us an interpretation, he sidesteps it!

– But the classics of psychoanalysis, from Freud to Lacan, offer you all the keys you could wish for, for locks which, you must acknowledge, he has already set about forcing.

189

– Precisely – for my liking, he has said both too much and too little.

– You seem to be in a bad mood. – *I usually am.* – It might be best if I kept my little story for another occasion. – *You mean, when I am not here?* – No, I don't mean that. – *Or are you afraid I will not be as kind to you, in private, as I would be in a crowded drawing room, with someone I didn't know?* – No, that's not the reason. – *Then be so good as to tell me what the reason is.* – It's because my little tale will not *prove* anything, any more than the one that has just bored you. – *Well, anyway, go ahead.* – No, no; you have had enough for today. – *Do you realize that, of all the ways people have of annoying me, yours is the one I detest most?* – And what is my way? – *Wanting to be entreated to do what you are dying to do anyway. So my friend, I beg you, I implore you: go on and enjoy yourself.* – Enjoy myself! – *Begin, for God's sake, begin.* – I will try to be brief. – *That will do no harm.*

Here, a little out of malice, I coughed, I spat, I took out my handkerchief, I blew my nose, I opened my snuffbox, I took a pinch of snuff; and I heard my good friend mutter, 'The story may be brief, but the preliminaries are certainly long.' It crossed my mind to call a servant and pretend to send him on an errand. But I refrained; and I began: . . .²

Once upon a time there was an all-powerful male, lord and father of a wandering horde, who thought nothing of massacring, castrating or banishing his sons in order to be left alone to enjoy all his females. One day, the banished brothers joined together, killed the father and ate him; in this way they assuaged their hatred, but also their love, since they identified with him by taking in his body. But very quickly they began to feel guilty and were seized with remorse. They repudiated their actions. And what the father had once stopped them from doing, by the very fact of his existence, the sons from now on prohibited to themselves; the dead father became more powerful than he had ever been during his lifetime . . . .

– But that's *Totem and Taboo* that you're spouting now!

– Let me finish.
– Pointless. Another little story . . . .
– Had I not said?
– And which no more proves . . . .
– Or which no less proves.

Notes

Introduction

1. The French second edition appeared only in the 1990s. So far it has been translated into Spanish (1981), Slovene (Ljubljana 1985) and Serbo-Croat (Belgrade 1987). Parts of it appeared in German (in the journal *Wo es war*, vols 1 and 2, Vienna 1986). His major paper 'The Polyphemus Case' is due to appear in the forthcoming second volume in the SIC series, *Cogito and the Unconscious* (ed. R. Salecl and S. Žižek), Durham, NC: Duke University Press.

2. 'But the phenomenon of Orientalism as I study it here deals principally, not with a correspondence between Orientalism and Orient, but with the internal consistency of Orientalism and its ideas about the Orient . . . despite or beyond any correspondence, or lack thereof, with a "real" Orient,' (Said, 1979, p. 5). 'And when I attempt to go and look behind what I believe to be the point from which, over there in that other world, it looks at me, it is myself and our world that I find in the end' (see p. 25).

3. It is nevertheless odd that Said keeps silent about Montesquieu, Grosrichard's starting point and essential reference, who was, after all, the author of one of the most important and influential books of 'Orientalist fiction', *The Persian Letters* (1721). He is mentioned only twice (pp. 119, 133), both times while enumerating a number of different authors.

4. Grosrichard dwells for some time on its early form in Aristotle, but leaves out, for example, its vast deployment at the time of the Crusades, or in the Renaissance, which present somewhat different problems.

5. 'Going through (traversing) the fundamental fantasy' is one of Lacan's famous formulas designed to conceive the end of analysis. 'Going through' the fantasy leads to the experience that the fantasy, as the support of the subject's desire and enjoyment, is groundless and contingent, and that it only covers a void. It entails what Lacan has called 'subjective destitution'. To be sure, this is not to be accomplished by a book.

6. In a wider sense this raises the intricate problems of the 'ontological status' of fantasy, something that puzzled Freud in the early stages of psychoanalysis. He

first took the fantasies, involving the 'primal scene' in one form or another, to be reflections of real events in early childhood, but he soon realized that the status of this event was precarious, that the same consequences could follow even if it did not take place, and that the 'primal scene' had, rather, the status of a phantasmic retroactive construction. If it initially seems that one is dealing with firm reality on one hand and imaginary fictions on the other, then the reality of fantasy undermines this division: astonishingly, it can easily pass from one side to the other; there is a sort of real in fantasy which escapes this alternative but nevertheless produces very tangible effects.

7. The spontaneous tendency to use despotism as an allegorical depiction of some present situation has also accompanied the publication of Grosrichard's book. Much to the astonishment of its author, it was immediately read as a *roman à clé*, a parable of a real psychoanalytic organization, the Paris Freudian School, with Lacan at its centre.

8. It should also be pointed out that the fantasy bridges, with an equally surprising ease, the divide between the conscious and the unconscious: Freud often speaks of unconscious fantasies, and insists that these follow the same logic as conscious 'daydreaming', so that one stumbles on the same structure at the opposite ends of the psychic apparatus. (See, for example, 'Hysterical Phantasies and their Relation to Bisexuality' (1908a, *Pelican Freud Library*, vol. 10), and Laplanche and Pontalis (1986) for an overview.)

9. The reality of fantasy also seems strangely neutral as to the psychic structure of its users:

> The contents of the clearly conscious phantasies of perverts (which in favourable circumstances can be transformed into manifest behaviour), of the delusional fears of paranoiacs (which are projected in a hostile sense on to other people) and of the unconscious phantasies of hysterics (which psychoanalysis reveals behind their symptoms) – all of these coincide with one another even down to their details. (*Pelican Freud Library*, vol. 7, p. 80)

So fantasy displays a curious obstinacy, perseverance and inertia under different guises, and the differences spring only from the different modalities of the subjects' bondings with it: perversion, psychosis and hysteria (as paradigmatic of neuroses), which Freud enumerates here, are precisely the three elementary structures of this tie.

10. 'Every extortion of surplus-value, every tribute of surplus labour, goes hand in hand with the subtle extortion of "surplus enjoyment", and a forced offer of love.' (p. 138)

11. There is a delightful aphorism by Stanislaw Jerzy Lec: 'Who knows what Columbus would have discovered if America hadn't stood in his way!'

12. '. . . what motivates the function of knowledge – its dialectic with enjoyment' (Lacan, 1991, p. 38). 'It is impossible not to obey the command which is there, at the place of the truth of science – *Continue. March. Continue to know always more*' (ibid., p. 120).

13. This is what Lacan tried to formalize in his conception of university discourse. Obviously his notorious theory of the four discourses relies precisely on this remark by Freud, providing it with a formal elaboration. To the three Freudian impossible professions (discourse of the Master for government, university dis-

course for education and the analytic discourse), he added the hysterical discourse, which can be seen, in our perspective, to rely on the supposition of a 'subject supposed to desire'.

14. 'In its structure as I have defined it, the phantasy contains the (− phi), the imaginary function of castration under a hidden form, reversible from one of its terms to the other' (Lacan, 1989, p. 322).

15. See Note 5 above.

16. See also, for example: 'Sharpening the paradox to its utmost – to tautology – we could say that *desire itself is a defence against desire*: the desire structured through fantasy is a defence against the desire of the Other, against this "pure" trans-phantasmic desire (i.e. the "death drive" in its pure form)' (Žižek, 1989, p. 118). I am indebted to the work of Slavoj Žižek for many insights in this Introduction.

17. The concept of 'the subject supposed to believe', proposed by Michel de Certeau, was elaborated by Rastko Močnik (1986). See also Žižek (1989), pp. 185–7.

18. The servant's attitude can be seen as sharing the structure of what psychoanalysis has pinpointed as obsessional neurosis:

> In fact the obsessional subject manifests one of the attitudes that Hegel did not develop in his dialectic of the master and the slave. The slave has given way in face of the risk of death in which mastery was being offered to him in a struggle of pure prestige. But since he knows that he is mortal, he also knows that the master can die. From this moment on he is able to accept his labouring for the master and his renunciation of pleasure in the meantime; and, in the uncertainty of the moment when the master will die, he waits. (Lacan, 1979, p. 99)

The implication is that the servant's impasse is ultimately not the master who hinders his enjoyment; rather, it springs from the servant's fantasy – the fantasy of the master's enjoyment, and of his death – which keeps him in servitude. He waits for the master's death, living in the expectation of the moment when he will finally be able fully to assume his subjectivity. He cannot kill the master – he became a servant in the first place because he could not do this – so he can only hope for the master's death – that is, he can live only a death-in-life until the death of the master. The servant responds to the deferment of the master's death by econom-izing his own death, and the deferment of enjoyment turns out to be a 'royal road' to it. (For a further elaboration, see M. Dolar, 'Lord and Bondsman on the Couch', *The American Journal of Semiotics*, vol. 9/2–3, 1992, pp. 69–90.) One should add that the mechanism of power based on the 'subject supposed to enjoy' basically implies, in analytic terms, the position of the obsessional neurotic as the model of the subject.

19. '*Your freedom or your life!* If he chooses freedom, he loses both immediately – if he chooses life, he has life deprived of freedom' (Lacan, 1979, p. 212). Montesquieu would say the same concerning the dilemma of honour: either to die or to be unworthy of life. One can find many literary examples, e.g. Byron: 'To die a prince – or live a slave – /Thy choice is most ignobly brave!' (Ode to Napoleon Bonaparte).

20. This is also the paradox which troubled Montesquieu: how is it that Asian nations, reputedly cowardly and given to bodily pleasures, display such an astound-ing equanimity in the face of death, surpassing the bravest of Europeans?

References

Freud, Sigmund (1915) 'Observations on Transference-Love', in James Strachey, ed., *The Standard Edition of the Complete Psychological Works of Sigmund Freud*, London: Hogarth, vol. 12, pp. 157–74.
—— (1973–86) *The Pelican Freud Library* (ed. A. Richards), vols 1–15, Harmondsworth: Penguin.
Lacan, Jacques (1979) *The Four Fundamental Concepts of Psycho-Analysis* (ed. J.-A. Miller, trans. A. Sheridan), Harmondsworth: Penguin.
—— (1989), *Écrits. A Selection* (trans. A. Sheridan), London: Tavistock/Routledge.
—— (1991) *L'envers de la psychanalyse. Le Séminaire XVII* (ed. J.-A. Miller), Paris: Seuil.
Laplanche, Jean and Pontalis, Jean-Bertrand (1986) 'Fantasy and the Origins of Sexuality', in Burgin, V., J. Donald and C. Kaplan (eds) *Formations of Fantasy*, London and New York: Routledge.
Mannoni, Octave (1969) *Clefs pour l'Imaginaire ou l'Autre Scène*, Paris: Seuil.
Marx, Karl and Engels, Frederick, *Collected Works*, London: Lawrence & Wishart, vol. 35.
Močnik, Rastko (1986), 'Über die Bedeutung des Chimären für die *conditio humana*', *Wo es war* 1, Ljubljana–Vienna.
Said, Edward W. (1979) *Orientalism*, New York: Vintage.
Žižek, Slavoj (1989) *The Sublime Object of Ideology*, London: Verso.
—— (1991) *For They Know Not What They Do*, London: Verso.

Part I

1   The Unnameable Threat

1. See Boulainvilliers, *Histoire de l'ancien gouvernement de la France*, 1727.

2. Thus we can read, in *Les Soupirs de la France esclave* (1689–1690), probably penned by Mézeray: 'In the present government, everything is of the People. We no longer know the meaning of quality, distinction, merit or birth . . . .'

3. La Bruyère also uses *despotic* as an adjectival noun; for example: 'There is no homeland in the despotic' (ch. 10, para. 4, 7th edn).

4. Ibid., para. 27 (7th edn).

5. *Nouvelle Héloïse*, second preface, Pléiade, vol. II, p. 24: 'Ever since all natural feelings have been stifled by extreme inequality, the vices and misfortunes of children have come from the iniquitous despotism of fathers.'

6. Aristotle, *The Politics* trans. T. A. Sinclair, revised Trevor J. Saunders, 1992, Harmondsworth, Book III, 1278b30.

7. Ibid., Book I, 1254a17.

8. Ibid., Book I, 1255b4.

9. Ibid., Book I, 1252a34.

10. Ibid., Book I, 1255b20.
11. Ibid., Book III, 1277b7.
12. Ibid.
13. Ibid., Book III, 1277a33.
14. Ibid., Book I, 1255b30.
15. Here we can grasp one of the essential features of despotic mastery: its necessary *splitting*. The real master never makes himself visible as such in person, but always through the eyes and lips of his minister; he is present only in his representative, and commands only through someone who speaks in his name.
16. Étienne de La Boétie, *Discours de la servitude volontaire*, Paris, Bordeaux, P. Bonnefon, 1892, p. 5s.
17. *The Politics*, Book I, 1255b16.
18. Ibid., Book III, 1279b4.
19. Ibid., Book V, 1311a8.
20. See, for example, *Lettre au marquis de Mirabeau* (26 July 1767).
21. *The Politics*, Book V, 1310b40.
22. Ibid., Book III, 1285b33.
23. Ibid., Book III, 1287a23.
24. Ibid., Book III, 1288a15.
25. It is here that the father resembles him, in his relation to his children.
26. *The Politics*, Book III, 1277b7.
27. Ibid., Book III, 1288a15.
28. Ibid., Book IV, 1295b13.
29. Ibid., Book IV, 1295a17.
30. Ibid., Book V, 1314a12.
31. Ibid., Book V, 1315a12.
32. Ibid., Book V, 1314b18, 1315a40.
33. Ibid., Book III, 1285a16.
34. Ibid., Book VII, 1327b18.
35. *Les Six Livres de la République*, II, ii, p. 200. Quoted by R. Derathé, in 'Bodin et Montesquieu' (*Theory and Politics, Festschrift zum 70. Geburstag für C. J. Friedrich*, Martin Nijhoff, p. 68).
36. *The Social Contract*, Book III, ch. 10: 'The tyrant is he who thrusts himself in contrary to the laws; the despot is he who sets himself above the laws themselves.'
37. See, among others, A. Geufroy, *Brière Description de la cour du Grand Turc*, Paris 1543; or J. Gassot, *Le Discours du Voyage de Venise à Constantinople*, Paris 1550, who take a very severe view of the regime. More admiring descriptions of the Sultan are given by P. du Fresne-Canaye (*Le Voyage au Levant*, 1573, reprinted H. Hauser, Paris 1897) and Ogier Ghislain de Busbec, the Flemish Papal legate (*Turcicae legationis epistolae quatuor*, Paris 1581).
38. See P. du Fresne-Canaye, who was a Huguenot. Among those who defended the Turk in one way or another during the sixteenth century, along with Montaigne, we can mention Bodin, R. de Lussinge, P. Charron or Guillaume Postel (*De la République des Turcs, et, là où l'occasion s'offrira, des mœurs et lois de tous les Muhamedistes*, Cosmopolite, Poitiers 1560). Postel speaks very admiringly about the education of the young princes (I, pp. 30–37), and he is one of the few in his day to present the Muslim religion in a relatively positive light.
39. On these last points, see, among others, articles by R. Derathé ('Les

philosophes et le despotisme', in *Utopies et Institutions au XVIIᵉ siècle*), and S. Stelling-Michaud: 'Le Mythe du despotisme oriental', *Schweitzer Beiträge zur algemeinin Geschichte*, 18–19 (1960–61).

40. *La Vie quotidienne à Constantinople au temps de Soliman le Magnifique et de ses successeurs*, Hachette, 1965, p. 89.

41. P. Jean Coppin, *Le Bouclier de l'Europe ou la Guerre sainte*, written in 1665, published in 1686 (Lyon, Le Puy), p. 7.

42. Ibid., p. 4.

43. *Voyages et Observations du sieur de La Boullaye le Gouz, gentilhomme angevin*, Paris 1653.

44. Ricaut, *Histoire de l'état présent de l'Empire Ottoman* (London 1669), French trans., Amsterdam 1670, pp. 2, 3. This is one of the sources for Racine's *Bajazet*.

45. Ibid., p. 5.

46. Tavernier, 'Voyage en Perse', in *Voyages dans l'Indoustan . . .*, 1665, vol. I, Book V, ch. 14, p. 646.

47. The copious literature on this question was catalogued and commented on by P. Martino (*L'Orient dans la littérature française au XVIIᵉ et au XVIIIᵉ siècle*), Hachette, 1906; M.-L. Dufrenoy (*L'Orient romanesque en France, 1704–1779*, Montreal, Beauchemin 1946); C.-D. Rouillard (*The Turks in French History, Thought and Literature*, Paris 1942).

48. 1669, the Embassy of Suleiman Muta Ferraca; 1684 and 1686, visit of ambassadors from Siam; 1715, the visit of Mehemet Riza Beg, 'ambassador' of Persia, which was a topic on everyone's lips (see M. Herbette, *Une ambassade persane sous Louis XIV*, Paris 1907); Saint-Simon describes this visit in his *Mémoires*, Hachette, 1857, p. 292).

49. In 1684, Giovanni Paolo Marana began the publication, in French, of *L'Espion du Grand Seigneur, et les relations secrètes envoyées au Divan de Constantinople, découvert à Paris pendant le règne de Louis le Grand*. This work was such a success that it was repeatedly reprinted up until 1756, with the title *L'Espion dans les cours des princes chrétiens, où l'on voit les découvertes qu'il a faites dans toutes les cours, avec une dissertation curieuse de leur force, politique et religion*. Below its title, the Dutch publishers of the *Persian Letters* added: 'In the vein of *L'Espion dans les cours*'. See Martino, *L'Orient . . .*, p. 284.

50. See, for example, Guerineau de Saint-Peravi, *L'Optique, ou le Chinois à Memphis*, Paris 1763.

2 The Concept of a Fantasy

1. Montesquieu, *Persian Letters*, trans. C. J. Betts, Penguin, 1973 (Usbek to Ibben, letter 37).

2. Montesquieu, 'Some Reflections on the Persian Letters', *Persian Letters*, p. 283.

3. On this question, see J. Ehrard, 'Le despotisme dans les *Lettres Persanes*', *Archives des lettres modernes*, no. 119.

4. Montesquieu, 'Some Reflections on the Persian Letters', *Persian Letters*, p. 283.

5. Usbek to Rhedi, letter 146.

6. Ibid. Montesquieu is referring especially to the consequences of John Law's bankruptcy.

7. Roxana to Usbek, letter 156.

8. The closing letters (147–61), which concern the final events in the seraglio, are spread at intervals from 1717 to 1720. The last one, in which Roxana confesses her betrayal and announces her death, is dated 'the 8th of the first moon of Rabia, 1729'. It therefore slightly antedates letter 146 from Usbek to Rhedi, cited above.

9. Usbek to Rhedi, letter 146.

10. Usbek to his wives, letter 154.

11. Usbek to the chief eunuch, letter 148.

12. Montesquieu, 'Some Reflections on the Persian Letters', *Persian Letters*, p. 283.

13. In the final exchange of letters between Usbek and his seraglio, we see the emergence of all the features of what *The Spirit of Laws* will describe as despotic power: the determination of actions by passion, the power of the letter, the contempt of his executors and its elision with the will of the despot, etc.

14. On this point, see Muriel Dobbs, *Les Récits de voyages, sources de L'Esprit des lois' de Montesquieu*, Paris 1929, repr. Slatkine, 1980; Robert Shackleton, *Montesquieu, a Critical Biography*, Oxford 1961; and R. Derathé, in the introduction and notes to his edition of *L'Esprit des lois* (Garnier, 1973).

15. Anquetil-Duperron (*Législation orientale*, 1778) writes: 'The reflections of M. Montesquieu have in some way defined ideas about the nature of despotism. Since then, he has only been copied, and no one moreover has further explored this subject but him.' (Quoted by F. Weil, in 'Montesquieu et le despotisme', *Actes du Congrès Montesquieu* at Bordeaux, 1955.)

16. Voltaire, *Essai sur les mœurs*, ch. 197.

17. Voltaire, *Pensées sur le gouvernement*, no. 22, in *Œuvres complètes*, Garnier frères, 1885, vol. 23, p. 530.

18. Voltaire, *Supplément (1) au Siècle de Louis XIV*, in *Œuvres complètes*, vol. 15, p. 111.

19. On this point see Louis Althusser, 'Montesquieu, Politics and History', in *Montesquieu, Rousseau, Marx: Politics and History*, trans. Ben Brewster, Verso, London 1902.

20. *Supplément (1) au Siècle de Louis XIV*, pp. 113–14.

21. Voltaire, *Commentaire sur l'Esprit des lois*, in *Œuvres complètes*, vol. 30, p. 409.

22. Voltaire, *Essai sur les mœurs*, ch. 93, 'l'État de la Grèce sous le joug des Turcs'.

23. Voltaire, *Dialogues entre A, B, C*, in *Œuvres complètes*, p. 323.

24. Voltaire, *Pensées sur le gouvernement*, no. 22, p. 530.

25. Voltaire, *Essai sur les mœurs*, ch. 93.

26. Ibid., ch. 93.

27. Voltaire, *Commentaire sur l'Esprit des lois*, p. 409. Here, Voltaire is thinking of what Montesquieu writes in Book II, Chapter 4: 'The most natural, intermediate and subordinate power is that of the nobility. This in some measure seems to be essential to a monarchy, whose fundamental maxim is, no monarch, no nobility; no nobility, no monarch; but there may be a despotic prince.'

28. Voltaire, *Supplément (1) au Siècle de Louis XIV*, p. 114.

29. Ibid.

30. On this point, see in the *Actes du Congrès Montesquieu* at Bordeaux (1955), the articles by F. Weil ('Montesquieu et le despotisme') and P. Vernière ('Montesquieu et le monde musulman'). See also F. Venturi, 'Despotismo Orientale', *Rivista storica italiana*', no. 72, 1960; and the articles already cited by S. Stelling-Michaud and R. Derathé. We know that the publication of Anquetil-Duperron's *Législation orientale*, in 1778, would contribute conclusive arguments on this point, showing that 'a system of despotism has been constructed which nowhere exists in reality', but which, as Stelling-Michaud notes, legitimates not the claims of the nobility, but the imperialist and colonialist postulates of the European States; if indeed, within despotism, territories belong *exclusively* to the despot, as former conqueror, then those who vanquish anew become legitimate owners in their turn.

31. Montesquieu, *The Spirit of Laws*, 1777 trans. by Thomas Nugent, Hafner Publishing Company, New York 1949, Book III, ch. 6.

32. Ibid., Book III, ch. 8.

33. Ibid., Book III, ch. 1.

34. Ibid., Book III, ch. 3.

35. Ibid., Book III, ch. 4.

36. Ibid., Book XII, chs 25–8.

37. Thus, 'honour, which, like a monarch, reigns over the prince and his people' (Book III, ch. 10). And how is honour corrupted? Chapters 6 and 7 of Book VIII show that this happens when it ceases to be inscribed in a relation of reciprocity, since this disequilibrium applies both to the monarch and to his subjects. It should be added that the corruption of the principle has as a symptom an excess of simulacra. A monarch becomes a despot when he scorns his subjects, and the sign that he scorns them is that he overwhelms them with marks of dignity: 'when honour is set up in contradiction to honours, and when men are capable of being loaded at the very same time with infamy and with dignities' (Book VIII, ch. 7). Likewise, the subjects become slaves when they scorn the prince to the point where they see in him a power that is 'boundless and immense'. This is not respect for him, but the opposite; it is, quite precisely, a crime of 'high treason against the prince' (ibid.).

38. Montesquieu, *Considérations sur les causes de la grandeur des Romains et de leur décadence*, in *Œuvres complètes*, Pléiade, vol. 2, ch. 22, pp. 15–18.

39. See, for example, *Spirit of Laws*, Book II, ch. 4.

40. *Considérations . . .* , p. 203.

41. *Spirit of Laws*, Book VIII, ch. 10.

42. Ibid.

43. *Persian Letters* (letters 89, 90).

44. This is indeed the dilemma imposed by honour: 'of either dying, or being unworthy to live' (*Persian Letters*, letter 90).

45. To the point where despotism and monarchy can seem imperceptibly different (in their effects): 'Though the manner of obeying be different in these two kinds of government, the power is the same' (*Spirit of Laws*, Book III, ch. 10).

46. Ibid., Book VIII, ch. 10 (emphasis added).

47. Ibid., Book V, ch. 14.

48. Ibid.

49. Ibid.

50. Ibid., Book XV, ch. 7.

51. Ibid., Book XVII, ch. 1: 'Political servitude does not depend less on the nature of the climate than that which is civil and domestic.'

52. Ibid., Book XV, ch. 7. This is why, monstrous though it is, despotism is in its way a 'perfect' government for Asia, if we can agree with Usbek that the most perfect government 'is the one which attains its purpose with the least trouble, so that the one which controls men in the manner best adapted to their inclinations and desires is the most perfect' (*Persian Letters*, letter 80). But at the same time, contradictorily, such a government is the worst, precisely because it is in conformity with natural inclinations instead of going against them.

53. *Spirit of Laws*, Book XIV, ch. 2.

54. The man 'who is soon weakened and overcome by his initial efforts, and languishes on the very field of victory, lying buried, so to speak, beneath his own triumphs.... It is to this state of debility that we are always reduced by the large number of wives we have, which is more likely to wear us out than to satisfy us' (*Persian Letters*, letter 114).

55. *Spirit of Laws*, Book XVI, ch. 6. Polygamy leads to love against nature between women as well as between men. We will return to this paradoxical phenomenon, where the extreme affirmation of virile mastery meets its extreme 'deviation'.

56. In despotic education: 'Everything ought to depend here on two or three ideas; hence there is no necessity that any new notions should be added. When we want to break a horse, we take care not to let him change his master, his lesson, or his pace. Thus an impression is made on his brain by two or three motions, and no more' (ibid., Book V, ch. 14).

57. Ibid., Book XIV, ch. 3. In despotic Russia, a woman is certain of being loved by her husband only if she is beaten, as is made plain in a letter from Nargum to Usbek (*Persian Letters*, letter 51).

58. *Spirit of Laws*, Book XIV, ch. 3.

59. *Persian Letters*, letter 89.

60. Usbek to Rhedi, *Persian Letters*, letter 113.

61. *Persian Letters*, letter 112.

62. Ibid., letter 113. In his edition of the *Persian Letters* (p. 236) P. Vernière notes that 'this "catastrophic" theory of the universe most likely comes from that strange work by Thomas Burnet, *Telluris theoria sacra originem et mutationes generales orbis nostri complectens* (London, 1681)'.

63. *Spirit of Laws*, Book XIV, ch. 5: 'The legislators of China were more rational'; for they understood that 'the more the physical causes incline mankind to inaction, the more the moral causes should estrange them from it'. Sade takes up this idea; compare Juliette's melancholy on the summit of Vesuvius when she is faced with the traces of a natural phenomenon once vital and now extinguished (she, too, must have read Burnet). From this perspective the Sadeian hero is necessarily 'anti-despotic'. He or she always acts as if compelled – admittedly through crime – to restore to nature a vitality which it has lost.

64. *Spirit of Laws*, Book III, ch. 10. Subsequently, N.–A. Boulanger wrote, at the beginning of his *Recherches sur l'origine du despotisme oriental* (1761):

> It is in these sorry regions that we see a man bereft of will kissing his chains; bereft of any certain fate or any property, and adoring his tyrant; bereft of any

knowledge of men or ideas, and with no other virtue but fear; and what should well amaze us and provoke reflection is that there men carry servitude to the point of heroism, unthinking of their own existence and blessing with a reverent imbecility the savage whim that frequently deprives them of their lives; probably the only thing they own but, according to the Prince's law, a thing which should belong to him alone, to dispose of as it pleases him.

65. *Spirit of Laws*, Book VIII, ch. 6: 'Monarchy usually degenerates into the despotism of a single person; aristocracy into the despotism of several; democracy into the despotism of the people', we read in a fragment (see *Dossier de l'Esprit des lois*, Pléiade, vol. II, p. 1048).

66. On this point, see the article by R. Derathé already cited.

67. *Spirit of Laws*, Book VIII, ch. 8.

68. Ibid.

69. The Turk continued to be a matter for concern up until the end of the eighteenth century; but his ambitions of conquest in Europe had died out in the sixteenth. For the Turks, the eighteenth-century wars with Austria or Russia were defensive wars in which it was a matter of safeguarding their vast empire against threat.

70. 'The King of France is old. There is no case, anywhere in our history, of a king having reigned for such a long time. They say he possesses in a very high degree the talent of making himself obeyed: he governs his family, his court, and his country with equal ability,' wrote Usbek on the 7th of the moon of Muharram, 1713 (*Persian Letters*, letter 37). On Montesquieu's critique of the absolutism of Louis XIV, see Badreddine Kassem, *Décadence et Absolutisme dans l'œuvre de Montesquieu*, Droz (Geneva), Minard (Paris), 1960, Part I, ch. 1, and Part III, ch. 14.

71. *Spirit of Laws*, Book XIX, ch. 14.

72. Ibid., Book XV, ch. 9.

73. Ibid., Book I, ch. 2.

74. Ibid., Book I, ch. 3. Holding an anti-contractualist conception of law, Montesquieu refuses to posit the transition from a state of nature to a state of society as a problem; the reason is that unlike Grotius, Hobbes, Locke and Rousseau, he regards society not as being in opposition to the state of nature, but as deriving from it:

> Every discussion of international law that I have ever heard has begun with a careful investigation into the origin of society, which seems to me absurd. If men did not form societies, if they separated and fled from each other, then we should have to enquire the reason for it, and try to find out why they lived apart from each other: but they are all associated with each other at birth; a son is born in his father's home, and stays there: there you have society, and the cause of society. (*Persian Letters*, letter 94. See also letter 104, and the *Traité des devoirs* [1725]).

75. *Spirit of Laws*, Book XI, ch. 4.

76. In the eighteenth century, China was contrasted with Turkey. Grimm (*Correspondence*, November 1785) records one of Louis XV's ministers, when consulted on reforms to be introduced in France, answering that there was a need 'to inoculate the French with the Chinese spirit' . . . .

77. 'De la politique', in *Complete Works*, vol. I, p. 112. Supported by countless examples, Montesquieu demonstrates here that those who have been seen as 'great statesmen' were only potential despots. He repeated this in *The Spirit of Laws* in relation to Richelieu: 'If this man's heart had not been bewitched with the love of despotic power, still these arbitrary notions would have filled his head' (Book V, ch. 10, p. 55).

78. In other words, Machiavelli's *Prince* is simultaneously shocking and peerless. Montesquieu's anti-Machiavellism has been rightly emphasized. It comes up in the *Persian Letters* (letter 94) as well as in the critiques of alleged 'political realism' (*Traité des devoirs*): 'It is Machiavelli's madness that he told Princes how to uphold their greatness through principles which are necessary only in despotic government', we read in the *Dossier de l'Esprit des lois* (p. 996). But if, as Montesquieu himself shows, despotism is present at the heart of all political power, every prince must, to some extent be a Machiavellian prince. Despite his declarations of principle, Montesquieu's entire *œuvre* confirms Bayle's judgement on *The Prince*:

It is surprising that there are so few people of the opinion that Machiavelli teaches Princes no dangerous lessons in politics; for it is instead Princes who have taught Machiavelli what he has written. It is the study of the world, and the observation of what goes on in it, and not some empty meditation at a desk, that have served as Machiavelli's masters. Whether his books are burned or rebutted, translated or commented upon, they will make not a jot of difference to government. By unhappy and grievous necessity it must be so that Politics prevails above Morality' (*Dictionnaire*, 3rd edn, 1720).

79. *Spirit of Laws*, Book VIII, ch. 6.
80. Ibid., Book VIII, ch. 7.
81. Usbek to Solim, *Persian Letters*, letter 153.
82. I shall deliberately set aside China and Japan, restricting myself almost entirely in the following pages to the accounts of travels in the Mogul Empire, especially in Persia and Turkey. This is where Oriental despotism appeared in its purest form in the eyes of Western travellers of the Classical period. From these innumerable tales, I have selected the ones which seemed the most representative. These are not always the most original or the most objective ones, but they are those in which the public believed, because it wished to believe in them.
83. Descartes, *The World*, trans. Michael Sean Mahoney, Abaris Books, New York 1977, p. 49.

Part II

3 The Gaze and the Letter

1. Jean, chevalier Chardin, *Voyages en Perse* (originally published London 1686), Amsterdam, 1711, vol. II, p. 214. This same scene is described by Tavernier.
2. Montesquieu, *Mes Pensées*, no. 1794, *Complete Works*, Pléiade, vol. I, p. 1429.

Montesquieu kept to this formulation, which is to be found elsewhere in the *Pensées* (no. 1794), and in *The Spirit of Laws*.

3. Chardin, *Voyages*, vol. II, p. 214: 'The right of succession belongs to the oldest son, unless he is blind. But the king usually has the sceptre handed on to the one of his choosing, by blinding his eldest sons.'

4. Xenophon, *Cyropaedia*, trans. Walter Miller (2 vols), Loeb Classical Library, London: Heinemann, Cambridge, MA: Harvard University Press, 1914 (reprinted 1968), p. 317.

5. Ibid., III, ch. 2.

6. *Journal et Correspondance* de Gedoyn 'le Turc' (1623–25), Paris, 1909, p. 127.

7. G. Thévenot, *Voyages . . . en Asie et en Afrique*, Paris 1989. See also Ricaut, *Histoire*, ch. 11, French translation, p. 89.

8. Jean Dumont, Baron de Carlscroon, *Nouveau Voyage du Levant . . .*, The Hague 1694, letter XIII, p. 194.

9. Baudier, *Histoire génerale du sérail et de la cour du Grand Seigneur, empereur des Turcs* (1623), 2nd edn, 1626, p. 37.

10. Du Vignau, *État présent de la puissance ottomane*, 1687, p. 21.

11. Tavernier, *Voyages*, vol. II, p. 486.

12. See, for example, the pages in Antoine Galland's *Journal*, Constantinople (1672–73), on the emergence of the Great Lord, whose brilliance defies imagination: 'If only Mademoiselle de Scudéry had been able to create something like this in her imagination [etc.] (*Journal*, ed. Schefer, 1881, vol. I, p. 122).

13. Xenophon, *Cyropaedia*, VIII, ch. 1, p. 325.

14. *The Embassy of Sir Thomas Roe to India 1615–49 as Narrated in His Journal and Correspondence*, Oxford University Press, 1926 edn, ed. William Foster, p. 87.

15. N.–A. Boulanger, *Recherches*. In a note he adds: 'There is scarcely a sovereign in Europe who, unwittingly, does not still affect to appear with this ceremonial regularity in the manner of the Orient' (section XVII).

16. Roe, *Embassy*. In the *Lettre à M. Chapelin* which follows his *Voyage dans l'Indoustan*, Bernier describes the terror with which the people of Delhi were gripped during an eclipse of the sun in 1666.

17. *Cérémonies religieuses*, vol. VI (quoted by Boulanger, *Recherches*, section XIII).

18. Tavernier, *Voyages*, vol. II, Book II ('Voyage des Indes'), ch. XVIII, p. 488.

19. *Spirit of Laws*, Book III, ch. 10.

20. Rousseau, *The First and Second Discourses and Essay on the Origin of Languages*, trans. Victor Gourevitch, Harper & Row, New York 1986, p. 241.

21. Montesquieu, *Spirit of Laws*, Book XIX, ch. 27.

22. Chardin, *Voyages*, p. 211.

23. In 1615, George Sandys (*Sandys Travels . . .*) speaks of a population of 700,000; in 1640, the Venetian *Bailo* Alvise Contarini speaks of a million. On this question, see Robert Mantran, *Istanbul dans la seconde moitié du XVIIe siècle* (A. Maisonneuve, 1962), p. 44.

24. Tournefort, *Relation d'un voyage du Levant*, Paris 1717, vol. II, letter 13, p. 35.

25. Ibid., vol. I, letter 12, p. 465.

26. There are a few little Indian kinglets, writes Baudier, who only ever speak to one man: 'And that man receives any request made to the king through the mouth

of fifty individuals who speak it one to the other, until it reaches him' (Baudier, *Histoire générale*, p. 38).

27. *Persian Letters*, letter 80.

28. Guer, *Mœurs et Usages des Turcs*, Paris 1746, vol. II, Book IV, p. 17.

29. Bernier, *Voyages au Cachemire . . .*, 1655, vol. II, p. 45: 'Letter to Mons. de la Mothe Le Vayer containing the description of Delhi and Agra, capital cities of the empire of the Great Mogul': 'The king cannot say one word, however unwarranted, but it is forthwith taken up, and certain of his highest-ranking Omerhs raise their hands aloft, as if to receive heaven's benediction, straight away crying: "Karamat, Karamat! A Wonder, he spoke a Wonder!"'

30. Tavernier thus describes the 'audience' of the ambassadors at Constantinople: 'Everything took place in great silence, and the Great Lord answered nothing, leaving it to the charge of the Grand Vizier to say a few words as leavetaking to the ambassador, who retired with a deep bow, without showing his face and without turning his back until he was out of the room' (*Voyages*, ch. 6, p. 453).

31. Baudier, *Histoire générale*, p. 37.

32. Baudier adds: 'Scarcely in all of history shall one find a single example of Monarchy or Republic in which the highest have commanded so imperiously and have been obeyed so promptly, as are the Turks; their letters exude only threats, and speak no other language but that of cruelty' (ibid., p. 14).

33. Chardin, *Voyages*, vol. II, ch. 7, p. 261.

34. Ibid.

35. A 'grammarian' like De Brosses saw in them the distinctive features of the 'Oriental' (which is to say Semitic) languages; by effectively omitting the vowels from their writing, the ancient Orientals indicated that these languages are 'languages for the eyes', while ours are, rather, 'languages for the ear' (*Traité de la formation mécanique des langues*, 1765, vol. II, p. 48, quoted by G. Genette in *Mimologiques*, Seuil, 1976, p. 90).

36. Du Vignau, *État présent*, p. 90.

37. Thévenot, *Voyages*, ch. 35. This same scene is described in unvarying terms by almost all the authors.

38. Du Vignau, *État présent*, p. 84.

39. Chardin, *Voyages*, vol. II, ch. 7, p. 261. 'The Great Lord [in Turkey] is a long way from being absolute in the manner of the King of the Persians', he adds. This does not seem to be Ricaut's perception: 'It is neither virtue, nor merit, nor nobility of blood which makes the Bacha, it is only the favour of the Sultan, who can without ado create one from the least of his soldiers' (*Histoire*, ch. 16, p. 127), or that of Dumont, Baron de Carlscroon: 'Disregarding the pashas of long standing, [the Great Lord] sometimes takes a mere *chiaous*, or even a cook, as has been seen, and in a single day raises him to the dignity of Grand Vizier' (*Nouveau Voyage*, letter XIX, p. 274).

40. Montesquieu, *Spirit of Laws*, Book V, ch. 16. See also ch. 19: 'In despotic governments . . . they indiscriminately make a prince a scullion, and a scullion a prince.'

41. Tavernier, *Nouvelle Relation de l'intérieur du sérial du Grand Seigneur*, 1712, ch. 15, p. 493. Similarly in Persia, where reversals of fortune are always 'prodigious and terrifying', 'for in an instant a man will find himself so entirely bereft that he has nothing left to him' (Chardin).

42. Montesquieu, *Spirit of Laws*, Book V, ch. 14.
43. Ibid., ch. 16.
44. Ibid.
45. Ricaut, *Histoire*, p. 81.
46. There is never any *image* on this seal, stresses Baudier (*Histoire générale*, pp. 178–9):

Nowhere do we read that any Turkish emperor had for his weapons and seal anything other than Arabic characters and words; moreover, these men whose words are not cast to the wind, like those of several other Princes, but engraved, have . . . subjugated the Empire of Constantinople, ravished that of Trebizond, conquered Egypt, pacified Palestine, Damascus, Pamphylia, Cilicia, Caramania.

47. Montesquieu, *Spirit of Laws*, Book V, ch. 19. This omnipotent character of the name, which has become independent of the man who bears it, is a characteristic feature of despotism; monarchy is lost and the king becomes a despot whenever 'his ministers make use of his name to do all things' (see *Dossier de l'Esprit des lois*, p. 997).
48. Or rather, plumes and tunics, which are a part of the panoply of signifiers available to the Master for elevating or annihilating one or other of his subjects.
49. Montesquieu, *Spirit of Laws*. Book VIII, ch. 6.
50. Bernier, *Voyages au Cachemire* . . ., vol. II, p. 312. 'Everything there is in ruins, desolation or barbarism', writes Paul Lucas on his arrival in Persia.
51. Du Vignau, *État présent*, p. 12. One cannot but be reminded of the critiques of urban density and the depopulation of the countryside, which developed in the eighteenth century.
52. Montesquieu, *Spirit of Laws*, Book V, ch. 13.
53. Tavernier, *Relation de l'intérieur du sérail*, ch. 8, p. 464.
54. Chardin, *Voyages*, p. 257.
55. Ibid., p. 258.
56. Bernier, *Voyages au Cachemire* . . ., vol. II, p. 312.
57. Tavernier, *Relation*, p. 382.
58. Tournefort, *Relation*, vol. II, letter 13, p. 5.
59. Tavernier, *Relation*, p. 382.
60. Chateaubriand, *Travels to Jerusalem and the Holy Land*, trans. Frederic Shoberl (Henry Colburn, London 1835), vol. 1, p. 272.
61. Ibid., p. 273.
62. 'The sun is the emblem of the great kings; everyone also knows that the sun in its entire form is that of the device of our great Monarch, and all those who have been in Persia, or who know of the particularities of that country, are not unaware that a rising Sun behind a Lion is the hieroglyph of the Princes who reign there.' (Chardin, *Le Couronnement de Soleiman Troisième, roi de Perse*, Paris 1671.)'
63. Montesquieu, *Spirit of Laws*, Book V, ch. 14.

4 The Machine

1. Ricaut, *Histoire*, ch. 11, p. 80.
2. Tavernier, *Relation*, pp. 385–6. The same thing goes for Persia, if we are to believe what Chardin reported (*Voyages*, p. 213). Montesquieu summed up this dilemma perfectly in two sentences: 'In a despotic state, where the prince's will is the law ... how could the magistrate follow a will he does not know? He must certainly follow his own.' And 'As the law is the momentary will of the prince, it is necessary that those who will for him should follow his sudden manner of willing', p. 65.
3. Thévenot, *Voyages*, ch. 35.
4. Tournefort, *Relation*, vol. II, letter 13, pp. 3–4.
5. La Rochfoucauld, *Maxims*, p. 73.
6. Tournefort, *Relation*, vol. II, letter 13, p. 5.
7. Ibid., p. 26.
8. The expression is Chardin's, with reference to the *Khans* (provincial governors) in Persia.
9. Hence the image of the torrent, which, if it: 'overflows one side of a country, on the other leaves fields untouched, where the eye is refreshed by the prospect of fine meadows' (Montesquieu, *Spirit of Laws*, Book III, ch. 9, p. 27).
10. Chardin, *Voyages*, p. 235.
11. Aristotle, *The Nicomachean Ethics*, trans. H. Rackham, Harvard University Press, Heinemann, Loeb Classical Library, 1926 (reprinted 1975), 7II and 7IV.
12. La Boétie, *Discours*.
13. The princes of Asia remain overgrown children for ever, and, surrounded by women and eunuchs, seeing nothing which would give them an example of what a man worthy of the name is, 'they become Kings having grown older with no knowledge of what it is to be Kings, amazed when they at first leave the Seraglio, like people arriving from another world, or emerging from an underground cave' (Bernier, *Histoire de la dernière révolution des états du Grand Mogul*, Amsterdam 1699, p. 194). We shall return to this matter of the Prince in Asia.
14. Montesquieu, *Spirit of Laws*, Book V, ch. 14.
15. Chardin, *Le Couronnement de Soleiman Troisième, roi de Perse*.
16. 'They heard it tranquilly said that Habas had died without making any testament, and accepted with satisfaction the man who had been elected in his stead; there was no one to be seen who was either much saddened or rejoicing; and there was no one who took it upon himself to find any fault with what was taking place, far less to rise up against it; everything went as a matter of fact....' (Ibid., p. 159)
17. Montesquieu, *Spirit of Laws*, Book III, ch. 1.
18. *Persian Letters*, 80. Here, Montesquieu is probably prompted by A. Galland, who puts it in these terms:

> As if it had been a voice emerging out of thin air, or an Oracle descending from Heaven, the demand that had been made by the rebels gave way to the latter ... everyone repeated the words of a common consent; nothing else was heard throughout the whole of this assembly but the name of Sultan

Mustapha. (*La Mort du Sultan Osman ou le rétablissement de Mustapha sur le Throsne,* Paris 1678)

19. Montesquieu, *Persian Letters*, 103.

20. On the 'eternal' nature of despotism, despite of – or rather, because of – the ephemeral nature of the despot, see Chardin, who writes of the coronation of 'Safié' after the death of Abbas: 'It seemed to me at that time that Ispahan was a Republic in the manner of Plato's, raised above fortune, and exempt from the accidents which work upon mortal things' (*Voyages*, p. 159).

21. Spinoza, *Tractatus Theologico-Politicus*, trans. from the Latin, N. Trübner & Co., London 1868, p. 324; Montesquieu, *Spirit of Laws*, Book XIX, ch. 27; Rousseau, second *Discourse*, dedicatory epistle.

22. Montesquieu, *Persian Letters*, 103.

23. Montesquieu, *Spirit of Laws*, Book V, ch. 11.

24. Ibid., Book V, ch. 14.

25. Ibid.

26. Ibid., Book II, ch. 5.

27. Montesquieu, *Mes Pensées*, p. 1440.

28. Montesquieu, *Spirit of Laws*, Book IV, ch. 3.

29. We know that hydraulic automata of this kind are used as a metaphor by Descartes in order to explain the relationship betwee the body and the soul in perception. Here, too, it is very much a question of a relation of power, of a structure akin to that of a prince over his subjects, as Spinoza would emphasize.

5 The Sword and the Book

1. Chardin, *Voyages*, ch. 2.

2. Ricaut, *Histoire*, I, ch. 2, p. 6.

3. There is the same idea in Chardin or Bernier with reference to the Mogul.

4. Tavernier, *Voyages*, vol. III, p. 384.

5. Ibid., p. 387.

6. P.J. de La Porte, *Tableau de l'Empire ottoman*, Paris 1757, p. 86 (J. de La Porte summarizes and often reproduces the text of the earlier works).

7. Likewise in Persia; Chardin compares the corps of the *coulars* (which means 'slaves') (*Voyages*, II, p. 228) to the famous Mamelukes of Egypt, who were all Christian renegades. In 1757, P. de La Porte notes that this form of recruitment has more or less disappeared in Turkey, where only 'natural Turks' are taken (*Tableau*, p. 74).

8. P. de La Porte, *Tableau*, p. 74.

9. Tournefort, *Relation*, vol. II, letter 13, p. 4.

10. At least until the beginning of the seventeenth century.

11. Bernier and Tavernier tell us that the Mogul Empire is made up of idolatrous peoples, but that its emperor is Mahommedan.

12. Montesquieu, *Mes Pensées*, no. 1475.

13. Montesquieu, *Spirit of Laws*, Book XXIV, ch. 3.

14. Du Vignau, *État présent*, p. 20.

15. Chardin, *Voyages*, p. 206.
16. Ibid., p. 207.
17. Ibid.
18. Baudier, *Histoire générale*, ch. 4.
19. Chardin, *Voyages*, pp. 274–5.
20. Ibid., p. 209.
21. Montesquieu, *Spirit of Laws*, Book III, ch. 10.
22. Chardin, *Voyages*, p. 212.
23. Ibid., ch. 15, p. 285.
24. Tavernier, *Voyages*, p. 403.
25. Montesquieu, *Spirit of Laws*, Book XII, ch. 29.
26. Gedoyn 'le Turc', *Journal*, p. 127.
27. In his *Histoire générale de la religion des Turcs* (1626), which will be the principal reference for the seventeenth century (Book III, ch. 1, p. 331).
28. Tournefort, *Relation*, vol. II, letter 14, pp. 106–7.
29. Tavernier, *Voyages*, p. 404.
30. For example, by undertaking some kind of manual labour, like gardening (Guer, *Mœurs et Usages*, Book IV, vol. II, p. 16).
31. Ricaut, *Histoire*, Book II, ch. 3, p. 195.
32. Chardin, *Voyages*, pp. 285–6.
33. Tavernier, *Voyages dans l'Indoustan*, vol. II, Book II.
34. Tournefort, *Relation*, vol. II, p. 35.
35. Ricaut, *Histoire*, Book I, ch. 2, p. 9.
36. Ibid., pp. 10–11.
37. Sade, *Juliette*, trans. Austryn Wainhouse, Grove Press, New York, 1968, p. 733.
38. Boulanger, *Recherches*.
39. See Tournefort, who makes no bones about adding: 'The chapter written by Rabelais with a somewhat agreeable title would be a great help to them if it were translated into their language' (*Relation*, vol. II, letter 14, p. 65).
40. Baudier, *Histoire . . . de la religion des Turcs*, Book II, ch. 1, p. 134.
41. Montesquieu, *Persian Letters*, 97.
42. Chardin, *Voyages*, p. 318.
43. Baudier, *Histoire générale*, p. 135, records that 'whoever has read the aura a thousand times will go to Paradise'.
44. P. Michel Nau, *L'État présent de la religion musulmane*, Paris 1684, p. 53.
45. Chardin, *Voyages*, p. 29. 'I always have on me over two thousand passages from the holy Koran; tied round my arm I have a little packet containing the names of more than two hundred dervishes; the names of Ali, Fatima, and all the saints are concealed in over twenty places in my clothes,' says Rica in the *Persian Letters*, 143.
46. Tavernier, *Nouvelle Relation de l'intérieur du sérail . . .*, 1712, ch. 15, pp. 519–21.
47. 'There is no other God but God, and Mahommet is his prophet.' Father Nau illustrates his point by telling the story of what happened to a Frenchman captured by some Turks; as if in jest, they had challenged him to speak this formula. The Frenchman took up the challenge, whereupon he was regarded as a Mahommedan and obliged to obey the Law (*L'État présent*, p. 61).
48. Montesquieu, *Spirit of Laws*, vol. II, Book XXV, ch. 2 (see also *Persian Letters*, 75). We find this idea in Spinoza's *Tractatus Theologico-Politicus* with reference to the first Hebrew State.

49. Montesquieu, *Spirit of Laws*, Book V, ch. 14.
50. Baudier, *Histoire . . . de la religion des Turcs*, p. 323.
51. 'The K has a right over my life, but he has none over my religion; this is why I would prefer him to have me die than to have me drink', was the answer given by a vizier to the emperor of Persia (Chardin, *Voyages*, pp. 208–9).
52. Montesquieu, *Spirit of Laws*, vol. II, Book XXIV, ch. 14, pp. 35–6.
53. Ricaut, *Histoire*, Book II, ch. 8. In the French translation (which is more an adaptation) of the work by A. Reeland on the religion of the Mahommedans published in Latin in 1705, we find this note:

> The Mahommedans tell us that before all things, God created this *Table* of his decrees, and then he createde the *Pen*. That this Table is made of a single precious stone of vast size; that the Pen is also made from a Pearl, which has a crack that distils the light, the true *Ink*, which God uses, or rather do his Angels, to record his Words and his Deeds. (*La Religion des Mahométans, exposée par leurs propres docteurs A . . . . Tiré du latin de M. Reeland*, The Hague 1721)

54. Montesquieu, *Spirit of Laws*, Book V, ch. 14.
55. Montesquieu, *Mes Pensées*, no. 2186. Montesquieu adds: 'In our climates, where power is moderate, our actions are usually subject to the dictates of prudence, and our good or bad fortune is usually the outcome of our own counsel. We do not have in our minds the idea of blind fate. In novels of the Orient, you see men repeatedly led by this blind fate and this unbending destiny.' There is something in this resembling a doctrine of relationships between politics and literature, which is also to be found in the preface of the *Persian Letters*, and can unexpectedly illuminate many aspects of literary production in the eighteenth century – from the epistolary novel to *Jacques the Fatalist*.
56. Chardin, *Voyages*, p. 312.
57. Montesquieu, *Spirit of Laws*, Book V, ch. 16.
58. Chardin, *Voyages*, p. 316.
59. Ricaut, *Histoire*, Book I, ch. 2, p. 9.
60. Tournefort, *Relation*, vol. II, letter 12, p. 3.
61. Ricaut, *Histoire*, Book I, ch. 2, p. 9.
62. The declared aim of Father Nau, in his *État présent de la religiion musulmane*, is to expose the idolatory which it hides under its mask of monotheism: 'I shall demonstrate . . . that the Mahommedans have no knowledge of the true God, and that the one they worship is only an Idol which they raise up in their imagination' (*Avertissement*).
63. Baudier, *Histoire générale*, ch. 2, p. 29.

6 Mahomet Beside Himself

1. See Baudier, Prideaux, Gagnier, Belon, etc.
2. Jean Gagnier, *La Vie de Mahomet, traduite et compilée de l'Alcoran . . .*, 1723, 2nd edn, 1732, vol. II, p. 317.

3. Michel Belon, *Les Observations de plusieurs singularités et choses mémorables* ..., 1554, Book III, ch. 10.

4. Baudier, *Histoire* ... *de la religion des Turcs*, p. 3.

5. Recorded by Bayle in the *Dictionnaire historique et critique* ..., 3rd edn, 1720, article on 'Mahomet', p. 1864.

6. A. Ducellier, *Le Miroir de l'islam* (Muslims and Christians in the East, 7th–11th centuries), Julliard, 1971, p. 193. The Koran was not directly known at Byzantium before the ninth century (was there even any Greek translation?). The main source of information about the Muslim religion was still the writings of Jean Damascène. See Ducellier, p. 194, *passim*; and A. Th. Khoury, *Les Théologiens byzantins et l'islam*, 1969.

7. See *Le livre de la loi au Sarrasin* (fourteenth century), or the famous *Roman de Mahon* [Mahomet] of which Alexandre du Pont's 1258 rendering became renowned: 'Mahon' was none other than a cardinal who had been refused the papacy. To take his revenge on the Church, he went to Arabia, sold his soul to the Devil, and founded a new religion from scratch.

8. This was the version which Bibliander was still disseminating, in adapted form, in 1543. On these last points, and the place of Islam in medieval thought, see M.-T. d'Alverny, *Deux traductions latines du Coran au Moyen Age* (1947–48) and U. Monneret de Villard, *Studio dell' Islam in Europa nel XII e nel XIII secolo (Studi e testi)*, 110, Vatican City 1944.

9. His *Alcorano di Mahometto* (1547), along with an essay on Mahomet and his religion, is an important source for Montesquieu. On this question of the relationship between Islam and the Christian West, see Norman Daniel, *Islam and the West*, Edinburgh 1960.

10. We owe the first French translation of the Koran (1647) to Du Ryer; it was to stand as an authority until that of Cl. Savary in 1783. In between, a translation by G. Sale had appeared in London, along with a foreword, according to R. Blachère, this was the first genuinely historical and objective account of the context in which Mahomet's preachings developed, in the seventh century. The work was an instant success, and was translated into French and German.

11. There were numerous subsequent editions: 1632, 1640, 1741 ....

12. Baudier, *Histoire* ... *de la religion des Turcs*, p. 20.

13. There has been a long debate (up until the present day) about the existence and identity of this *éminence grise*, and there has also been a view of him not as a heretical Christian monk but as a rabbi from Mecca (see Gardet, *L'Islam, religion et communauté*, Desclées, 1970).

14. By, among others, the very serious Grotius (*Vérité de la religion chrétienne*, vol. VI).

15. Baudier, *Histoire* ... *de la religion des Turcs*, p. 35.

16. Ibid., p. 28.

17. Ibid., Book I, ch. 2, p. 60.

18. Ibid., Book III, ch. 1, p. 330.

19. Ibid., Book I, ch. 1.

20. Baudier is still referring to the twelfth-century translation, which draws on a Toledan version. According to him, the Koran then in circulation (the Bibliander edition) was bowdlerized in order to spare the reader embarrassment.

21. Ibid., Book II, p. 141.

22. A. Prideaux, *La Vie de l'imposteur Mahomet*, 1699, p. 221.
23. Ibid., p. 97 and *passim*.
24. Baudier, *Histoire . . . de la religion des Turcs*, Book I, p. 40.
25. Ibid., p. 245. See also Nau, *État présent*, p. 42.
26. Baudier, *Histoire . . . de la religion des Turcs*, p. 250.
27. Ibid., Book II, ch. 1, p. 130.
28. Ibid., p. 131.
29. Hoornbeck, in Bayle, *Dictionnaire*, p. 1856. Similar descriptions of Mahomet's paradise are to be found in all the authors of the period.
30. 'He believed that he could set himself up in the shadow of so many divisions, merely by inventing a new religion that would have something in common with all of those he sought to destroy, and that through it he would reunite divided minds, and bond them to the author of this reunion' (Prideaux, *Vie*, p. 18).
31. Nau, *État présent*, p. 31.
32. *Le Fanatisme, ou Mahomet le Prophète* (composed in 1736, performed in Lille in 1741, in Paris in 1742, and withdrawn after three performances; staged again in 1751).
33. Letters from 1741, *passim*; see Martino, *L'Orient dans la littérature française*, p. 218.
34. *Mahomet*, Act II, Scene 5.
35. Ibid., Act II, Scene 3.
36.
   For the mind to reflect becomes sacrilege.
   Mortals make so bold in a place far from me
   As to judge for themselves and believe what their eyes see.
   Whosoever dares think is not born for my creed;
   For only silent obedience is glory indeed (III, vi).
37. Ibid., Act I, Scene 4.
38. Ibid., Act II, Scene 4.
39. Ibid., Act V, Scene 4.
40. By his own account, having been compelled by the Kabal of Jansenists an their *convulsionnaires* to withdraw his play after three performances, in 1742.
41. He would be followed on this point by, for example, Rousseau: see *Essay on the Origin of Languages*, ch. 11; fragment of a draft of the second *Discourse*; and especially the *Lettre à Christophe de Beaumont* (Pléiade, vol. IV, p. 982).
42. Reeland refers to the notes of Don Martino Alfonso Vivaldo in his notes on D. P. de la Cevalleria's book *Le Zèle du Christ contre les juifs et les mahométans*.
43. *Le Zèle du Christ contre les juifs et les mahométans*, p. 94.
44. 'Mahommedanism is founded on the knowledge of the true God, creator of all things, on love for one's neighbour, on the cleanliness of the body and the serenity of life. There is an abhorrence of Idols, and their worship is scrupulously forbidden', wrote Tournefort.
45. P. Ludovico Maracci, *Alcorani textus universus . . .* , followed by a second volume entitled *Refutatio Alcorani*, Patavii, 1698.
46. Reeland, *La Religion des Mahométans*, para. 133.
47. Boulainvilliers, *Vie de Mahomet*, Amsterdam 1731.
48. Ibid.
49. Bayle, *Dictionnaire*, p. 1854.

50. Ibid.
51. Ibid.
52. Ibid.
53. *Commentaire philosophique sur ces paroles de J.-C.: 'Contrains-les d'entrer'*, 1686.
54. Ibid.
55. He presents a long 'extract' from Chardin's *Voyage en Perse* in the *Nouvelles de la République des Lettres* of October 1686.
56. Chardin, *Voyage*, p. 312.
57. Bayle, *Commentaire philosophique*, p. 1159. This is followed by a quotation from Jurieu, taken from the *Apologie pour la Réformation*, vol. II, p. 55: 'We can say with truth that there is no comparison at all between the cruelty of the Saracens against the Christians, and that of Papism against the true faithful.'
58. Montesquieu, *Spirit of Laws*, Book XXIV, ch. 4.
59. See P. Vernière, *Spinoza et la Pensée française avant la révolution*, PUF, 1954, p. 447s.
60. 'I shall examine, therefore, the several religions of the world, in relation only to the good they produce in civil society, whether I speak of that which has its root in heaven, or of those which spring from the earth' (*Spirit of Laws*, Book XXIV, ch. 1).
61. *Spirit of Laws*, Book XXIV, ch. 4.
62. Ibid., Book XXIV, ch. 3.
63. See Saint Thomas Aquinas: Mahomet 'did not bring forth any signs produced in a supernatural way, which alone fittingly gives witness to divine inspiration ... Mahomet said that he was sent in the power of his arms – which are signs not lacking in to robbers and tyrants' (*Summa contra Gentiles*, trans. Anton C. Pegis, University of Notre Dame Press, London/New York, 1975, Book I, ch. 6, p. 73).
64. Reeland, *La Religion des Mahométans*, p. 158.
65. Bayle, *Dictionnaire*, p. 1864.
66. Bayle, *Nouvelles de la République des Lettres*, April 1685. Cited by R. B. Oake ('Polygamy in the *Lettres Persanes*', in *The Romanic Review*, 1941), with a reference to Voltaire's remarks in the *Essai sur les mœurs*, which is formulated in the same terms.
67. See R. B. Oake, *ibid*. Montesquieu makes reference to Leyser in the *Persian Letters*, 35.
68. *Isaaci Vossii Observationum Liber*, London and Rotterdam 1685 (see also Bayle, *Nouvelles de la République des Lettres*, January 1985).
69. Letter 94.
70. *Spirit of Laws*, Book XVI, ch. 2.
71. Ibid., Book XVI, ch. 4: 'I confess that if what history tells us be true, that at Bantam there are ten women to one man, this must be a case particularly favourable to polygamy. In all this I only give their reasons, but do not justify their customs.'
72. Ibid., Book XVI, ch. 2. Montesquieu was aware of the boldness of this explanation, which was inserted only in 1757, after his death.
73. See pp. 42–3.
74. *Spirit of Laws*, Book XVI, ch. 9: 'Of the Connection between domestic and political government.' See also Book VII, ch. 9, and Book XIX, ch. 15 (and Annex): 'One naturally follows the other: the despotic power of the prince is connected with the servitude of women; the liberty of women with the spirit of monarchy.'

75. See *Spirit of Laws*, Book XIV, ch. 2. The peoples of the south of Asia (Russia and China offer a specific problem) are 'indolent, effeminate and timorous' (Book XVII, ch. 3).
76. Letter 155.
77. *Spirit of Laws*, Book XXIV, ch. 3.

Part III

7 The Anatomy of the Seraglio

1. *Bajazet* (1671) was not the first tragedy performed in France with a Turkish or Oriental theme; starting with Bounyn's *La Soltane* (1561), the number stands at more than fifteen (see Martino, *L'Orient dans la littérature française*, Part I, ch. 1, p. 33; and Part II, ch. 1). But for reasons – both internal and external – which are easily understood, it is Racine's tragedy which constitutes a landmark.
2. *Bajazet*, second preface.
3. Ricaut, *Histoire*, ch. 17, p. 138.
4. *Bajazet*, second preface.
5. R. Mantran furnished proof of this in his thesis 'Istanbul dans la seconde moitié du XVIIe siècle' (p. 249).
6. P.J. de La Porte, *Tableau*, p. 147.
7. Guer, *Moeurs et Usages des Turcs*, vol. II, Book IV.
8. Ibid., p. 61.
9. 'For I do not reckon as men the black Eunuchs who have been made monsters by their deformities of body and of face', adds Tavernier (*Nouvelle Relation du sérail*, ch. 16, p. 530).
10. Ibid.
11. Chardin, *Voyages*, p. 275.
12. Ibid., p. 280.
13. See, besides the collection by various authors edited by H. Bergues (*La Prévention des naissances dans la famille*, INED–PUF, 1960), work by J.-L. Flandrin (*Familles*, Hachette, 1976), or Edward Shorter (*The Making of the Modern Family*, Basic Books, New York 1975).
14. In the seraglio at Ispahan: 'it is widely reported that the most ghastly abominations in the World are committed: suppressed pregnancies, forced abortions, newborn infants deprived of life, by refusing them milk or by some other means . . .' Once the girls of the seraglio have had children, they are never given in marriage, and for this reason they fear the king's favours more than they desire them: 'The wiles which are used to avoid pregnancy, and the enormities which are committed in order to prevent childbirth, are the stuff of a thousand tales told on these things' (Chardin, *Voyages*, pp. 277–8).
15. See Baudier, *Histoire générale du sérail*, vol. I, ch. 9.
16. L. Deshayes, Baron de Courmenin, *Voyage du Levant*, 1624, p. 176.
17. See Bernier: 'One of the main causes of poverty and bad government, of the depopulation and decline of the Empires of Asia, is that the children of the

Kings are brought up only among women and eunuchs who are often merely wretched slaves from Russia and Circassia [etc.]'; they remain 'arrogant overgrown children',

> indulging in certain childish manners which are even more tiresome and disgusting, or else in cruelties, but cruelties of a blind and brutal sort, and in a base and vulgar drunkenness, or else in unbounded senseless luxury, or ruining the body and the mind with their concubines, or leaving everything to throw themselves into the pleasures of the hunt like flesh-eating animals, ... in short always casting themselves into some altogether unreasoned and extravagant extremity according to the direction of ... their natural impulses or the first thought put into their heads. (*Voyages au Cachemire*, p. 194)

We should remember that Bernier was a medical doctor in the faculty at Montpellier.

18. Chardin, *Voyages*, p. 215.

19. See the *Politique tirée des propres paroles de l'Écriture Sainte*, Book V, Article 4.

20. See Bossuet, *De l'instruction de Mgr le Dauphin*. In the appendix we can read this letter, where the famous tutor justifies his harshness in relation to his august pupil, who is guilty of grammatical errors, with these arguments:

> It is, without question, shameful for a prince, who must have order in everything, to fall into such errors; but we look higher when we are thus made so angry, for we do not blame so much the fault itself as the lack of attention which is its cause. This lack of attention makes you now confuse the order of words; but if we allow this bad habit to age and be strengthened, when you come to manage, not words but things themselves, you will upset all their order. You speak now against the laws of grammar; you will then scorn the precepts of reason. You misplace words now, you will then misplace things, you will reward instead of punishing, and you will punish when reward is called for.

21. See Bossuet, *Politique* . . ., Book II, 9; and 'Lettre au Pape Innocent XI', of 8 March 1679 (in *De l'instruction de Mgr le Dauphin*).

22. See pp. 67–8 above.

23. See Tavernier, *Nouvelle Relation*, pp. 380, 177; or Ricaut, *Histoire*, ch 5, p. 17.

24. Without any doubt, this is the one which is secretly dreamt of by the eighteenth-century educators. By way of simple reference, let us here recall that Rousseau's Émile is supposed to be an 'orphan', with this detail: at the end of his education, in a great solemn declaration to his governor, Émile concludes: 'This, my father, is my chosen course.' In a first draft, Rousseau had written: 'This, my master, is my chosen course' (*Émile*, trans. Allan Bloom, Basic Books, 1979; Penguin, 1991, p. 472; this alteration was noted by Lecercle in *Rousseau et l'Art du roman*). This implies a complete redefinition of paternity, of which we shall have a great deal to say further on.

25. Ricaut, *Histoire*, ch. 5, p. 46 (emphasis added). See also Tavernier, *Nouvelle Relation*, p. 382, etc.

26. See, among the earliest informants: Nicolas de Nicolay, *De l'institution des azamoglans*, in *Discours et Histoire véritable des navigations, pérégrinations, voyages de M. de N.*, Antwerp 1568 (trans. into several languages).

27. Ricaut, *Histoire*, p. 49.

28. Tournefort, *Relation*, vol. II, letter 14, p. 12.
29. Tavernier, *Nouvelle Relation*, p. 447.
30. Tournefort, *Relation*, vol. II, letter 14, p. 14.
31. Baudier, *Histoire générale du sérail*, Book II, ch. 3.
32. De La Porte *Tableau*, p. 187.
33. Tavernier, *Nouvelle Relation*, p. 458.
34. Ibid. In A. Boudhiba's *La Sexualité en islam* (PUF, Paris 1975) there are numerous references, drawn from religious texts, to this discipline of the body and the ritual purifications (see particularly pp. 63–8). On the superstitious respect held for everything relating to the letter, see above, and the observation by Galland noting that when the scribe 'sharpened the sticks to write in Turkish he would carefully keep the shavings and make sure that they did not fall upon the ground, from fear, he said, lest something drawn from an article destined to form the characters in which the Koran is written might be sullied by falling to the ground' (*Journal du séjour à Constantinople*, 1672–1673, Ch. Schefer, 1881, vol. I, p. 163).
35. Tavernier, *Nouvelle Relation*, ch. 7, p. 459. Tavernier remarks that formerly the pages wore only flimsy linen in the bath. 'But since it was noticed that they made abuse of this, and that the beautiful young boys would tear off each other's linen as they frolicked, so as to see their nakedness, ever since only linen sewed upon them from waist to feet is used in the bath.'
36. See 'Le Saint pédagogue', *Ornicar?*, no. 2, March 1975.
37. Baudier, *Histoire générale du sérail*, Book II, ch. 3, p. 126.
38. Tournefort, *Relation*, vol. II, letter 13, pp. 14–15.
39. Montesquieu, *Spirit of Laws*, Book IV, ch. 3.
40. Ricaut, *Histoire*, ch. 5, p. 48.
41. Helvétius, *De l'Esprit*. 'Discours troisième', ch. 12, where, moreover, we find a celebrated example of the effects of castration (almost real, in this case) on character. It is Boileau's: when he was only a child,

> a turkey pecked him several times on a very delicate part of his body. Boileau was troubled by this for the rest of his life; and hence that austerity, that dearth of feeling which is discernible in all his works. . . . His satire on ambiguity, his admiration for Arnaud, and his epistle on the love of God – these perhaps we owe to the accident which had befallen him; so much is it true that it is often imperceptible causes which determine the whole conduct of life and the whole course of our ideas. ('Discours troisième', ch. 1)

42. Of these two languages, Marx studied one, and Lacan provides the elements for studying the other. (On this point, see P. Legendre's, *L'Amour du censeur* and *Jouir du pouvoir*.)
43. The phrase is J.-A. Miller's, and it serves as a title for his article on Jeremy Bentham's Panopticon, *Ornicar?*, no. 3, May 1975.
44. De La Porte, *Tableau*, pp. 107–8.
45. 'In the history of the Turks, "commanding the cord" is the despatching of mutes armed with an imperial patent authorizing them to strangle the person to whom it is addressed. . . . When the man is dead, they cut off his head, flay it, stuff it and put it in a magnificent green velvet bag, and present it like this to the emperor' (*Encyclopédie*, article on 'Cordon').

46. *Encyclopédie*, article on *Diltsis*, signed De Jaucourt, who follows Tournefort to the letter.
47. Tournefort, *Relation*, vol. II, letter 13, pp. 19–20.
48. Ricaut, *Histoire*, ch. 9, p. 65.
49. B. Lamy, *La Rhétorique ou l'Art de parler*, fourth edition, Book I, p. 3.
50. See Abbé Deschamps, *Cours élémentaire d'éducation des sourds et muets*, 1779, preface.
51. This language of the mutes in the seraglio is different, both in its means and in its purpose, from another 'sign' language (that of the salaams), which we will discuss below.
52. Tournefort, *Relation*, vol. II, letter 13, p. 20.
53. Chardin, *Voyages*, pp. 275–7. To explain this difference, Chardin has recourse to 'the naturalness of lust to the Persian climate . . . which is generally hot and dry, to the point where the movements of love are felt more greatly, and there is greater capacity for responding to them'. Hence the violent passion for women, and a jealousy which is 'stronger than in neighbouring countries, in which it seems plainly that love is felt less':

> I always find the cause or the origin of the customs and habits of the Orientals in the quality of their climate; having observed on my travels that, since customs follow the temperament of the body, in accordance with Galien's remark, the temperament of the body follows the quality of the climate; so that the ways or habits of Peoples are in no wise the effect of pure Whim, but of certain causes, or certain natural necessities, which one only ascertains after precise research.

These are observations which Montesquieu will bear in mind.
54. 'All the girls who are locked up in it must have been captured in the enemy countries of the Ottomans' (Poland, Russia, Muscovy, Circassia, etc.). 'The Turks, the Greeks and the Armenians, who are subjects of the Great Lord, cannot be locked up in it' (De Vignau, Sieur des Joannots, *Secrétaire turc*, Paris 1688, p. 214).
55. Ibid.
56. Baudier, *Histoire générale du sérail*, ch. 11, p. 61.
57. See ibid., ch. 11, p. 62S; L. Deshayes, Baron de Courmenin, *Voyage du Levant*, p. 165.
58. Tournefort, *Relation*, vol. II, letter 13, p. 22.
59. Saint Augustine, *De Bono Conjugali*, XVII, 20 (emphasis added) [The Good of Marriage', in Saint Augustine, *Treatises on Marriage and Other Subjects*, ed. Roy J. Deferrari, Catholic University of American Press, Washington, DC 1955, pp. 34–5]. See also *De Nuptiis et concupicienta*, I, ix, 10.

8 The Guardian of the Thresholds

1. Ricaut, *Histoire*, ch. 9. This same explanation is given by all the travellers.
2. On the trade in eunuchs, see Tavernier, *Nouvelle Relation*, p. 389. 'In the kingdom of Butan, every year twenty thousand eunuchs are made to be sent for sale to diverse States' (Ancillon, *Traité des eunuques*, 1707).

3. Chardin, *Voyages*, p. 284.
4. Ibid.
5. Ibid.
6. Ibid. Everything Chardin has to say here can be found in Montesquieu's *Persian Letters*.
7. Of the black eunuchs in Persia, Chardin says besides that they are 'grey'.
8. Tavernier, *Nouvelle Relation*, p. 397. These black eunuchs in the seraglio at Constantinople, 'come from Tyro, where they have been educated to serve under the supervision of the Bassa who is its Vice-Regent' (Baudier, *Histoire générale*, ch. 11).
9. Tavernier, *Nouvelle Relation*, pp. 390–91. The white European is, of course, the standard of reference for judging degrees of beauty (or degeneration) in a people. This, for example, is one of Buffon's criteria in the 'Variétés dans l'espèce humaine', the final chapter in his *Histoire naturelle de l'homme*.
10. P. de La Porte, *Tableau*. Fatmé writes to Usbek:

When I married you, my eyes had not yet seen a man's face; you are still the only one whom I have been allowed to see, for I do not count as men those horrible eunuchs, whose least imperfection is that they are not males. When I compare the beauty of your face with the ugliness of theirs, I cannot help thinking myself happy. I cannot imagine anything more delightful than the wonderful beauty of your body . . ., even if I were allowed to choose from all the men who live in this city, the capital of nations: Usbek, I swear, I should choose no one but you. There can be nobody on earth who deserves to be loved except you. (Montesquieu, *Persian Letters*, 7)

11. Baudier, *Histoire générale*, ch. 11.
12. Ibid.
13. Terence, *Eunuchus*, prologue, V, 44–5.
14. Ancillon, '*Traité des eunuques, in which are explained all the different kinds of eunuchs, what rank they have held, and what importance has been attached to it. . . . The chief object of this study is whether they are fitted for Marriage, and whether it should be allowed them to marry*', by M. . . . D. . . . sl., 1707.
15. See, for example, *La Magnifique doxologie du festu*, 1610, by Sébastien Rouillard, the author of a *Grand Aulmosnier de France* (a catalogue of all the hospitals and lazarets in France being of Royal foundation): a work of great value (1707).
16. J. Passerat, *Rien*; Duvergier le Jeune, *De rien et du néant*; J. Balthazar Schupp, *De Usu et Praestantia nihili*, etc.
17. Ancillon, *Traité*, ch. 5, p. 23.
18. A prejudice which can be attributed to the depravity of our tastes, Rousseau would say, one which goes against nature and the imperatives of population. He goes on to say:

the advantage of the voice in the castrati is offset by many other losses. These men who sing so well, though with neither warmth nor passion, upon the stage, are the worst actors in the world; they lose their voice very early, and take on a disgusting stoutness; their speech and diction is worse than that of true men, and there are even letters, such as the *r*, which they cannot pronounce at all. (*Dictionnaire de Musique*, Article on 'Castrato')

19. Ancillon, *Traité*, ch. 5, p. 19.
20. See Ancillon. But Ricaut, too, discussing Turkish marriages: 'They have yet another kind of marriage among them, if one can give it such an honest name; this is the marriage of a eunuch with a woman, I mean a eunuch who has nothing left at all; yet they take several wives, and with them practise a certain strange and brutal sensuality' (*Histoire*, ch. 21, p. 278).
21. Saint Augustine, *City of God*, Book VI, ch. 10.
22. Under the Justinian Code (reinforced by Leo): 'a man who made a eunuch was regarded as a notary or scrivener perpetrating a false document; the place where this act had been committed was regarded as the scene of a crime of lèse-majesté' (Ancillon, *Traité*, ch. 9, p. 77). But the Cornelian law (under Hadrian) 'de sicariis et veneficiis' said: '*Si puerum quis castraverit et* preciosorem *fecerit...*' ('If a child is castrated, giving him *more* value...').
23. Matthew 19: 12. There are three kinds of eunuchs: 'For there are some eunuchs, which were so born from their mother's womb: and there are some eunuchs, which are made eunuchs of men: and there be eunuchs, which have made themselves eunuchs for the kingdom of heaven's sake. He that is able to receive it, let him receive it.'
24. This voluntary mutilation, which was already condemned under civil law, was officially condemned by the Church at the Council of Nicaea (352). This formally prohibited membership of the clergy to any *voluntary* eunuch.
25. Voltaire, *Essai sur les moeurs*, Introduction, para. 12.
26. Ibid.
27. Ibid.

It is not at all from any principle of health that the Ethiopians, the Arabs and the Egyptians were circumcised. It is said that they had a foreskin of excessive length; but if a nation can be judged from an individual, I have seen a young Ethiopian who was born outside his homeland and had not been circumcised; I can affirm that his foreskin was exactly like ours (Ibid., para. 22).

28. Ibid., para. 30. See also *Dictionnaire philosophique*, Article on 'Idole, Idolâtre, Idolâtrie', Garnier, 1967, pp. 240–41.
29. *Journal de médecine*, vol. VIII, 1758, p. 268S, 'Observation sur un homme qui s'est fait l'opération de la castration sans accident fâcheux', by M. Maistral, doctor at the Quimper hospitals; and vol. IX, 'Observation sur un religieux hermite qui s'est fait la castration', by M. Laugier, doctor of medicine in Paris, who adds a further observation.
30. *Journal de médecine*, vol. IX, p. 521, 'Lettre à M. Vandermonde ... sur la guérison d'un homme qui s'est coupé tout ci qui caractérise son sexe', by M. Louis, deputy head surgeon of the Charité hospital in Paris.
31. Chardin notes: 'the Persians call eunuchs *coja*, a word which means old man, either because they manage and govern domestic affairs, as do the old, or because they can make no more use of women than can the oldest of people' (*Voyages*, p. 283).
32. The Bororo's statement of identity which declares: 'I am a macaw' is no more a matter for surprise than the declaration 'I am a doctor', or 'I am a citizen of the French Republic', and doubtless represents fewer problems of

logic than the proclamation: 'I am a man', which, in its full sense, can mean no more than this: 'I resemble the one upon whom, by recognizing him as a man, I base my own recognition as such.' (Lacan, L'Aggressivité en psychanalyse, in *Écrits*, Seuil, Paris 1966, pp. 117–18)

33. Ancillon, *Traité*, II, ch. 6 (sixth objection, reply).
34. Ibid., ch. 1 (first objection, reply).
35. Saint Augustine, *De Bono conjugali*, I, III, 3, p. 13.
36. Ibid., II, ix, 9.
37. *The Being of the Beautiful, Plato's Theaetetus, Sophist and Statesman*, trans. and with commentary by Seth Bernardete, University of Chicago Press, 1984, 268c–d.
38. Ibid., 243b.
39. 'It seemed to me as if you had been born for a second time, leaving a state of slavery in which you would always have to obey and entering one in which you would issue commands', writes the first eunuch to Jahrum, one of the black eunuchs, recalling the moment of his castration (Montesquieu, *Persian Letters*, 15).
40. See P. Legendre, *L'Amour du Censeur*.
41. Montesquieu, *Persian Letters*, 34. Chardin points out that in Persia it is a black eunuch who guards the door of the Treasury. As the guardian of everything which is of value for an economy of *jouissance*, is it not equally he who creates value? Guillaume Postel had observed earlier that in Turkey: 'the Treasurer of the said place [the seraglio], whose name is Chasnandar Bassi', is also deprived of his 'planter of nature' (*De la République des Turcs*, vol. III, pp. 11, 69).
42. Montesquieu, *Persian Letters*, 22.
43. Of course, it will be said that in Asia it is necessities of climate which have imposed constant vigilance over women, and that this vigilance could be entrusted only to eunuchs. But we have seen that the eunuch is 'already definitively' beyond this merely utilitarian role.
44. Tournefort, *Relation*, vol. II, letter 13, p. 19.
45. Ricaut, *Histoire*, ch. 8, p. 66.
46. Ibid., p. 66.
47. L. Deshayes, Baron de Courmenin, *Voyage du Levant*, p. 156.

9 The Other Scene

1. Chardin, *Voyages*, p. 213.
2. Du Vignau, Sieur des Joannots, *Secrétaire turc*. Let us remember that in Persia, the queen mother is the titulary custodian of the Seal.
3. Quoted by Ancillon, *Traité*, I, 8, p. 65.
4. Ricaut, *Histoire*, ch. 18, p. 149.
5. On Monday 25 April 1672, he noted in his journal, in relation to the departure on a military campaign: 'I was assured that it had been decided that the Pashas would take no ichoglans with them on this campaign, lest their softness and their charms might prevent them from fulfilling their duties.'
6. Baudier, *Histoire générale*, ch. 14, p. 155s.
7. Ricaut, *Histoire*, ch. 6, p. 59.

8. Chardin, *Voyages*, p. 279.

9. Ibid., p. 280.

10. La Boullaye le Gouz, *Voyages et Observations*, Book I, ch. 14, p. 33.

11. Baudier, *Histoire générale du sérail*, ch. 15, pp. 159–60.

12. Baudier, *Histoire générale de la religion des Turcs*, Book II, p. 282.

13. Ricaut, *Histoire*, ch. 7, p. 62.

14. See Guer, p. 412; Du Vignau, *Secrétaire turc*, p. 5.

15. Du Vignau, *Secrétaire turc*, pp. 6–7.

16. Ibid., p. 20.

17. These hieroglyphs had already impressed the Greeks and the Romans of Antiquity, and they invented some to decorate their own monuments. They supplied Cesare Ripa with the model for his *Iconologia* (1595), a code and encyclopaedia of abstractions figured in sculpture, which was universally adopted for almost two centuries. On all these points, see Madeleine V. David, *Le Débat sur les Écritures et 'hiéroglyphe aux XVII* et XVIII* siècles*, SEVPEN, Paris 1965; and E. Iversen, *The Myth of Egypt and its Hieroglyphs in European Tradition*, G.E.C. GAD, Copenhagen 1961.

18. William Warburton, *The Divine Legation of Moses* (1737–41) (probably trans. into French by Léonard de Malpeines, as *Essai sur les Hiéroglyphes des Égyptiens* (1744). We find Warburton's theses on the history of writing summed up in the article 'Writing' in the *Encyclopédie*, as well as in the article 'Hieroglyph' (the author is De Jaucourt).

19. Rousseau, *Essay on the Origin of Languages*, ch. 1, p. 243.

20. Tournefort, *Relation*, vol. II, letter 13, p. 19.

21. Du Vignau, *Secrétaire turc*, 'Catalogue' of salaams, nos 33, 92, 54.

22. Ibid., p. 12.

23. Ibid., p. 14.

24. Ibid., p. 16.

25. Ibid., p. 22.

26. Ibid., pp. 19–20. It will be apparent that by uncovering the principles of composition and interpretation of the salaams, Du Vignau provides one of the essential keys to the interpretation of Egyptian hieroglyphs (which is also, for Freud, one of the 'keys' to the interpretation of dreams). But in his time no one knew how to decipher those hieroglyphs, precisely because it was imagined that they depended only upon mimesis, without the introduction of the phonemic relationship. Thus, in comparing the salaams to hieroglyphs, Du Vignau is simultaneously right and wrong. Wrong because, as he shows, the salaams are in the nature of a puzzle, not of a hieroglyph (in the sense understood at the time). But right since, to our informed eyes, it is indeed with hieroglyphs that the salaams can be compared. From this perspective, the obscure Du Vignau becomes the unknowing and unknown precursor of the illustrious Champollion. . . .

27. Ibid., p. 19.

28. Du Vignau, *État présent de la puissance ottomane*, p. 214.

29. 'Kings turn men into coins to which they assign what value they like, and which others are obliged to accept at the official rate, and not at their real worth' (La Rochefoucauld, *Maxims*, p. 114).

30. Rousseau, Second Discourse, p. 197.

31. *Nouvelle Héloïse*, II, xiv, Pléiade, vol. II, p. 236.

32. Ibid., p. 231.
33. *Persian Letters*, 156.
34. Diderot, *Les Bijoux indiscrets*, ch. 18.
35. Ibid.

Wo es war

1. Freud, Letter to Fliess, 3 December 1897, in *The Complete Letters of Sigmund Freud to Wilhelm Fliess, 1887–1904*, trans. and ed. Jeffrey Moussaief Masson, The Belknap Press of Harvard University Press, Cambridge, MA, 1985.
2. An allusion to an image in Goethe's *Faust*, Part II (see letter to Stefan Zweig, 6 June 1932, in *Letters of Sigmund Freud*, ed. Ernst L. Freud, trans. Tania and James Stern, The Hogarth Press, London 1961).
3. Freud, *The Future of an Illusion*, trans. W.D. Robson-Scott, The Hogarth Press, London 1928, pp. 54–5.
4. What is perpetual motion? In Classical terms, it is a motion *whose effect must be supposed to be more powerful than its cause*. This is a manifest absurdity, like the one Leibniz perceives as the outcome of the laws of shock discovered by Descartes in the second part of the *Principia* (see Leibniz, *Animadversiones in partem generalem Principiorum Cartesianorum*, article 36).

Epilogue

1. Diderot, *This Is Not a Story*, trans. P.N. Furbank, Oxford University Press, 1993, p. 17.
2. Ibid., p. 18.

Translations from Verso

T.W. Adorno
In Search of Wagner
Translated by Rodney Livingstone

T.W. Adorno
Minima Moralia
Translated by E.F.N. Jephcott

T.W. Adorno
Quasi una Fantasía
Translated by Rodney Livingstone

Giorgio Agamben
Infancy and History
Translated by Liz Heron

Louis Althusser
For Marx
Translated by Ben Brewster

Louis Althusser
Philosophy and the Spontaneous Philosophy of the Scientists
Translated by Ben Brewster et al.

Louis Althusser
The Spectre of Hegel (Early Writings)
Translated by G.M. Goshgarian

Marc Augé
Non-Places
Translated by John Howe

TRANSLATIONS FROM VERSO

Etienne Balibar
The Philosophy of Marx
Translated by Chris Turner

Etienne Balibar
Spinoza and Politics
Translated by Peter Snowdon

Georges Bataille
The Absence of Myth: Writings on Surrealism
Translated by Michael Richardson

Jean Baudrillard
America
Translated by Chris Turner

Jean Baudrillard
Cool Memories
Translated by Chris Turner

Jean Baudrillard
Fragments: Cool Memories III, 1991–95
Translated by Chris Turner

Jean Baudrillard
The System of Objects
Translated by James Benedict

Jean Baudrillard
The Transparency of Evil
Translated by James Benedict

Walter Benjamin
Charles Baudelaire
Translated by Harry Zohn

Walter Benjamin
One-Way Street
Translated by Edmund Jephcott and Kingsley Shorter

Walter Benjamin
Understanding Brecht
Translated by Anna Bostock

Walter Benjamin
The Origins of German Tragic Drama
Translated by John Osborne

Norberto Bobbio
Liberalism and Democracy
Translated by Martin Ryle and Kate Soper

TRANSLATIONS FROM VERSO

Momme Brodersen
Walter Benjamin
Translated by Malcolm Green

Guy Debord
Comments on the Society of the Spectacle
Translated by Malcolm Imrie

Guy Debord
Panegyric
Translated by James Brook

Régis Debray
Media Manifestos
Translated by Eric Rauth

Midas Dekkers
Dearest Pet
Translated by Paul Vincent

Gilles Deleuze and Félix Guattari
What Is Philosophy?
Translated by Graham Burchell and Hugh Tomlinson

Jacques Derrida
Politics of Friendship
Translated by George Collins

Hans Magnus Enzensberger
Political Crumbs
Translated by Martin Chalmers

Hans Magnus Enzensberger
Mediocrity and Delusion
Translated by Martin Chalmers

André Gorz
Capitalism, Socialism, Ecology
Translated by Chris Turner

André Gorz
Critique of Economic Reason
Translated by Chris Turner

Ernesto Che Guevara
The Motorcyle Diaries
Translated by Ann Wright

Jean-Claude Guillebaud and Raymond Depardon
Return to Vietnam
Translated by John Simmons

TRANSLATIONS FROM VERSO

Siegfried Kracauer
The Salaried Masses: Duty and Distraction in Weimar Germany
Translated by Quintin Hoare

Fritz Kramer
The Red Fez
Translated by Malcolm Green

Henri Lefebvre
Introduction to Modernity
Translated by John Moore

Pierre Macherey
In a Materialist Way
Translated by Ted Stolze

François Maspero
Roissy Express
Translated by Paul Jones

Carlos Monsiváis
Mexican Postcards
Translated by John Kraniauskas

Mario Perniola
Enigmas
Translated by Christopher Woodall

José Pierre, ed.
Investigating Sex: Surrealist Discussions 1928–32
Translated by Malcolm Imrie

Jacques Rancière
On the Shores of Politics
Translated by Liz Heron

Viramma, Josiane Racine and Jean-Luc Racine
Viramma: Life of an Untouchable
Translated by Will Hobson

Paul Virilio
Open Sky
Translated by Julie Rose

Rudi Visker
Michel Foucault
Translated by Chris Turner

Breinigsville, PA USA
06 March 2011
257011BV00001B/194/P